The Divine Circle of
LADIES MAKING
MISCHIEF

Also by

Dolores Stewart Riccio

CHARMED CIRCLE

CIRCLE OF FIVE

The Divine Circle of
LADIES MAKING
MISCHIEF

DOLORES STEWART RICCIO

KENSINGTON BOOKS
http://www.kensingtonbooks.com

KENSINGTON BOOKS are published by

Kensington Publishing Corp.
850 Third Avenue
New York, NY 10022

All Kensington titles, imprints and distributed lines are available at special quantity discounts for bulk purchases for sales promotion, premiums, fund-raising, educational or institutional use.

Special book excerpts or customized printings can also be created to fit specific needs. For details, write or phone the office of the Kensington Special Sales Manager: Kensington Publishing Corp., 850 Third Avenue, New York, NY 10022. Attn. Special Sales Department. Phone: 1-800-221-2647.

Kensington and the K logo Reg. U.S. Pat. & TM Off.

ISBN 0-7582-0986-X

First Kensington Trade Paperback Printing: April 2005
10 9 8 7 6 5 4 3

Printed in the United States of America

To Joan Bingham,
a friend for all reasons

Acknowledgments

With warm appreciation to some wonderful people . . .

Thanks to all the dear friends and family who have formed my ideal of friendship over the years.

Thanks to the Saturday morning circle. Their faces change from time to time, but their hearts keep on offering patient listening, helpful insights, and constant support.

Thanks to my editor, Audrey LaFehr, whose guidance and enthusiasm have meant so much, and to Kensington copy editor Margaret Jarpey for her care and thoroughness.

Thanks to my daughter, Lucy, for her own special magic.

Thanks to my husband, Rick, who inspires and encourages me in every word.

Chapter One

"I've never been married to an honest man before." Heather Devlin idly paddled her float through the pool's chlorine blue to reach the champagne cooling in a bucket on the ceramic stairs. "Unlike my three avaricious ex's, I had to do some fast talking to get Dick to leave that Spartan bachelor den above his animal hospital and move into my place." She gestured toward her handsome Federalist mansion with the widow's walk perched on top.

"And I've never had a guy who was true," I reflected, although I had only one ex for comparison. Trailing my left hand through the water, I gazed fondly at the emerald engagement ring, chosen (Joe had said) to match my eyes. At that moment, however, Honest and True were elsewhere, knights-errant on their quixotic quests. Heather's Dick Devlin, a holistic veterinarian and charismatic speaker, was presiding at a fund-raiser for an animal sanctuary in Utah. My Joe Ulysses, a ship's engineer for Greenpeace, was somewhere on the Tasman Sea where activists were assembling to protest the shipping of nuclear fuel by the British—which was about as far away as a lover could roam, all the way around the globe.

Heather and I were left to bask in the hot eye of July and drift around Heather's new pool, built as a miniature replica of the Hearst mansion's, only without the half-draped Grecian statuary that might have seemed a bit over the top in the puritan atmosphere of the town of Plymouth, with its unwritten but inflexible sumptuary laws. A hidden CD player was broadcasting "Margaritaville" and "Cheeseburger in Paradise" while a cacophony of barking and yelping rose from time to time from the fenced enclosure behind the house. Heather never has less than seven or eight canine companions in residence, usually the neediest cases out of Animal Lovers, the no-kill animal sanctuary she supports with her trust income. Her triple garage has been converted into posh sleeping quarters for the larger breeds; smaller mutts sleep in the mansion's conservatory.

Heather and Dick's wedding had been a "canine companions welcome" event, with each of the white-shirted ushers holding one of Heather's crew on leash, and her bloodhound, Trilby, serving as ring bearer. All the canine guests had been requested to wear the white bow ties provided at the gate. My own mutt, Scruffy, bathed and blow-dried to perfection for the festive occasion, had taken a dim view of the elastic collar and tie, scratching mightily with his newly clipped nails to shred the offending item. *Real dogs don't wear cute stuff* was his point of view.

"Speaking of husbands," Heather said, topping up her flute and reaching out to fill mine. "An interesting couple has moved into the Stickley place—you know, that sprawling old house up the road with the great gardens." No matter how many times a property changed hands in bedrock New England, to the natives it always retained the name of its original owner. "It's mostly on one floor, which is convenient, since she's in a wheelchair, rather twisted up, poor dear," Heather continued. "She's an illustrator and painter, and he's a writer, a handsome blond, bearded devil— seems absolutely devoted to her. Kelliher. Brian and Maeve. They're working on a book together: *Living the Druid Life*. And they have several companion cats, as well. I feel they're our sort, don't you?"

Second only to the companionship of one's beloved, a girlfriend like Heather with a taste for gossip is a great comfort. My girl-friends, as it happened, are Wiccans, a circle of five kindred souls. So Heather was right. A couple of Druids with a bunch of cats were definitely our sort. "You've met them, then? Tell me more."

"They bought the property a couple of months ago, but there was a problem right off the bat, so they've only been fully moved in for about three weeks," Heather continued. "I had an imme-diate good feeling about them when I drove by and saw a bevy of cats sunning themselves on the roof. Even though I don't believe in letting cats roam freely outdoors—so dangerous for the poor things! Anyway, I brought over a few loaves of Portuguese bread, a couple of bottles of good red, some catnip mice, and a package of your all-natural fleabane. A basket from the Wiccan Welcome Wagon, if you will. I meant just to leave the stuff on the doorstep and scram, but Brian caught me at it and insisted I come in. They were just having tea. It was herbal tea, too—just like something you'd concoct—and there was a plate of crescent moon cakes."

"That sounds sympatico. What problem right off the bat?"

"Maeve had some kind of physical setback. A week in Jordan Hospital and another week at Manomet Manor Rehabilitation Center. Well, you know—that was right about the time when there was an unpleasant rumor making the rounds, Brian said. Maybe nothing to it, but he got her out of there in a hell of a hurry anyway."

"A rumor about some convalescents dying rather suddenly, as I recall. Respiratory failures. Heart attacks. Suspicious circum-stances."

"That's the one."

"Stone followed up on that, questioned the director, the nurses and aides. Dr. DeBoer was mad as hell about the unfavor-able publicity, but who're you going to sue for a rumor? As DeBoer put it, his hospital's full of sick people, and sick people sometimes die. Phil says it's a question of whether there's enough evidence to warrant exhuming the bodies in question. Most relatives are against it." Phillipa Stern, part of our Wiccan circle, is married to

Detective Stone Stern, which makes it that much easier for us to keep our fingers on the pulse of crime in Plymouth. This is fortuitous, because from time to time, we find ourselves involved in crime fighting, and Stone is a reluctant but dependable resource.

"I think I've had just about enough sun, Heather," I could feel by the heat of my skin that I was beginning to burn. Heather's a bronze goddess type, but my skin is fair and vulnerable. "And I know I've had enough champagne."

At that moment something large and furry hurled itself through the air and into the pool, toppling both of us off our floats, spilling the champagne, and having an instant cooling effect on my overheated body. A golden retriever was splashing around us with an expression of absolute ecstasy. "That's Honeycomb," Heather explained, pulling herself gracefully out of the pool. I followed, wringing the chlorinated water out of my mop of hair. "She must have squeezed past the new housekeeper again. Honey adores the pool—don't you, you big, sweet baby!"

From a basket of water toys near the water's edge, Heather selected a dilapidated tennis ball and tossed it into the pool. Honeycomb swam furiously to retrieve it.

We wrapped ourselves in terrycloth robes and slid our feet into thong slippers. "I wouldn't mind a cup of black coffee before I drive home," I suggested. Honeycomb padded out of the pool's shallow end and dropped the sopping ball into Heather's hand.

"Up to the house, then," Heather said. "Lucrezia will make us some espresso. A double shot of that should clear up the champagne mist."

"I have to admit I never believed you'd find another housekeeper who'd put up with your mutts tracking muck over your rugs. She must be a good-natured soul."

Heather laughed. "Not on your life. She's deeply Sicilian and fanatically clean, but she needed to get out of Boston. I didn't inquire too closely, but there's definitely a story there. She's a couple, actually—comes with her brother Caesare. Well, she says he's her brother, and what do I care, since he appears to be a gifted gardener. That's him, over behind the dog yard, trying to coax life back into those crooked apple trees. But the main thing is, Lucrezia is a fabulous cook—you'll die for her pastries. And my mutts, as you call them, seem to be impervious to the evil eye."

Heather's so-called dog yard is an ample stretch of lawn with several large maples offering an oasis of shade for panting canines and a fountain set low to the ground bubbling over with cool water. I could see Caesare among the apples trees beyond—a compact, wiry, swarthy fellow. Lucrezia, when I met her shortly afterward, proved to be a five-foot dynamo with arms as muscular as her brother's and a distrustful expression. In her severe black dress and a white chef's apron, she reminded me of Joe's mother, the redoubtable Athena, whom I'd met last year when he took me to Greece to be presented to his family, and vice versa. I thought sadly of the late lamented Ashbery, stamping around in her corduroy pants and Wellingtons. Heather's longtime housekeeper and friend had been blown up with an explosion that took out the back of the Morgan mansion. The newly rebuilt dream kitchen surely ought to please even the wary Lucrezia. After all, it had impressed Phillipa. And as a cookbook author (and sometime poet), she was no slouch when it came to well-equipped kitchens.

Heather introduced me formally to her housekeeper as "Cass Shipton of Shipton's *Earthlore Herbal Preparations and Cruelty-Free Cosmetics*. She'll love to hear all about Sicilian herb lore, especially healing plants and love potions." Lucrezia's thin-lipped smile didn't reach her eyes. "Ah, *signora*, those are only for the *strega*." She slapped down a plate of delectable cream-filled and pine nut-crusted goodies, then bustled away, picking up discarded rubber bones and tennis balls and throwing them into her apron as she went.

"That went well," I commented. "What's *strega*?"

"I don't know. Some kind of country herbalist, I guess."

"I'm relieved to learn it's Lucrezia Malatesta and not Borgia," I said, sampling a tiny cannoli. The espresso and accompanying delicacies were all that Heather had promised. Jimmy Buffet's beach-bum concert having concluded, our snack was accompanied by some sprightly medieval folk music.

As I climbed into my Jeep Wagoneer a while later, I was feeling tranquil from head to toe. "Thanks for a marvelously decadent afternoon," I said. Her knack for living abundantly, almost carelessly, no matter how many times she'd been taken advantage of in the past, made a few hours with Heather more relaxing and certainly more fun than a full day's treatment at some luxurious spa. "I hope I get a chance to meet your Druid friends."

"Oh, you will, Cass, you will. I've invited them to our July Esbat. I think Maeve will be able to wheel around okay up there, don't you?" Heather's tanned arm waved vaguely toward the hill where she'd had a ring of great stones laid out last year. Surrounded on three sides by trees, it was wonderfully private, by far the most magical of our meeting places. The flat stone altar at the center of the ring was becoming imbued with the energy we raised in our ceremonies. Many a sacred site, from cathedrals to stone circles, had gained spiritual power from the chants and prayers of those who gathered there year after year.

"Druids. That's trees and Celtic stuff, isn't it? They ought to feel right at home joining our Esbat. I trust you consulted the others?"

"Oh, it's my turn to be hostess-priestess, and no one will mind meeting such a fascinating couple. But I will get on the phone today and check. The Kellihers are just dying to meet the circle. Brian's heard about us—old news articles and town gossip, I guess—and he hopes we can help to prove or disprove the suspicions about Manomet Manor. He's worried that Maeve might have to go back there—she needs some sort of physical therapy from time to time—and both of them sense a strangeness about the place. 'A touch of the weird,' Brian calls it."

"Here we go again," I said.

Before we could get ourselves involved in the Manomet Manor mystery deaths, however, my attention was diverted to other concerns, beginning with an unsettling Monday morning call from my youngest daughter in San Francisco. Cathy works in the theater whenever she's got a part and at odd jobs between productions. "Mother!" she exclaimed. "Something is *terribly* wrong with Becky. You must go to her *at once.*"

Even as I took into account Cathy's love of drama, this pronouncement was quite a shock to me. My older daughter, Rebecca, lives in Boston with her husband, Ron Lowell, so I see her fairly often. Added to that, I'm a clairvoyant. So how could Cathy, on the opposite coast, know that her sister was in trouble while I remained unaware?

"What do you mean?" I demanded. "What's wrong with Becky? I just saw her—oh, when was it? Easter! I just saw her at Easter, and everything was fine. And we've talked on the phone several times." Still, I felt a stab of maternal guilt skewer my heart. Shouldn't I have called more often?

"Well, to begin with, Mother, Becky's been a bit blue since the miscarriage, and—"

"Miscarriage! What miscarriage?" My voice got shrill. My hand went to my abdomen, massaging away the hurt. (Hadn't I felt that phantom pain telling me someone I love is hurting—right after Beltane?—and discounted it. I'd wondered who it could be at the time. Everyone I knew was fine.) "May? Was it in May?" I could hear my own voice rising to its highest register.

Breathe slowly and deeply, I ordered myself. *Stay calm.*

"*I* thought you'd have guessed, but Becky said you hadn't! Becky said it was too soon to tell you because you'd just make a big fuss, and then after she lost it . . . well, you'd have been hanging over her with herb teas, amulets, and so forth. She was only two months along . . . it wasn't the end of the world. Everything seemed fine, *really* it did. But *now* there's trouble with Ron."

"Trouble with Ron? What trouble with Ron?" Now I really was screeching and, worse, repeating phrases like a parrot.

"It was after he lost that little election he had his heart set on. State senator. He was all right for a while—until the plaintiff won that big harassment suit he was defending—Brigham Boat, was it? *Major* kick in the ego! I think that's when their relationship began to go sour. Becky's let a few little things slip."

"Not to me, she didn't." Why is a mother always the last to know? *Well, never mind that,* I told myself, *the important thing is to be there for Becky now.* "When did you speak to her last? What did she say that rang the alarm?"

"She offered to book tickets for me and Irene if we would come East for a visit. I suspect she feels the need of a confidante and a buffer. Well, Mother, you know we would *love* to be there for her, but as it happens I've just got myself a *wonderful* part in this O'Neill production that's starting rehearsals a week from today. And Irene's singing regularly at a club."

"That's great, Cathy," I murmured. "Don't worry about Becky. I'll find out what's going on there and do whatever I can to help."

"Oh, good. I thought you would." The relief in her voice lifted my spirits, too, as if a ray of sunlight had penetrated the gloom. I could see her in my mind's eye, my slender, golden Cathy, a perfect Titania.

"And what about you? Are you happy and healthy? I hope you've been eating better. The last time I saw you, a stiff breeze off the ocean could've blown you away." *I should be paying closer attention to my children,* I scolded myself.

Cathy's laugh was bell-like, too theatrical to be reassuring. "Oh, don't worry about *me*. Irene watches over me *day and night*. But there's one more little favor I want to ask of you, Mother . . ."

"Anything, darling. You know that."

"An old school friend called me from Quincy. Do you remember Rose? Rose Fiorella she was then. She's in *terrible* trouble—has to get out of the place she's staying, like, today or sooner. Would it be a *awful* imposition if I asked you to put her up, for one night only? She just needs to check out a few shelters and find one that will take her in."

"Shelters?"

"You know, battered women shelters. Her husband's going to *kill* her, or at least that's what he says."

I couldn't think of any role more thankless than inserting myself into a full-blown marital crisis, and now it seemed as if I was getting hit by a double whammy. But my relationship with Cathy was so tenuous and precious, I didn't want to deny any reasonable request she might make of me—although this was stretching "reasonable" a little. "Okay. Not to worry, darling. Do you want me to call her? Where is she?"

"What time is it there? Eleven-thirty? Probably on the bus by now. She'll be waiting for you to pick her up in Braintree. She's going to hang out at the mall until you get there. Just park and get a cup of coffee at the Food Court. Rose will find you. She says she remembers you *very well.*"

"Right. So it's all set up, then? Sounds really clandestine."

"Well, Rose's into some *really* serious shit. Sorry, Mother. And thanks a million. We'll talk again, real soon." Suddenly she was in a hurry to click off. I could hear someone in the background, indistinguishable words but an urgent tone.

"Sure, Cathy. You take care of yourself now." I knew I should say, "Break a leg," but I couldn't. My grandmother had taught me that "thoughts are things," and all my Wiccan experience had proved that to be true.

Scruffy danced around, begging, *Take me! Take me!* Not exactly aloud of course, but I always hear what he's thinking. So I explained that I couldn't leave him in the car in July while I waited to connect with Cathy's old school chum. He slumped down in front of the refrigerator, a favorite cool spot in summer, in an attitude of deep disappointment. All the world was contriving to make me feel guilty.

As I drove to the mall, I figured out how to manage everything. I'm a Libran, so I strive for balance and beauty. Or at least, a bridge over chaos. I'd get Rose settled in the guest room, then call Becky and make a date for lunch on Wednesday or Thursday. Surely by then Rose would have found herself a shelter and I could tend to the problems in my own family.

I parked near the Food Court entrance, bought a pricey cup of cappuccino at a Starbucks kiosk, and sat at one of the tables, wondering who I was looking for or, more accurately, who was looking for me. I'd hardly got to lick the cinnamon milk froth when a voice behind me whispered, "Mrs. Hauser? Cathy's mom?"

My former married name was like a chilly blast from the past. I turned in the voice's direction. *Rose Red*, was my first thought at seeing before me the frail young woman with raven black hair peeking out from under a flowered head scarf, skin like fresh cream, and a rosy blush across her cheekbones. She was wearing a long, loose gray dress. Her dark glasses didn't quite succeed in hiding the yellowed skin around one eye. In one hand she was holding a neon pink plastic gear bag, in the other a small boy's arm, and her grip on both had an air of desperate determination. "I'm Rose Abdul—but you might remember me as Rose Fiorella?— and this is my son, Hari." Rose's voice was harsh and low. I had to lean forward to hear her.

I'm going to have a word with that Cathy, was my second thought. "Rose . . . and Harry . . . hello. I'm Cass. Cass Shipton now. I hope you like doggies, Harry. There's a doggie at the house where you're going to spend the night." The boy, who looked about five years old, was in need of a good wash, his face and hands grubby, his shirt stained.

"Hari," the boy corrected me. His large brown eyes, fringed in black lashes, stared up at me sadly. "Mommy forgot my Pooh bear," he said.

I bet they're hungry, was my third thought. We were surrounded by attractive food booths, with their competing sweet and savory aromas. My mind's eye, the clairvoyant one, finally kicked in with a vision. It was just a man's face, suffused with rage, looming up over us in a threatening fashion. The image vanished an instant after it appeared, but I've learned to pay attention. It pushed me into deciding that a home-cooked meal would be best. I bundled Rose and Hari into my Jeep, and we took off immediately.

On the way home, Rose thanked me effusively but said little else about herself. "If you will allow me to use your phone, I'll start calling right away for a place to stay." Her raspy voice tried to sound self-assured. "We left in such a hurry, there was no time to make an arrangement. But I've worked as a lab technician, and I have friends and associates. I'm sure I can find something for us."

She sounded anything but confident.

Chapter Two

So, what have we here? . . . It's a smelly little person. Under my watchful gaze, Scruffy sniffed over Hari's hair, face, shirt, and sneakers. The little boy only giggled. Then he clutched the dog's shaggy fur with both hands and looked directly into his eyes, nose to nose. "What's your name?" he shouted.

"Doggie doesn't like that, dear," I warned Hari.

Although he'd had little experience with small children, Scruffy merely shook off the boy, none too gently. *Hey, who does this shortie think he is—alpha pup?* He stalked away for a long drink, followed by Hari, who was giggling again. Leaning over, Hari's head bounced upside down as he watched Scruffy lap up water.

"Look at how doggie drinks with his tongue, Mama!" Hari stuck his finger in the water bowl and splashed some water on Scruffy's nose.

"His name is Scruffy, and he likes to play ball. See that orange ball under the rocking chair? That's an old favorite."

"Play nice with the doggie, Hari," said his mother in her strange whisper. She stood drooping beside the kitchen chair like a wounded butterfly afraid to light anywhere.

"Would you like to see your room, Rose? Maybe you'd enjoy

relaxing for a bit while I make us a little lunch?" She looked ready
to topple over. July or not, it would be chicken soup for these two
waifs. *But first*, I thought, *Rose should put her feet up for a few minutes*. Without waiting for a response, I picked up her gear bag and
headed for the stairs. On the second floor of my old saltbox cottage are two matching guest rooms, sharing a bathroom, always
kept ready for my children's rare visits.

"I stay with doggie." Hari had claimed the orange ball and was
holding it up in the air, just out of Scruffy's reach.

"Play nice with Hari, Scruffy," I said.

Docilely, my guest followed me upstairs, where I led her to
the bedroom with pale rose wallpaper to match her name. We
Wiccans are into the Law of Sympathies. "Hari can sleep in the
other twin bed, if you like. There are some old toys in the chest
in the hall—maybe even a teddy. Let Hari help himself to anything he wants. Maybe a stuffed animal that will make him feel
comforted."

Rose had taken off her dark glasses. Her eyes were a soft
brown; around one of them, there were several ugly rings of yellow. For a few long moments, she stood looking at the room as if
spellbound. Then she turned around swiftly and threw her arms
around me. "Oh, you are so kind," she said in her strange voice.

I was sorry she did that, because as often happens with me,
when she touched me I absorbed more physically and sensed
more emotionally than I wanted to about Rose's troubled life, including a throat injury caused by being choked half to death. Was
that a commitment I felt coming on? "Lie down for a few minutes, Rose—I insist. I'll send Hari to get you when lunch is ready,
okay?"

She smiled wanly, nodded, and sat on the edge of one of the
twin beds. The open window between them had a white ruffled
Cape Cod curtain that gave the room an air of yesteryear, of more
innocent times. I'd taken the time to arrange a little bouquet of
fresh lavender blooms and tea roses in a milk-glass vase. A calming, cheerful scent. Rooms have their magic, too. I hoped this

one would confer a peaceful spirit. Rose swung her legs up, lay back, and closed her eyes with a sigh. I tiptoed away.

I found Hari climbing up on the living room window seat where Scruffy was sitting upright, gazing attentively out the bay window. It was nearly time for the mailman to ease along in his little white truck and stop at our mailbox. A good distance to the main road, the mailbox was nearly invisible behind a wall of pines, but the mailman's appearance would not go unheralded. Two noses pressed against the glass. Scruffy gave the child a look of disgust and moved as far away as he could. *Get a life, kid.*

"Hi, Hari. Come on in the kitchen with me, and we'll make lunch. Do you want to help set the table?"

The boy came obediently enough but put his hands behind his back when I handed him three soup spoons. "That's for girls to do," he said. Beneath those appealing dark curls, his eyes were self-assured, his little chin set stubbornly.

It wasn't my job to reeducate the child, but I did lay my hand softly on his head and say a few silent words, more or less a blessing. "May his mind be open to light, his heart to love."

Although she got busy calling right after lunch, not surprisingly, Rose's whispered pleas found no immediate place for herself and the boy at any of the shelters where she had contacts. There were waiting lists; they would get back to her. You don't often see someone actually wringing her hands, but Rose did exactly that, looking at me beseechingly. When Hari trotted after Scruffy onto the kitchen porch, she whispered, "It's very important that we hide somewhere. My husband . . ." She seemed unable to continue.

"Let me see what I can do." In the privacy of my office, I called Phillipa and explained the situation. "The girl is exhausted and desperate. She's been beaten in the past, and she's in fear of her life. Ask Stone if he can help, and let me know what he suggests, okay?"

"Did you say Cathy sent these people to you?"

"What could I do? When she called me, Rose and Hari were already on the bus to Braintree."

"You could say a few sharp words to Cathy, but I know you won't. Give me a few minutes."

Phillipa called back shortly. "Stone will meet you at the station, to have a photo taken of that eye and help the girl to get a restraining order. He'll set up an appointment with a friend at legal services. Get some judge to grant Rose a quickie temporary custody before the father can claim she's kidnapped the child. That's very important, otherwise Rose will find herself in deep trouble, maybe lose the kid. Did you say his name was Abdul? Another complication, I guess you know. Stone thinks maybe he can get her into a shelter here in Plymouth, at least within a day or two. It's a place that has the advantage of being not very well known, and the woman who runs it is a tigress. You'll love her."

"Oh, Phil . . . you're a lifesaver. And I mean that literally."

"Yeah, yeah. Pack them up, and I'll see you at the station. I wouldn't want to miss anything, you know."

With Stone to speed up the wheels of justice, our plans for Rose went ahead very smoothly. A place for her and the boy at St. Rita's House (so named because the commodious brick building had once been a convent) would be available by Thursday evening. Rose and Hari would stay with me until the shelter could take her. Rose assured me she'd told no one of her plans, had contacted only my daughter for help because Cathy was a school friend unknown to her husband Rasheed. Her call had been made from a pay phone using a phone card, so there would be no record on Rasheed's monthly statement. After her husband had threatened to kill her if she wouldn't go along with his plans to move his family to Saudi Arabia, she'd thought out her escape very carefully and didn't think it was possible that Rasheed could trace her to me.

On the strength of St. Rita's promise, I called Becky and made a date for lunch on Friday. She sounded pleased, not at all too busy to fit in some time for her mother, even though she was working full-time as an associate at Lowell, FitzGerald & Lowell, her husband's law firm.

"What's bringing you to town?" she asked. "I can't believe it's shopping."

I'm not known for my devotion to fashion, although I have smartened up some since I met Joe, particularly my lingerie—which gave me the idea to answer, "Just thought I'd get a jump start on my trousseau. Braintree Mall is no inspiration at all."

"Oh, Mom . . . is this it, finally? Ever since that Ulysses guy took you to Athens and you came back wearing the flashy emerald, we've all been holding our breath, waiting for an announcement of The Big Day. And waiting and waiting. Never mind; whatever you're up to, you can tell me about it over lunch. I know the most fabulous new place—The California Café."

"How about lunch at the Ritz, instead? My treat." Indeed it would be my treat—I loved the Ritz, even though the new owners kept chipping away at its former elegance.

"Mom, I know you'll just adore the café—it's such fun. And you have to try the mesquite-grilled rattlesnake sausage. You won't believe how good it is."

"True, I won't. Okay," I conceded, "but it's still my treat. And that Ulysses guy's name is Joe."

"Right, Mom. Keep weaving. See you on Friday."

Keep weaving, indeed! But I was at a loss to explain to myself why Joe and I hadn't set the date We'd certainly talked about it, laughed about it, dreamed about it. When could Joe arrange for a month off from saving the planet? Would I refrain from visions of villains during that same window of opportunity? Where would it be? Not Athens, for sure, although I have to admit that the memory of Joe dancing Zorba the Greek–style with his cousins certainly was a turn-on. Just thinking about it brought on a full-body rush of warmth that definitely wasn't a hot flash.

Then there was the question of who would officiate. Joe had been brought up in the Greek Orthodox church. I was a born-again

Wiccan, but I was also a middle-class gal who liked things to be sewn up legally. Perhaps a civil ceremony followed by a handfasting? We'd both been married before and had to get our divorce papers in order. And it would be really nice if I could also get all my children together for the ceremony. But afterward, how would they react when they witnessed Joe and me tying the knot—literally—in the old Wiccan way? I decided to sound out Becky, the most conventional of my three children.

When I'd talked to her today, Becky certainly hadn't sound stressed or depressed. On the contrary, she seemed to be the same confident, efficient young woman as ever, managing to combine marriage and a law career without breaking a sweat. I'd hung up with a hopeful heart. Maybe Cathy was just being over-dramatic. It had been known.

When the phone rang, I thought it must be Becky with some change in plan. My gift of clairvoyance rarely clues me in to who's at the other end of the line. Instead, my psychic sense saves itself for the really big stuff, like who's murdering whom. So I was surprised and thrilled to hear Joe's deep, sexy voice.

"Hello, sweetheart. God, do I miss you!" Although somewhat diluted by the distance it was traveling, his intimate tone touched my skin like a caress.

"Where are you, darling?" This is always my first question.

"Now, don't get upset, Cass. I just want you to know I'm all right. In fact, now that I'm talking to you, I'm fine. Do you want the good news or the bad news first?"

"What bad news?" I demanded.

"I'm in an Australian hospital," Joe said. "Rather a nice hospital, and we'll be out in a day or two—nothing to be concerned about. They offered me a chance to phone home, and I was delighted to take advantage of the opportunity. I really needed to hear your voice."

"What's the medical term for 'nothing to be concerned about'?"

"Costochondritis. Grazed hip needed a few stitches. All fixed up now, but there are a few formalities. . . ."

"Costo what?"

"It's like a punch in the ribs. A little cortisone fixed me up."

"Are you in trouble with the law? Shouldn't you have called an attorney . . . I guess it's solicitor there."

"Greenpeace looks after that. Not to worry, sweetheart."

"So, what did you do this time? As an engineer, aren't you supposed to stay with the ship and keep your head down?"

"Yes . . . well . . . I made the error of offering to man one of the inflatable boats trying to blockade the nuclear shipment. Hey, I wasn't the only lunatic. I was joined by a member of the New South Wales Parliament. But then two of the protesters leapt into the sea to hold up a banner right in front of the freighter—only about four hundred meters away. Its skipper had to take evasive action. One of the kids got swamped, and I jumped in to give him a hand."

"Oh, Joe . . ." I wailed. "That was very brave, and quite sappy."

"I know . . . I know . . . 'She loved me for the dangers I had passed.' But you haven't asked me about the good news yet."

"Tell me now. I can't wait."

"I'm coming home. I'll be there in—let's see—four to five days."

"Oh, darling . . ." I felt an upsurge of such indescribable longing—and such sweet satisfaction in the way Joe had said "coming home," as if I had become his home.

"Now tell me about you," Joe said. "All quiet and serene? Just a little sedate spellworking with the girls?"

I laughed. "Oh, that is so sexist. 'Girls' indeed! And when has my life ever been serene? Cathy has sent me an abused wife and her son to hide. Becky's got some kind of marital difficulties—we're having lunch on Friday. There's an Esbat coming up at the full of the moon, which is next Tuesday. Heather's invited a couple of Druids as guests. Husband and wife. She's in a wheelchair. He wants us to look into some suspicious deaths at—"

"*Jesu Christos*, sweetheart! Please don't get into anything dangerous. No crime solving until I get back there to . . ." Joe's voice was breaking up. I couldn't hear the rest of his words, and maybe that was just as well.

"Listen, darling, this isn't a great connection, so let's say good-bye for now. Call me when you know your flight! I love you."

" . . . love you . . ." were the last two words I heard before the line went dead.

By Wednesday evening, Rose had her restraining order and a glimmer of hope that she might free herself from her husband, Rasheed, before he could make her a virtual prisoner in Saudi Arabia. Insisting on taking over the cleanup detail after dinner, Rose handed Hari two ginger cookies from the jar on the counter and shooed him into the living room to watch TV "with the big bushy dog."

That kid can't hang on to anything. Scruffy followed Hari's trail of cookie bits with scornful attention.

I took the opportunity to check my computer for orders. My son, Adam, the computer whiz who lived too far away in Atlanta, had set me up with a Web site, catalog, and on-line business capability that had enlarged my customer base and my income in a most gratifying way. My office, in what used to be the borning room, a cozy nook next to the kitchen, looked out on a graceful cluster of white birch through which I could see the Atlantic in all its moods. Soon I was pleasantly immersed in printing out orders I would box up later. The "Sweet Dreams" Moon Pillows were on a roll, Love Potion XXX (a massage oil) was getting to be a real hot item, and my own special tea blends were perennial favorites. Printing out a rush order for Quiet Child Tea, I made a mental note to present a box of that calming bedtime drink to Rose. Clearly, this was an upsetting time for her son.

So it was that neither Rose at the sink nor I at my computer was keeping a close eye on Hari, who had become bored with the early evening cartoons. As I reconstructed the scene later, the cookies gone, Scruffy had sneaked away for a quiet nap in my bedroom, which was on the first floor, but he was soon tracked down by his new nemesis. The phone was on my night table. Hari knew his numbers and had been taught how to call home. The clever little boy had paid attention, too, when we were driving away from Braintree Mall. Just to make Rose feel more comfortable, I'd chatted away about Plymouth and my house on Black Hill Point. Maybe he didn't get it all just exactly right, but apparently it was close enough. When the little boy put the phone receiver back, he must have left it a little askew, which is how I found it much later. After exploring my bedroom (a person who lives alone can always tell if someone has been fooling around with her stuff), Hari ran upstairs to forage in the toy chest built in under the slanted ceiling.

Not yet recovered from the exhaustion that comes from acting brave while feeling terrified, Rose started upstairs early to get ready for bed, meeting Hari coming down. The boy carried a battered teddy and a book, *Make Way for Ducklings*, which he ordered his mother to read to him. Taking Rose's hand, he turned to say, "Night, night, Scruffy. Night, night, Aunt Cass. Daddy is going to bring my Pooh bear."

Rose smiled at me over his head. "Maybe we'll find you a new Pooh some day soon. Wouldn't you like that?"

"No!" Hari said, kicking the stair rise. "No, no, no!"

Chapter Three

Tomorrow I would certainly be tied up with the needs of my houseguests, so after Rose and Hari went to bed, I carried the printed orders down to my cellar workroom. Sturdy pine shelves, once filled with a winter's supply of my grandma's home-canned fruits and vegetables, now housed dried herbs, essential oils, beeswax, charcoal, unbleached linen, and the products I created from them.

In the center of this fragrant room was an ancient scarred gate-leg table over which hung a cord with a green-shaded lamp that did not shine as far as the cobwebby corners. A little spooky at night, but I was used to it. Sometimes when I stared at the brass scales softly reflecting the lamplight, I'd be transfixed with one of those instant visions that trouble me from time to time—revelations that never seemed to be good news. I purposely avoided fixing on the gleaming brass that night, which was mistake number two.

Often Scruffy would come down to keep me company, lying under the table, sighing if I took too long. Here I assembled and boxed the new orders, inserted packing slips, and pasted on my preprinted labels.

It was after midnight when I began stacking the finished orders to bring them upstairs for mailing tomorrow. With my arms full of packages, I became aware of a barely audible rumble under the table. *Some stranger is outside, and he's up to no good,* that low growl warned me. Scruffy sprang out from under the table, his fur standing on end in a stripe down his back. *Just let me outdoors, Toots. I'll frighten the living daylights out of him.*

But we never got to surprise the stranger. Quite the reverse.

Just as I put one foot on the first stair, Scruffy in the lead as usual, stalking his prey on padded paws, there was a crash of glass overhead. The cellar door, tucked away beside the kitchen fireplace, was almost but not entirely closed. Abandoning the sneaky approach, Scruffy hurtled up the stairs, barking loudly, and crashed into the room. Wood banged wildly against fieldstone. A platter fell to the floor. Dropping the packages, I rushed after the dog, just in time to see that a man's arm was reaching through the broken glass of the back door. With one magnificent leap straight across the room, Scruffy caught the intruder's sleeve in his teeth. The man screamed, the shirt tore, and Scruffy fell onto his rump.

Let me out! Let me get him! Leaping up instantly, Scruffy's lip curled back, and he commenced growling and clawing at the door.

"Daddy! Daddy!" Hari came running down from the second floor, tears streaming down his face. "Was that my daddy? Did you hurt him, you naughty doggie?"

"No way, Buster," I said to Scruffy. Snapping the leash that always hangs by the back door onto the dog's collar, I pulled him away from the broken glass on the floor. "I'm calling the cops."

Rose rushed down from the bedroom—white-faced, barefooted, wearing only a sleep T-shirt. Seizing Hari in her arms, she plunked down on the stairs and hung on with surprising strength even when he flailed and yelled for his daddy.

We could hear the footsteps of someone running away, at least as far as the pines. I grabbed the kitchen wall phone but got no dial tone. Of course—the intruder had cut the wires. My handbag was hanging on the knob in back of the open dining room door. Cursing the delay, I fished out my cell phone and, with a shaky finger, punched in nine-one-one. "This is Cassandra Shipton on Black Hill Point. Someone just tried to break in. Yes . . . yes . . . smashed the glass in my kitchen door. Please get a cruiser here right away. I think he ran into the pines up near the road. Hurry—maybe you can catch him."

I wanted to call Stone, too, but the dispatcher told me to stay on the line until help arrived. "I'm contacting the cruiser now," she said. "Is anyone hurt?"

"No, no one is hurt. But hurry, please. He may come back."

Within a few minutes the driveway was jammed with two cruisers and an off-duty policeman driving his own Chevy. At one in the morning, crime was at a low ebb in Plymouth. Scruffy had both paws on the kitchen windowsill, ears alert, scanning the darkness, his trophy sleeve abandoned. Hari's voluble protests had diminished to a rising and falling whine. To prevent his running outside, Rose was still holding him close. I picked up the sleeve Scruffy had dropped and held it up for her to see. It seemed to me there was a flash of recognition in her eyes.

"Just keep Hari inside and watch out for that broken glass. Everything will be all right now. Don't you worry." Grabbing the end of Scruffy's leash, I pushed aside the mess of broken glass with my shoe and hurried out to meet the patrolmen and describe the incident. One of the guys was grinning as if he'd just been invited to a party. Another was waving a drawn gun and looking around nervously, ready to shoot at the first moving shadow. They didn't inspire confidence. I needed Clint Eastwood, and they'd sent me Austin Powers. "I have a young woman staying with me. It may have been her husband. There's a restraining order."

Meanwhile Scruffy seemed to think he'd been invited out to bring down the intruder single-pawed and was lunging forward repeatedly if unsuccessfully. *Hey, Toots, let me at him. I'll run him down faster than these big guys. They couldn't smell their way out of a paper bag.* Truth be told, I was tempted to let the dog go, if only to lead the officers in the right direction. I was more than a little annoyed at how long it took them to get moving. I feared that Rasheed would be long gone. All he would have to do is to lose himself in the woods between my house and Phillipa's place. Surely he took off as soon as the first cruiser arrived. I wondered where he had parked his car, making a mental note to ask Rose for a vehicle description.

Later, when the clumsy search for the intruder had petered out, Rose was questioned by one of the officers. She insisted that the man couldn't be Rasheed, that her husband didn't own a shirt that matched the plaid sleeve, and there was no way for him to know where she was staying.

"Oh, Rose," I said. "Who else?"

Her small chin went up in a determined fashion. Hari had quieted in her arms but was not too exhausted to assert, "Daddy said he'd bring my Pooh bear."

No point in waking Stone now, I decided. But when I called early the next morning, I got Phillipa instead. "Stone's gone already to have a talk with the M.E. Another death at Manomet Manor. Elderly man, a little senile, no close family apparently."

My clairvoyant sense clicked in. In one eye blink, I saw a Valkyrie nurse with shoulder-length blond hair and a smile that turned down at the corners. She was coming at me with something that looked like a hypodermic needle raised like a weapon to strike. Funny, I thought. Most women's mouths turn up. There was something strange about her eyes too, a fold of flesh that made them seem to slant downward like her mouth. An instant later, the vision disappeared.

Feeling nauseous, I dropped into a kitchen chair. I really didn't have the energy to deal with this now. I shook my hands to dispel the negative image, while Phillipa rattled on, unaware.

"Dr. DeBoer—he's the director—signed the death certificate, respiratory failure, and in the absence of family, arranged for a cremation, to be paid for by the old guy's trust. But there was some kind of screwup with the funeral home, and the M. E. got into it. He called Stone—he's not so sure about the cause of death and wants to do a lab workup."

"Tell Stone to check out a full-figured blond nurse with a mouth that turns down. Her eyes, too. See if the recently departed gent happened to be in her care."

"Oh sure, Cass. He's going to love that. Is that what you wanted to tell him?"

"No. That was what came to me while you were talking. And talking. I called for help. We had some big trouble here last night." I told her about our break-in; that I needed to get Rose somewhere safer.

"Well, enough about the Manor, then. Stone's probably seen the reports of your break-in, but I'll check when he calls in later. I'm sure he can make arrangements to get those two refugees into St. Rita's immediately. Boy, you can't stay out of trouble for two minutes, can you?"

"You could be a little more sympathetic, Phil. The window in my kitchen door is shattered, and my guests are not holding together very well, either."

"Of course I'm sympathetic," she asserted. "You can always count on me for a little sisterly support and superior tarot divination, you know that. It's such an adventure just being your friend. You're aware, aren't you, that a glass-paneled door is an invitation to a break-in?"

"Yes, but I like the view."

"Well, you'd better get your protective spells into gear, then. Got any red candles?"

"Ah, protection with passion. I like that idea." I drifted away into thoughts of Joe's Mediterranean eyes, his brawny arms, his tantalizing beard, his mouth. . . . It would be a good thing to have Rose and Hari settled safely somewhere else before my lover came home.

So I have to admit I breathed a sigh of relief the next morning, when I turned my charges over to the doyenne of St. Rita's.

Stone's "tiger" turned out to be a dove—Serena Dove, a fine-boned, olive-skinned woman with wild, wiry gray hair, a sweet smile, and shrewd, bright eyes that didn't miss a trick.

"Come in, friends. . . . Come in. We'll take good care of you, never fear," Serena said, gently taking the pink gear bag out of Rose's hands. Before we left the house, I'd slipped some special tea blends into that bag, along with a Moon Pillow stuffed with protective herbs and a lavender-scented candle—a Wiccan first-aid kit.

Rose smiled tentatively and allowed herself to be drawn into Serena Dove's calm aura. Hari hung back, a finger in his mouth, Cathy's old teddy bear under his arm. "You, too, little boy. You'll find some new pals here—just about your age, too." Serena had a soft, soothing voice, just this side of hypnotic, but that alert gaze moved on to consider me. She would have a talent for appraisal, but so did I. We tussled psychically for a moment, then called it a draw. "I've heard about you, Cassandra, from Stone. Some interesting things. You and his wife Phil and some other local women. And I know you had an incident at your house last night."

"Yes, it was very upsetting for Rose, and especially for Hari. I'm not absolutely sure, but I believe that our midnight visitor may have found us through a telephone call. Something to be on guard against." I nodded toward Hari, who had interested himself in a few children's books lying on the coffee table. He grabbed one, then darted back to be close to his mother. "I would say we're no longer incognito."

"You have to dial nine to get an outside line here. And we're prepared for unwanted visitors. Hiding identities isn't what we do, although if it becomes necessary, we know how to reach an underground that specializes in that sort of thing. Instead, we take full advantage of the law. I believe Rose already has a re-straining order and temporary custody. A date's been set for a more permanent custody arrangement. Her husband will be present at that hearing, of course," Serena warned. "She will have to face him in the courtroom. I'll be there with her."

"So will I. And I'll be bringing reinforcements. Just let me know when." I turned to Rose, who was looking slight and vulnerable, Hari leaning on her leg as if taped to it. But when I hugged the girl, I could feel the firmness of her resolve like a slender steel rod strengthening her backbone. "You're all right now," I said. With all my psychic energy, I was visualizing a protective white light surrounding Rose and her boy. "Blessed be."

The California Café was not the Ritz. But, then, neither was the Ritz anymore. I got the impression of a dizzying array of orange and pink zigzags. The slightly acrid smell of overworked grills and roasted garlic wafted into the waiting area. And there was something weird about the acoustics. Voices rose in a furious babble, mingled with a clash of cutlery and accompanied by soft rock a bit louder than was comfortable. Perhaps the noisy atmosphere was meant to create an air of excitement, a feeling of being at the center of a party.

We waited twenty minutes for our table, shouting at one another over the din as we stood in line, keeping our conversation on subjects suitable for sharing with a crowd of strangers. Becky didn't rag me about getting married. I didn't ask her what was wrong at home. Besides, it was a joy just to see her. She was wearing her chestnut brown hair in a new way, a short, stylish flip. Impeccably groomed in a navy suit, navy hose, and navy pumps, she carried a maroon briefcase that was almost feminine, and no handbag. But I'm her mother—I saw the shadow in her blue eyes.

Once we were seated, there was the business of the waiter reciting a long list of "specials," everything from rare tuna burgers to roasted ostrich filet, and taking our order for drinks. Becky ordered a Cosmopolitan; California Chardonnay for me. I would wait for the first fortifying sip before beginning to pry with a gentle guile. Meanwhile we studied our menus, whose size and content resembled an atlas of the world.

Mercifully, the drinks came quickly. "Cathy called me Monday," I began. The wine had a faintly corky taste.

"She's got some kind of wonderful new part in an O'Neill thing." Becky's Cosmopolitan looked delicious. I wanted to ask what went into it, but I feared to digress and lose my point.

"Yes. That's why she couldn't come out to visit you. She and Irene."

Becky flushed ever so slightly. "I miss her."

"I do, too. I wonder if she wouldn't do better in New York. That's where most of the theater hopefuls go."

"Someone in that bunch she was running with talked her into San Francisco. Los Angeles would have made more sense. I think she just wanted to get away. Far away." Becky took a sip of her drink and turned the page of her menu. I fancied that "from her mother" hung in the air unspoken. *All right, then. Let's get into it.*

"And what about you? How are you doing? Any lingering depression?"

She looked up, a quick, savvy glance. "So . . . Cathy told you . . . what?"

"Never mind Cathy. Why didn't you tell me?"

"Oh, that. I just missed a month, that's all. Before I could say anything, it was over."

"Becky, I want you to promise me that you'll let me know right away the next time you get pregnant. Will you do that?"

Her sadness was unmistakable. Not only in her eyes, but in the line of her brows, the set of her mouth, normally so cheerful. "There may not be a next time," she said.

"You and Ron are having problems?"

"Wait until I get hold of that Cathy. . . . I think I'll have the Angel Hair Pasta with Prawns. How about you?"

"Oh, anything except the rattlesnake. That's fine. You haven't answered my question."

"Honestly, Mother. Spare me the third degree. Is this why you suddenly needed to come to Boston to shop for your trousseau? And, by the way, when *are* you getting married?"

We were both saved from answering by the appearance of the waiter.

"Have you ladies decided? Need a few more minutes?" His eyes flicked to Becky's empty glass. "Another Cosmopolitan?"

Becky nodded curtly and gave him our order. "And bring us two Warm Hazelnut-crusted Goat Cheese Salads." Deliberately, she began chatting about the case she was working on, some corporate tax maneuver that would have put any reasonable person to sleep. It wasn't until we were having double espressos and tiny sorbets frozen inside orange skins that the first break came.

"They ought to give us miniature ice picks with these," I complained, hitting at the sorbet with the point of my spoon. A morsel flaked off and instantly melted.

"Sometimes I think Ron is seeing someone else," Becky said, her gaze fixed on the frozen dessert in front of her. "It's like I *know*, but I don't really. I suppose that doesn't make sense."

"Actually, it does make sense, dear. A husband and wife are so close that there's a kind of natural telepathy at work."

"Of course, *you'd* say that. You've always known everything that was going on with us."

"I wish. But my insights are only glimpses. Often I'm blind to the most important things. Your miscarriage is a case in point." I wondered if Becky had inherited a little of my clairvoyance. None of my children, so far, had revealed any signs of that gift. Mine had come, I felt sure, from my grandmother, so maybe psychic gifts did skip a generation.

"Oh, I feel so foolish, but I find myself checking up on him— you know, searching his pockets, examining his laundry, checking his credit card receipts. It's so despicable, I just hate myself." She thrust her spoon at the sorbet with disgust.

"I'm so sorry. It's awfully difficult to live in a state of suspicion, I know. Have you considered just asking him right out? This notion of yours didn't arrive out of the blue. Do you know how intuition works?"

"Yes, you've told me many times. It's little things that go by too fast for the ordinary five senses to pick up on. But I don't need intuition to tell me that he doesn't find me sexually attractive anymore."

"Oh. I see. Do you think he may be afraid to put you through another mis— Or maybe he's feeling unsure of his own performance?"

"No."

I didn't ask her how she knew that. "What are you going to do?"

"I don't know. I have to decide. Please don't do anything hokey like spells and magic stuff."

"I won't even advise you—how about that?"

She laughed. The ice was broken, and even the sorbet was melting a bit. "That will be the day," she said as we dug into our desserts.

"All I ask is that you let me know if you're okay and what's going on, and most of all, if there's anything I can do to help, short of full-scale voodoo," I said. Of course, I would say a few words for Becky when our circle raised a cone of power at the next Esbat. But "to keep silent" was part of the spell.

The rest of our luncheon talk was warm and confiding, with fervent assurances on both sides that we would stay closer in future. But I knew that life has a way of interfering with such well-meant promises. I only hoped I left Becky feeling less alone.

Driving home in the glaze of commuter traffic, I resisted the impulse to visit some well-deserved hex on Ron. Not even a little one, like hemorrhoids. Not that I was sure my hexes would work—although strange things had happened in the past when I didn't watch myself closely. What I was sure of is that "thoughts are things" and—the first rule of Wicca—evil thoughts come back to the sender threefold. "Harm no one, and you may do as you will."

Chapter Four

The Esbat of the Thunder Moon was aptly named. As the magnificent moon of July rose over ominous black clouds on the horizon, thunder rumbled in the distance. The sultry air was heavy with negative foreboding. I hoped Maeve's wheelchair was safely grounded—it was a fair distance from the stone circle on the hill to the safety of Heather's sturdy house.

We five, with the Kellihers as guests, had gathered to celebrate the full moon in the ancient Wiccan way. Heather Devlin (née Morgan), being hostess, was therefore priestess of this celebration. Still wrapped in that honeymoon glow, she herself shone with a warm radiance as she cast and consecrated the circle. A fire leaped at its center where a flat gray rock served as our altar. With a bronze braid of hair nearly reaching her waist and a green linen dress belted in the medieval fashion, she could have passed for Maid Marian—especially when she raised her silver-handled athame to invoke the four powers. From the east, the inspiration of air. From the south, the energy of fire. From the west, the healing of water. And from the north, the oneness of earth. My aromatic herbs, arranged earlier in the crisscrossed wood, surrounded us in heady scents.

Phillipa had written our invocations, and now as she listened to Heather speak the cadenced phrases, she leaned forward, listening intently. With wings of dark hair and a wicked smile to match her wit, there was more than a hint of the dark goddess Hecate to Phillipa. Bringing her own unique talent to our circle, she was one of those tarot readers who could hardly look at a spread of cards before making some amazing psychic leap. Ask her to read at your peril! And her poetry had that same authority; words spoken now by Heather to align ourselves with the Eternal Spirit that lights the Moon, the Sun, and all our lives.

As always, it was pretty awesome and never failed to send a small thrill of anticipation down my spine. I glanced over at Maeve Kelliher, curious about her reaction. Sketchbook in her lap, she appeared to be transfixed in unblinking attention. When her hand snaked out over the wheelchair's arm, Deidre took hold of it in a reassuring way. "You okay?" she whispered.

"She's fine," Brian whispered back, smiling at his wife fondly. "Throes of creative inspiration."

"Heather uses her dagger almost like the Druid sword," Maeve murmured.

"Athame," Deidre explained in low tones. "Wiccan ritual knife. But don't you worry, it's not supposed to be used to cut anything, or be clipped to our belts for a trip to the supermarket. It's just for meetings."

Comfort was something Deidre was used to doling out, like cookies. Although her mop of blonde curls and baby blue eyes made her seem a child herself, she was mother to four, the latest only a few months old. Fortunately, energy ran high in Deidre. Besides the demands of family life, she was an arts and crafts queen, too—expert in everything from needlepoint to woodburning to throwing a mean little pot. She also created anatomically correct poppets and amulets with surprising attributes. Her husband, Will Ryan, a local fireman, was still under the impression that our circle meetings were some kind of women's craft exchange or Magic Chef party—which wasn't all that far from the truth.

"Right now I could use a chair like Maeve's—my knees are

killing me," Fiona whispered fiercely in my ear. The oldest among us, our local librarian, Fiona, once a flower child and still a free spirit, was our serendipitous finder, whether accidentally laying her hand on some obscure pamphlet with just the information that was wanted, or dowsing with her crystal pendant to discover a missing person. Even more notably, she was also mistress of the Glamour, able to change her appearance with a shift of consciousness that had us all envious—especially when her podgy little self would suddenly metamorphose into a regal presence.

It was Fiona who'd brought us together a few years ago for a "women's study group," but it was the discovery of Wicca that had bound us to one another—our own brand of Wicca, a religion with no dogma and no governing body. Its simple ethic was to revere the earth and all living things; its creed offered free will as long as no harm be done to another. There are holy days, based on the old pagan fetes of the earth's yearly cycle, and there's a sense of the goddess as well as the god in the Deity. We were looking for something that had been lost along the way to civilization—the power of the female and, of course, the alchemy of transformation—popular magic!

"Druids observed the same holy days. And theirs was an equal-opportunity priesthood—women officiated as well as men," Brian was saying. "All that, and tree magic, too." Leaning against a thick old maple, hanging on to Maeve's chair as if it might take off without him, he looked like a blond god of the woods—the Green Man himself! What a handsome devil, I thought. From across the stone circle, Phillipa raised a slim black eyebrow and winked at me—reading my mind again!

In contrast to Brian's vigor, Maeve appeared pale and plain, although there was a sweetness to her expression that seemed to radiate from her inner being. A mass of brown curly hair was her best feature, but her face was angled by illness, and there were blue smudges under her hazel eyes. Flipping open her sketchbook, she began to draw Heather, catching the play of firelight and moonlight on her long hair, her patrician cheekbones, and the upraised athame in her hand. Although done very quickly, the sketch caught the essence of Heather and the occasion in a few bold strokes. I was impressed.

With Maeve's crippled body and Fiona's aches and pains on our minds, that evening we were concentrating on healing, passing the elaborate white work candle that Heather, our candle-magician, had created for us. She'd filled it with tiny seashells and silver charms, the surface decorated with gold-painted runes meaning Goddess-knows-what. We offered our wishes to the altar's flame; I had written several on small folded slips of paper—for Becky, for Rose, and for Maeve and Fiona.

After visualizing our wishes, we began to pass the energy of our bodies from hand to hand, clockwise, slowly at first, then faster and faster, until it seemed too powerful to contain. At last, with a signal from Heather, we threw up our arms, releasing the cone of power into the night air. The ominous overcast had completely obscured the full moon. At that very moment, the rain began, just a few refreshing drops, but a flash of lightning illuminated the sky, the thunder following rather more closely than was comfortable. We were, after all, standing under the trees.

"Let's get out of here—fast!" Phillipa voiced it for all of us. Hastily, Heather dispersed the circle with her athame, and Deidre quenched the fire. We ran for the house just as the rain began to pelt us heavily. Phillipa took Fiona's arm, helping her along the path.

Brian pushed Maeve's chair so fast he outdistanced all of us. With each heavy step he trod, a word thudded forth. "This has been a truly . . . amazing . . . interlude."

Stamping into Heather's marble-floored entry hall, we shook off droplets like a pack of wet dogs. Just as that image popped into my head, Heather's canine crew began to stir. A muffled cacophony of barking ensued. "Where are all the little critters hiding tonight?" I asked Heather.

"Tucked up in their kennels and the conservatory. They're a

bit overwhelming, and their buffet manners leave a lot to be desired. Speaking of which, let's open the wine!" Heather shepherded us into her Victorian red living room, handsomely furnished by generations of sea captains. Mercifully, Heather's AC made her home an oasis in the July sweats.

"Oh, this is heavenly," Fiona sighed, falling onto a velvet fainting couch with her hand laid gracefully to her forehead, fingers curled outward. Clearly, she was ready to be waited on.

I brought her a glass of the delicate Moselle that Heather had opened. "Here, m'lady—something to lubricate those old bones. Do you want me to fix you a plate?" Heather's new housekeeper had laid out a delectable spread for us before disappearing into her private rooms. My clairvoyant sense, however, kept jumping in with flashes of Lucrezia's door opening a crack and her ear pressed against it.

"Oh, *would* you?" Fiona breathed. Was she indeed changing before my eyes, becoming opulently curved instead of dumpy? Her figure on the couch swam in my vision, in and out of glamour. The carroty-gray braids coiled around her head took on a regal glow. Even her fingers seemed slimmer and longer, more expressive as she stretched out her arm and several silver bracelets rang together like small bells.

"Fiona, you are too much!" Phillipa was seeing what I saw.

"Jealous . . . jealous . . ." Deidre laughed at the two of us.

Brian was getting a plate for his wife. I had the impression that, even with his back turned, he was keeping an eye on Maeve. The strength of their mutual love was almost visible to me, like a silver bond that stretched from one to the other wherever they were.

I could hear Maeve explaining to Fiona that she'd been on crutches or in a wheelchair ever since she was three, a victim of childhood polio. We were all listening, of course, while trying to look as if we weren't—curious about the cause and extent of Maeve's handicap. Fiona was insisting that Maeve take two of her several bracelets, which were carved with magical symbols.

"They'll do you a world of good, dear." Never mind that they hadn't cured Fiona.

"How's the book going?" I asked Brian.

"The text is finished, but I still find myself puttying it up here and there." Brian peered closely at a tiny apricot pastry, decided it would do, and added it to the plate. "We try to keep her salt intake low, to ward off edema," he explained. "Maeve's got two more illustrations to go, the Yule log and whatnot. Moving took a big chunk of our time and energy. Then with Maeve winding up in the hospital, it's a wonder we're in as good shape as we are. Deadline's October 30th."

"Oh, heavens. Three whole months!" I said.

"It goes by damned fast," he said, his brows knitting into one across his intense blue eyes. Maybe it was the wiry blond beard, but it was easy for me to picture him in another time frame, wearing a roughly woven, hooded garment.

Impulsively I asked, "Do you ever wear Druid regalia?"

He smiled. It was a smile that would melt any woman's bones, and her inhibitions as well. "When the occasion calls for it," he said. "Perhaps one day . . ."

Before I could hear more, however, Maeve gave a soft cry, and Brian hurried away to her. "Oh, Brian," she exclaimed. "Fiona is going to check herself into Manomet Manor this fall, too, at the same time as me. She's going for the pain management clinic, and some intensive physical therapy. And we're both going to do the aquatic therapy, too. I'll feel so much better knowing I'll have a friend in that weird pink palace. We can commiserate about the terrible food and Nurse Roughneck's massages."

"Oh no," Phillipa cried out. "Fiona!" I wailed. "I feel a *big* cloud of suspicion hanging over the Manor. I hope you're listening, too, Maeve. Brian?"

"I'm not happy about this, either." A spasm of pain or guilt crossed his face. "I have to be in New York for a conference with our editor, and Maeve can't be persuaded to go with me. She insisted it would be an ideal time for her to take some physical therapy at the Manor. Maeve wants to be able to do more with crutches or a walker. Believe me, I've tried to reason with her." He smiled at his wife affectionately. "She's a stubborn little thing!"

"Oh, we'll be fine," Fiona said, waving her hand in the air as if to dismiss all our concerns. "You girls are such worrywarts. You all know I can take care of myself. I'll miss dear Omar Khayyám of course, and Persians are so sensitive. But then I thought, Heather will see that my old fellow gets sympathetic care at her shelter. I understand the cat house is quite jolly."

"Great Goddess," exclaimed Deidre, glancing with alarm at the bulging, old green reticule from which Fiona would never be parted. It lay on the floor beside the couch, spilling out a fan of esoteric pamphlets. "You're *not* bringing that nasty Colt forty-five!?"

"One of the most useful things Rob Angus Ritchie ever gave me," affirmed Fiona, patting the suspicious lump in the bottom of her reticule. "Officer's model, too. Never leave home without it."

"I didn't hear that," said Phillipa. "If I heard that, I'd have to speak to Stone about it."

"Just because you're hitched to a detective," Heather said as she moved gracefully around the room refilling glasses from the second bottle she'd opened, "you don't have to go all law-and-order on us. No need to worry, Fiona. Omar will get five-star treatment at Animal Lovers, plus the company of any number of fascinating females. All spayed, but nonetheless frolicsome. Maybe you'll decide to take one or more home with you? A nice little harem for Omar?"

Deidre pulled me away in the direction of the food so that she could lean over and whisper, "Don't you think this sudden onset of arthritis in Fiona has something to do with little Laura?"

Fiona's niece Belle MacDonald, having borne a baby out of wedlock, had parked the child with Fiona in order to go off un-encumbered to Harvard Law School. Laura Belle, a.k.a. "Tinker Belle," had soon become the joy of Fiona's solitary life, and her formerly chaotic home evolved into a child-centered haven. But the inevitable parting had happened much sooner than anticipated. Last spring, in an attack of maternal guilt, Belle reclaimed her adorable little daughter with the morning-glory eyes. Since her parents had sold their Iowa farm and moved East, Belle persuaded them to take over Fiona's role. Even worse, jealous of the child's love for Fiona, Belle had become very stingy about visits. Fiona was devastated.

"Yes, I'd made that connection, too. I've tried all my herbal remedies. Even the wintergreen rubs are doing nothing for her." Since I was standing there anyway, I refilled my plate with tiny prosciutto crescents and pine nut macaroons. "The situation is so complicated, I hardly know how best to word my spells. Maybe Tinker Belle ought be just where she is—with her natural mom. So I'm leaving it all up to the Universe of Infinite Solutions to sort out."

"Always the best way. And I'm saying a novena as well." Deidre was putting her chips on all the numbers. I often wondered how she juggled Wicca and the Church, but clearly she was untroubled by any sense of religious conflict. Or worries about her petite figure, either—she piled a pyramid of pastries on her plate.

"Not even Fiona will be able to smuggle a pistol into a medical facility," I said.

"I don't know. She's pretty resourceful."

"*I heard that,*" Fiona called over from her enthronement on the fainting couch. She was patting the arm of Maeve's chair. "I could use one of these on my bad days."

"Banish that thought," Phillipa said. "Your place is so crammed with stacks of books, we have to wedge through it sideways. Besides, haven't you been promised that the new drugs and a little physical therapy will soon have you whirling like a dervish?"

"If it's water exercise you need, ladies, my pool is available, and you are most welcome. If you don't mind sharing it with Honeycomb." Heather pulled back the drape to look out the bay window just as a bolt of lightning, simultaneous with an ear-splitting clap of thunder, struck something up on the hill. Every dog on the premises began barking or howling. "Of course, the pool, being outdoors, will have its drawbacks once fall comes. I wonder what the hell got hit?"

"We need to propitiate the gods," Brian said. "Hmmm. Let's see. A virgin sacrifice might do it." With the drapes opened, we could see another stab of lightning followed by a terrifying burst of thunder. I was standing beside the buffet with Deidre when the sudden brilliance in the sky gave me such a strange feeling I had to sit down.

"Well, don't look for a virgin here," Phillipa was saying as the room began to swim around me. "And besides, we suburban witches are too tenderhearted for that sacrifice sort of thing. Most of us make believe that our frying chickens were born in those little yellow plastic trays at the supermarket."

The warmly lit red walls, Phillipa's voice, and the storm all faded from my consciousness. I found myself in a dim blue corridor with a desk lighted by a green-shaded lamp at the end of it. There was a woman working at the desk, her blond head bent over some record sheets. A baby-faced man with an uptilted nose came out of the shadows behind her. He was wearing a white coat. As he leaned over her shoulder in the pool of light, I could see that his head was well-shaped, his light brown hair still thick but graying. Baby-face whispered in her ear. She looked up at him, laughing—her eyes had that downward slant that had come into my earlier visions. Getting up from her chair, the nurse took a key out of her pocket and unlocked a wall cabinet. I couldn't see what she was taking or putting back, but a moment later I saw her and the doctor enter one of the patient's rooms. His hand went under her skirt. Nuzzling his neck, she leaned against him as they went in the door. Smelling a strong, musky odor, I noticed I could almost read the room's number. Two something.

The next thing I knew, I was lying on the fainting couch and Fiona was standing beside me laying a cold cloth across my eyes. I knew it was her because of the tinkling bracelets. "Oh, damn, I didn't mean to do that," I said. My eyes opened to a circle of concerned faces and the familiar room spinning. Quickly I sat up to dispel the nausea.

"What did you see," demanded Phillipa. "Does anyone have paper and pencil?"

"I do," Maeve offered. "Here, use a page of my sketchbook."

"No, Maeve, you hang on to it," I said. "I'll describe the scene and the doctor while you draw your impression of my words. I don't know if what I saw has happened or will happen, but my feeling is, there was some sick combination of sex and death there." As I related the details of my vision, I could hear the bold sounds of Maeve's charcoal pencil.

"Cass is a clairvoyant," I heard Deidre whisper to Brian. "Every once in a while she keels over like this, and it's very informative. We've worked with the Plymouth Police, you know."

"Sure, they contact us on every major crime," Phillipa said. "And they tell us to stay out of it. But do we listen?"

"What the hell is going on in that place? 'Rehabilitation'—that's a laugh." Brian's voice was harsh with concern. "I'm damned sure I'm not allowing Maeve to go there ever again."

"Nonsense," said Maeve, quite firmly. Her legs might be weak, but there was a quiet determination in her tone. "It's a perfect opportunity for Fiona and me to do a little undercover work. Bit of a pun there. . . ." She giggled. Brian fumed.

Maeve was proving to be a girl after my own heart.

Chapter Five

Two days later, on an idyllic July evening, just as the sun was setting behind the pines and the whole sea was glowing with its reflection, Joe arrived in a Budget Rent-A-Car low-end Chevy. Ever since a letter bomb directed to our Wiccan apprentice, Freddie, had blown up his Hertz rental, he'd felt a tad unwelcome at their Logan Airport booth. *Hertz must be staffed with robots*, I thought, *not to appreciate a customer like Joe.* Not only was he handsome and sexy, he was what Phillipa called a mensch as well—a real grown-up man of strength, compassion, and integrity. They should be begging him to rent their Lincolns, waiving the insurance, rolling out the red carpet in the car lot. Well, my welcome would make up for all the inconveniences, and in consideration of that exhausting flight from Australia, I'd see that he got right into a comfortable bed—mine.

That furry-faced person is here again. Scruffy was always first at the window to check out visitors. I threw open the back door, and there was Joe, wonderfully tan and muscular, with a duffel bag slung over his shoulder that he instantly dropped to the porch floor. At once I was swept into his powerful arms for a long fiery kiss.

Scruffy registered his indifference to the homecoming hero by merely allowing himself to be patted while looking off into the distance with a bored expression. He was soon won over, however, by a brisk chest scratch and that fascinating duffel bag, scented no doubt with kangaroo, koala, and other delightfully exotic aromas.

Then Joe and I were locked in another clinch. The dog sighed heavily. *I suppose this means I'm to be booted out of the bedroom.*

"Right you are," I agreed when we came up for air. "As soon as I feed this guy. Aren't you hungry, darling? That airline food . . . And what about your ribs . . . and your hip. Are you in any pain?"

"Not now, honey." Whether he meant the food or the pain, I never found out, but his voice was deep and intimate. He kissed my neck and slid his lips around to the open collar of my shirt, his lower body pressing against mine. A hot thrill of desire flowed through me. Taking his hand, I led him into the bedroom, closing the door, making sure the latch was caught.

It was just getting dark, the sweet smell of phlox drifting through the open windows. We took off our clothes in the half-light, watching each other, connected heart and soul. Our love-making was like sailing off into another dimension where there were no borders between bodies and we were one universe together.

"Hmmmm. I guess your injuries haven't slowed you down much," I murmured, cradled in his arms. I'd been careful about not hugging him too tightly. The cut on his thigh was healing well, but what if an artery had been involved? "I missed you so much."

"And I missed you, honey. I thought about you all the time. Even when I was trying to stay afloat with my aching chest and bleeding leg, I was thinking, what am I doing in this damn cold ocean treading water? I ought to be on my way to Plymouth. I'm getting married to my angel—no offense. In my church, angels are divine beings with mysterious powers. So . . . when *are* we getting married? There's no reason to wait, except for a license."

"I like the simile. Wiccans believe in angels, too. Would that mean you're going to stay around for a while? Or were you plan-ning to wed, bed, and run. 'I do; wham, bam; thank you m'am.' "

He drew me against him for a kiss that was not an answer but was very sweet anyway. "It's my job," he said finally.

"You love it. And no wonder; it's heroic stuff, saving the earth."

He grinned. "No, it's you I love. When I'm saving the earth, I'm thinking of you." And he paused to give me charming evi-dence of that. "But there *is* a satisfaction to what we do. I can arrange to take more time off between assignments."

"Well," I said, stalling for time. Suddenly my independence seemed so precious, never having to explain an outrageous phone bill or a dented fender or a girls' night out making a little civic-minded magic. I forced myself to remember how lonely I'd been before Joe had dropped into my life, like a gift from the Goddess. "I want to get my family together for the ceremony, whatever kind we decide it should be. That's important to me."

"Is it possible? Isn't Cathy in California getting some big break in the theater?"

"Let me talk to everyone. What if we set the date for, say, Yule. Five months should give everyone time to make arrange-ments, including me."

"Yule. That's Christmas, right? Environmental emergencies should be at a low ebb at that time of year. We can take a nice long honeymoon somewhere tropical. And I know just the place. Traveling around with Greenpeace has its perks. You and I alone on a moonlit beach . . . a little rum, a little skinny-dipping . . ."

"Sounds like paradise to a New England gal," I said.

Wow! We had finally set a date. Well, not the exact day, but we'd definitely fixed on the season. Beautiful Yule, glowing festi-val of light and hope. Maybe I'd wear winter white and a circlet of holly in my hair, carry deep red roses. Embroidered by my imagination, the dress became velvet, with a trailing cloak trimmed with ermine. No, that wouldn't do. Heather would never speak to me again if I wore real fur. . . .

I didn't know what fantasies occupied Joe's mind while I went off on my little wedding-gown trip. Perhaps he was imagining me on the porch of a honeymoon hut filling his glass with champagne while wearing a see-through sarong—or some other improbable scenario. I'd better not wear white velvet, anyway. A formerly married woman with three grown children was definitely in way-off-white territory. If fact, maybe Merry-Matron green or Medicare blue would be a better choice.

"You're very quiet, honey. A golden doubloon for your thoughts."

"I was just thinking how lucky I am to have run into you on that endangered eagles controversy. It was definitely love at first sight. Or at least, lust."

"There was something about you that went right to my heart," he said. "I've always thought there was some witchcraft involved."

"It's magic all right. Watch what this voodoo can do," I said, running my hands over his chest and thighs and between his thighs.

But, yes, around ten-thirty, we were very hungry—and thirsty—when we emerged from the bedroom. A cranky Scruffy was lying on the tile in front of the refrigerator. He got up stiffly, glowering. *I've had to pee for hours. The least you could do is to move my bolster bed into the kitchen. We older dogs need our creature comforts.* I opened the kitchen door, and he stalked by me, then ducked through the pet door on the porch and ran down the stairs already barking at whatever might be out there. I prayed it wouldn't be a skunk, but I was feeling so beatific, I didn't think anything could faze me now.

While I cooked up a batch of peppers and eggs, Joe poured wine and turned on the little kitchen TV for the late news. The anchor Pete Ogle, with an appropriately somber expression, was reading from the teleprompter. "And tonight all Plymouth County mourns the unexpected passing of Plymouth's beloved Ilsa Sigridsson who touched so many young lives during her thirty years at Silver Lake, first as an English teacher and then as the high school's principal. Recovering from hip surgery at Manomet

Manor, the seventy-seven-year-old Miss Sigridsson, who also suffered from heart disease, succumbed in her sleep last night. We've been informed that a memorial tribute is already being organized by the present faculty of Silver Lake. And now"—Ogle brightened visibly—"right after the break, Russ Rainey will bring you tomorrow's weather. Another terrific summer day in store. . . ."

My bubble of contentment broke into several jagged pieces. "Well, I sure as hell hope they're going to autopsy the old dear," I exclaimed, slapping the spatula onto the counter and punching the toaster oven ON with a vicious poke. "That Manomet Manor is getting to be Plymouth's answer to the Bates Motel. And to think Fiona and Maeve are going to subject themselves to some crazy nurse's tender mercies. . . . Well, we'll see what we can do about that!"

Joe looked up from letting Scruffy in the back door, startled. "You said something about suspicious deaths on the phone last week. Is that the place? Why is Fiona going there? Who's Maeve? One of the Druids? I think you'd better catch me up . . . so I can keep you out of trouble."

Oh, boy . . . that sure smells good, Toots. Scruffy's nose sniffed the air appreciatively. He licked his chops. *Eggs are good for my coat, you know.*

I divided the eggs between two plates, leaving a small portion in the pan to mollify Scruffy, then gingerly removed hunks of hot French bread from the toaster oven. A long swig of wine calmed me down before we began to eat—or, rather, Joe ate while I regaled him with stories about the escalating number of deaths at the Manor that had piqued Stone's interest. I even told him about my bout of clairvoyance. But words can never quite convey the emotional punch of a vision. "Dr. DeBoer, the director, ought to be alarmed himself. It's surprising the prospective patients aren't reconsidering their options. There must be plenty of other rehabilitation facilities in Massachusetts," I concluded.

"Apparently, your friends haven't been warned off. Listen, honey, you have to leave this one for Stone to investigate. I wouldn't want to go off on another assignment with that worry hanging over my head. I'd go crazy imagining someone sticking a lethal hypodermic needle into my bride."

"Sometimes, when a friend may be in danger, a person just has to get involved. You know that." I dug into my eggs, secure in the knowledge that I'd scored a point there. Scruffy's nose rested on my foot, a devoted reminder that he was ready for his share of the midnight snack. "And when exactly are you going off on another assignment?"

"I'm not sure. Maybe two weeks. Maybe less. We left it that they'd page me."

I wondered how hard it was to hex a pager. Just a little psychokinesis. Our former apprentice, Freddie, had been a whiz at zapping electronics, but right after graduation, she'd headed down to Florida to check on how her younger brothers were faring in the care of their irresponsible mother and abusive stepfather. I tried to remember how she did the psychokinesis thing. "It's just a way of concentrating," she'd explained, which was like Tiger Woods saying, "It's just a matter of hitting the little ball into that hole." Her hands would actually get hot to the touch, and sweat would run into her eyes. Maybe I'd give it a try.

"You're going off into outer space again, honey." Joe emptied the rest of the wine into our glasses as I put the cooled frying pan on the floor for Scruffy. "What are you plotting now?"

I smiled and said nothing. Getting married or not, a woman's entitled to a few secrets.

Chapter Six

Grabbing an armful of fairy-godmother dolls off one of the chairs, Deidre stuffed them into a box to make room for me. Her sunny yellow kitchen overflowed with the products of her clever hands and unbounded enthusiasm for crafts. Once a hobby, the soft dolls she created were now being sold on selected Internet markets. I noticed this new model resembled Fiona to an amazing degree. Perhaps there was a box of Cassandra dolls hiding in one of her closets? That type of thing had been known.

"Sit right here, Cass. Coffee or iced tea?"

I remembered Deidre's coffee all too well. "Iced tea, please. Where's Bobby?"

"Pre-preschool. I know he's only four, but I need my mornings to get balanced, sort of." She stirred some brown powdery stuff into two glasses of water, added ice, and handed me one. Baby Anne, the latest live doll at the Ryan's house, banged on her little tray-table, screwing up her face in slow motion for a good cry. Deidre stuck a spoonful of something purple from a little jar into Annie's open mouth. "Eat up, precious." The baby's big blue eyes got round with surprise. I waited, fascinated, as this brand-new little person decided between swallowing the purple stuff or letting it ooze out the sides of her mouth. The sweet taste won. "That's Mommy's good girl!"

"These new creations are just fabulous," I said, picking one out of the box to examine it more closely. "I love its little coronet of red braids, the coat-sweater, and the tiny green reticule. No miniature Colt forty-five in there, I trust?" A little card hung around the doll's neck: *Hi! I'm Fiona, Your Fairy Godmother. You'll always be a princess to me. Whenever I wave my magic wand, your wishes are sure to come true.* The doll's round finger clasped a satiny sliver of wood with a sparkling point. "How are they selling?"

"I used authentic witch-hazel wood for that wand. All my dolls are doing fairly well, but, to tell you the truth, I still miss my old job at the mall. I even miss the commute, the feeling of being out and about all by myself first thing in the morning—which is not the same as toting three kids to school. The vitamin shop was just right for me. Sure, it wasn't easy to run that place and keep the hearth fires burning too, but I always managed fine. I hired good help at the shop—I could take a few hours off when I needed to. And if I do say so myself, I'm a whiz at time management." Deidre sighed that sigh of a woman who wasn't having it all.

"Before you know it, this little one will be in school like the rest," I reassured her. "Take it from one who knows how the years just zip by. You'll be really glad later that you had this time together."

"Okay, Model Mom. Don't you just wish you were back in a kitchen feeding strained plums to your own baby?" Deidre stuck another tiny spoonful into the now-willing rosebud mouth. Annie was the spittin' image of Deidre, with the same blond curls and mischievous sparkle in her eyes.

"Sometimes I do," I lied.

"Rumor has it that you and Joe have set a date." Deidre didn't look up, but I could detect a little smirk at the corner of her mouth. The diminutive spoon kept scooping up strained plums. Annie's eyes went all dreamy with contented knoshing.

"What rumor? You mean the psychic grapevine otherwise

known as cell-to-cell gossip? Yes, we're thinking about Yule, as I mentioned to Heather. She knows all the good shops in Boston where a gal can buy an over-the-hill wedding outfit. I'm thinking pastel satin."

"Pale mossy green—perfect with your eyes. Just tell me you're not planning to move somewhere, you know, like Gloucester or Greece."

"Why would I do that? I'm marrying a guy who's never going to be home, so I think I'll stay here where I have friends and herb gardens and an ocean right outside my windows."

"Right. Best of both worlds, I'd say." Apparently Annie'd had enough. She signaled her surfeit by batting away the spoon and giving the plum jar a baby-size karate chop. Deidre began mopping up the child, the tray, and the floor. "Are you going to write your own vows? What kind of ceremony are you going to have? Greek Orthodox? Reverend Peacedale? Handfasting?"

I'd been too busy dreaming up the wedding outfit to worry about the vows, so I said, "The vows will be pure poetry. The ceremony will be indisputably legal. And a frolicsome handfasting will follow. I think I'll ask Fiona to officiate. But that's a long time away. Listen, Dee . . . what I'm worrying about right now is Fiona and Maeve. Do you think you could whip up a couple of really powerful amulets for those two hardheads to wear while they're entombed in Manomet Manor?"

"Sure. I got some stuff from South America you wouldn't touch with a ten-foot athame, but I have it on good authority that it's got some big-time voodoo."

"No kidding. What's it called?"

"Something unpronounceable. *A-ga-wan-da-hoof* . . . or *poof*, I'm not sure which. I'll call them good-luck charms."

"Aren't they?"

"Well, if freezing the balls off your enemy isn't good luck, what is?"

"Whoa. Watch it. You aren't wandering off the white path, are you?"

"Hey, we're only talking *self-defense* here, not *off*ense. You probably heard about Ilsa Sigridsson's unexpected departure for Summerland?"

"It may have been perfectly natural, but then again, perhaps not." As a Libran, I often find myself giving this kind of wimpish but balanced response. I decided to abandon reason in favor of intuition. "Actually, the moment I heard Pete Ogle intoning the sad news I felt very strongly that Sigridsson had been given a push off the twig."

"Me too," Deidre said. "She was, of course, a real old battleax—just ask Will. During the last half of their senior year, she tortured the whole football team with *The Lady of the Lake*. Nonetheless, she ought to have been allowed to live out her life in dignified eccentricity."

"Do you know if she had a family?"

"Never married. You could check the obit for grieving relatives."

"I'm just wondering if she left her money to anyone."

"Good question. I bet she still had the first dollar she ever made pinned to her bodice. Not one for the high life, Ms. Sigridsson."

Our conversation was cut off by a high-pitched commotion in the backyard. "It's the mailman," Deidre said, opening the kitchen door to let in her two toy poodles, Salty and Peppy. Immediately, they checked out the baby's tray-table and the baby herself for tasty crumbs. Annie chortled at their tickling whiskers and clapped her hands.

"Why do all dogs hate mail carriers, do you suppose? You watch Annie for a minute, will you, while I run out to the mailbox."

"They carry suspicious bundles. Sure." As soon as Deidre banged out the door, I poured the rest of my powdered tea down the sink. From the window, I could watch her race to the post office box and back. No wonder she never put on a pound! She hardly ever stopped moving. No surprise that she missed the vitamin shop, which must have seemed like an oasis of peace and quiet.

A few moments later, she was back with a big grin and an armful of envelopes, which she spilled onto the diminutive kitchen desk, one of her stenciled creations with hearts and flowers on a blue background. "Checks in the mail—my favorite!"

Salty and Peppy were now sniffing my sandals with consummate interest, getting news of their nemesis, Scruffy, no doubt. "I'd better get going. It must be almost time for you to pick up Bobby." I looked around for a clock and found only the stove timer.

Deidre ignored it. Instead she looked out the window to where the sun had risen to the top of the jungle gym. "Not quite yet," she said. "I'll have the amulets ready for Lammas. Soak the cords in *Agawanda*-whatever, and add a couple of healing stones—innocent but potent. I'll bring one for everyone so it won't seem so directed, with an extra for Heather to give to Maeve. Lammas is at Phil's, right?"

"Actually, bring me an extra, too." *Now why did I say that?* Sometimes words just come out of my mouth without being routed through my brain. "You know how Phil revels in the harvest thing, whipping up loaves of bread and all. I hope the amulets won't be too much trouble. You're right, you *are* a whiz at management. How do you find time for everything?"

"Time out of mind, dearie. Or, rather, a trick of the mind. Have you ever noticed how time expands to fit whatever got done that day?"

"Yeah, but that's in retrospect." One of us was confused.

Deidre's Mona Lisa smile settled oddly on her cute face. "Not if you view it from between the worlds. Sometimes I have the feeling of actually stretching time—or maybe I should call it stepping into timelessness. Especially when I'm working on my dolls."

"Is that the Zen kind of 'flow' thing? I wouldn't mind learning that one. Considering a career as a Cosmic Time Manager?"

"Maybe it's Zen, but it's also Wiccan. I have to admit that stretching time is one of my talents. Well, not if I'm in the middle of a kid crisis. But other times, like on my good days."

A few minutes later, as I was driving home, I thought how there was more to Deidre than poppets and embroidered pillows. That time-stretching trick would be worth studying. Did every psychic skill lead to others? Look at Fiona—not only a finder, but also mistress of the Glamour. Did I have a latent talent, I wondered, beyond clairvoyance? I conversed with Scruffy, of course, but wasn't that a perfectly ordinary ability that everyone had? Dogs have very strong opinions that beg to be heard. Sometimes I even caught a word or two of Salty and Peppy's thoughts—like the way they despised their names and would much prefer to be called Louis and Marie. Or was that merely my imagination? *No way, Toots*, as Scruffy might say.

Chapter Seven

By the week before Lammas, Joe had my herb gardens weeded to perfection—no small job, especially the thyme beds infiltrated by crabgrass. He'd fixed the garage roof, painted the porch interior, and pruned the pines on the hill of their lower branches so that I could see the road. Now he was working diligently on repairing our rotting beach stairs, which might be a lifetime project, or at least a lifesaving one. One gets inured to the dangers one lives with, but in truth those stairs were hazardous to our health.

At the head of the stairs, we'd installed Joe's totem pole (a gift from grateful Native Americans in a logging dispute on the West Coast). I hoped the totem would have some big magic to keep the whole edifice from collapsing onto the sand below. Eagle, bear, and salmon gazed as impassively at the Atlantic as they had once surveyed the Pacific—symbols of air, earth, and water, a powerful combination. And I have a special fondness for eagles. Joe and I had met because of an endangered eagle crisis.

These weeks had been like another honeymoon for us. Absence really does make the heart grow fonder, and other parts, too. But as Joe began to work at a feverish pace on the stairs, it was obvious that he wanted to get the project finished before the pager summoned him elsewhere. I'd cast a number of baleful glances at that pager, but psychokinesis is not my forte.

Two days before Lammas, Joe got the summons to call Greenpeace International in Amsterdam. He was needed on the *SV Rainbow Warrior.* The ship would be supporting a flotilla of small boats carrying Nuclear Free Irish Sea banners to oppose a shipment of plutonium fuel. Joe's smile was rueful, but he didn't fool me. The light in his eyes said, "I love danger."

"Promise me you're going to stay out of the small boats this time," I demanded. "Last time it was a punch in the chest and a cut thigh, but next time it might be a broken leg or worse. You'll be stuck in an Irish hospital for Goddess knows how long. And you practically a bridegroom at last!"

He took me in his arms and assured me most convincingly that he would be the soul of caution, he would never leave the ship no matter what happened to the poor buggers in the little dingies. As we were in the bedroom anyway, his kisses and protestations soon led to one of those sensuous interludes so natural to deep summer afternoons. I may not have been deceived, but I was mollified most satisfactorily.

"By the way, Circe," Joe said at dinner—a beautiful candlelight dinner on the refurbished porch—"you dazzled me so completely I nearly forgot. I'm not the only one with a habit of sailing into harm's way. Now *you* have to assure *me* that you'll steer clear of trouble. No pursuing lethal medical workers, sparring with irate Saudi Arabian husbands, or any other villains that cross your bow, right? At least not until I get home again. It shouldn't be too long this time. The *Warrior*'s due for an overhaul right after this campaign is completed. Come hell or high water, I'll cruise to shore with her."

"Rose! Gosh, I haven't given a thought to that poor girl." These halcyon days with Joe were making me forget everything. I got up to fetch the coffee—a good strong brew. "I should have checked up on her at the shelter, to see if she's getting along all right and that husband of hers has stayed away. But I'll be careful, just as careful as you always are."

"That's what I'm afraid of."

Scruffy, supine under the wicker table, nudged my knee. *Hey, Toots, remember me? Any leftover pork chops?*

"Would I forget you!" I said.

"I hope not." Joe's tone was startled. I decided not to explain that I was talking to the dog.

Joe's flight to Ireland was scheduled for the next evening, but he'd have to return the Chevy and be at the airport a couple of hours early, and the drive into Logan would take an hour or so. I would *not* let him spend his next to last day in Plymouth working on those blasted stairs, so he never did get to replace the rotted wood in the last half-dozen steps.

I've found that guilt is a great energizer. That evening I packed up all my overdue orders so that I could mail them in the morning, then visit Rose at St. Rita's in the afternoon. Not only was I concerned about her and Hari, it would be nice to have some news for Cathy the next time we talked. Rose's plight was one thing my youngest daughter and I had in common when there wasn't a whole lot else.

I'd just got back from the post office when Phillipa came by with her usual basket brimful of the overflow from testing new recipes. Scruffy tried to get his nose in the basket, but Phillipa would not be lured by the slimy orange sponge ball he rolled toward her by way of distraction. She kicked it back and lifted the basket onto the safety of the kitchen counter.

I invited Phillipa to stay for lunch and to go to St. Rita's with me. She raised a winged eyebrow as I removed a plastic-covered bowl from the refrigerator. "Tuna salad?"

"Tarragon from my garden. Homemade mayonnaise," I countered.

"*Not* made with a fresh egg, I trust?"

"Doused with lemon juice. Guaranteed not to promote salmonella. I personally said a blessing over the food processor."

"Oh, well, then. What kind of bread do you have?"

"Are you accepting my kind invitation or not? Seven-grain with baby lettuce."

"Sounds good."

"Iced tea? Home-brewed, served with lemon slices and a sprig of mint?"

"All right. Where's Joe? I thought he might like these phyllo pastries."

"He left yesterday to keep the Irish Sea free of plutonium." I took out the breadboard and began to make sandwiches with Phillipa watching me closely.

"Here, why don't you let me do that. You can fix the iced tea. Don't you sometimes feel that Joe's missions make our little adventures pale into insignificance?"

"Sit, Phil. I *can* make a tuna sandwich. Personally, I don't feel the least bit insignificant. We're saving Rose from being buried alive in Saudi Arabia. And we have Manomet Manor to look into." I garnished the sandwiches with cornichons, tiny French gherkins—just like a photo from *Bon Appetit*. Phillipa was already making the iced tea and laying out a plate of pastries on the side. Scruffy took his accustomed place near my chair. Surreptitiously, I put a cheese pastry on my hand and held it under the table where he could crunch it up.

"Stop right there," Phillipa said. For a moment, I thought I'd got caught, but then she continued, "Stone wants us to keep our noses out of Manomet Manor."

"Yeah? And what did you think about Ilsa Sigridsson's surprise demise?"

"I thought it was a little fishy. I told Stone so. Especially considering that hefty bequest."

"Bequest? I knew it! Who to?"

"Dr. DeBoer. Sigridsson had been in and out of the Manor for years, convalescent from various surgeries, no one at home to look out for her. DeBoer is a handsome guy, if you like that florid fleshy look, and I understand he gave her a lot of his personal attention. Grateful patient, no relatives. And there was another bequest, too, to some favorite therapist. The bulk of the estate, however, goes to her church, the Lutheran one in Braintree."

"Stone ought to have a careful look at that will, when bequests were made and so on."

"Leave it to Stone, Cass. Truthfully, though, I told him the same thing."

We finished our lunch and stacked the dishes. "Sorry, fella. You're staying home to guard the house," I explained to Scruffy.

He sighed mightily. *Boring, boring. I need exercise every day, you know. Good muscle tone is my birthright—I'm a French briard.*

"Only on your mother's side. Your father was some traveling terrier of unknown origin. We'll go for a good run on the beach when I get home."

Promises, promises.

Rose was blooming—her pale cream pallor had warmed, the blush on her cheeks looked less feverish and more glowing, and her shy smile was all the prettier since her black eye had faded. Her son Hari was racing around like a young lord, but soon he was swept outside into a game of baby soccer with a few other young children and a sturdy red-haired woman. I noted that St. Rita's back lawn was enclosed by a high stone wall with decorative iron spears and a locked gate dating back to its convent days.

Serena Dove already knew Phillipa as the wife of that helpful detective who always could be counted on for protection in an emergency. After they'd said hello, I introduced Phillipa to Rose, who served us lemonade in the toy-strewn, fan-cooled living room.

"We're so proud of Rose," Serena said. "She's found herself a fine position locally as a lab technician." There was something both wise and comforting about Serena's smile. *A magic person*, I thought. "She'll be staying on here for a bit, so that Hari will have secure daycare until the custody business is no longer an issue. Fortunately, we're rather out of the way, and few people even know what we're about. Some may even think we're some kind of convent school."

"Rasheed would have come for his son," Rose said in her strained whisper, "if he knew we were here."

"But you have a restraining order. And temporary custody," Phillipa interjected.

"Rasheed believes a husband's right, a father's right, is above the law. That's why I'm so grateful to you and to Detective Stern for finding such a fine, safe place for us." She looked down modestly. I noticed that she was no longer wearing the flowered head scarf. "I'll be so pleased to work and contribute my share. It's been a long time—Rasheed did not approve—but my new employer is willing to give me a chance, not only to manage the little lab but also to help out with the pharmacy supplies."

"What grand news," Phillipa said. "Stone will be really glad to hear you're doing so well. Is it those two periodontists in Plymouth Center by any chance? I seem to remember they were looking for a girl."

"No," said Rose. "It's for a doctor, a very private facility. I hope Rasheed won't discover it. There's someone on Ms. Dove's staff—Ken, the gardener—who transports us girls in St. Rita's van. It seems that everything is working out so perfectly . . . I feel very lucky to have good friends." That was the first time I'd ever seen Rose looking genuinely happy. She refilled our glasses. It was real lemonade, sweet-tart and refreshing.

"Ken Wakahiro is not only a talented gardener," Serena said. "He's also a martial arts expert. One evening a week he gives the women a few pointers in self-defense. Builds confidence, you know, and rather equalizes things."

"Right on!" Phillipa said. "I wouldn't mind learning a few chops and throws myself."

"You're welcome to join us—both of you." But Serena's offer sounded less than wholehearted. In my mind's eye—one of those quickie visions that plague me—I saw her watching out the window as we drove away. For some reason, she was relieved to see us depart. Perhaps she didn't want any comfortable and perhaps talkative Plymouth matrons upsetting her charges. In some strange way, this place was still a convent. I wondered if she'd ever been the headmistress of a girls' school—or as a nun, responsible for novices. Yes, that was it. . . .

I zipped my lip. But in case I was tempted to pry, a distraction burst into the room. A fierce and muddy Hari threw himself into his mother's lap. "Give me a drink, Mommy!" he demanded. "I'm awful thirsty. That woman said I had to come in because Betsy got in my way."

"You mean Miss Dorothy, don't you, Hari," Serena Dove reproved.

"Hari, you didn't push the little girl, did you?"

Phillipa caught my eye. We got up and said our good-byes.

"Promise me you'll call if there's anything—anything at all—I can do to help you." I hugged Rose's thin shoulders.

We were walking down the stone stairs when Rose's raspy voice called after me, "Please thank Detective Stern for me again. It's all because of him that I have this wonderful home and a great job at Manomet."

Phillipa and I turned like two synchronized swimmers, and cried out in unison, "Manomet *Manor*?"

"Yes, that's the place. Didn't I say? Dear Dr. DeBoer was so kind as to hire me, and I'll try very hard to deserve his confidence."

"If we believed in coincidence . . ." Phillipa began.

"Which I don't," I amended. "I believe in Jungian synchronicity. And in my own view of the intentional universe. Perhaps it won't be a bad thing at all to have Rose in that little lab. Maybe it's even meant to be. Besides, I couldn't bring myself to throw cold water on her joyous announcement."

Phillipa sighed. "Me neither."

We were driving past the stretch of mostly pine forest between her house and mine that is very dear to us both. Because it includes an official wetlands and a pair of nesting eagles, it's now a nature preserve. Last year the town of Plymouth bought the woods and renamed it Jenkins Park, thus making this desirable property, which stretches from Route 3A right to the Atlantic shoreline, permanently safe from developers. As always, Phillipa and I were craning our necks for a glimpse of "our" eagles. That doesn't make for especially safe driving..

"Watch what you're doing," Phillipa snapped as I ran over the road's shoulder, crushing a tiny pine sapling. Nothing the Wagoneer couldn't handle. "Did you see anything?"

"No. Did you?"

"No. I only hope they haven't taken off anywhere."

"Those eagles know they've found a good home here. Plenty of dumb ducks and bluefish jumping practically into their beaks. And Rose has found a safe haven, too," I assured us both, lumping Rose in with other endangered species. I rather think optimistic statements influence the future, or at least, keep a person cheery and strong enough to face whatever happens.

"Red Riding Hood among the wolves at the Manor. It will be just grand. I can hardly wait to tell Stone."

"You see Rose as a storybook heroine, too. To me, she's always Rose Red.

"She does have a 'faerie' quality. Except for that frog voice."

After dropping Phillipa off, I drove back past Jenkins Park, noticing that a black pickup truck was parked on the same shoulder I had run over. I hoped it wasn't someone after the bayberries that I like to think of as my own private preserve. Although Heather has become our chief candle maker, always messing about with some new magical formula, I still like to make a few bayberry-scented candles in the fall for my own use.

Scruffy welcomed me with the usual complaints and wagging tail. Yes, I admitted, it was indeed past time for the promised walk. Taking the leash that hangs on a hook by the back door, I draped it around my own neck in case it would be needed but let Scruffy run free since we were headed for the beach. It was just four o'clock of a fine summer's evening. My herb gardens were still intensely fragrant with thyme, sage, and mint, although I'd already harvested lavender, meadowsweet, feverfew, and numerous others when they were in their prime. A pleasant breeze from the East ruffled the ocean. I wondered where Joe was at this very moment, perhaps just now joining the crew of the *SV Rainbow Warrior*. With my thoughts on Joe, I laid my hand affectionately on the totem pole at the head of the beach stairs and looked out at the water. Scruffy ran on down to the beach, no doubt looking for a good stick to tease me into throwing.

I heard a car door slam. Then pounding footsteps, an angry voice yelling behind me. "Where are they? Where are my wife and son?"

I whirled around, hanging on to the totem pole to steady myself. Although I'd never met Rose's husband—despite his having tried to break into my kitchen—I knew it must be he. Furious dark eyes, cropped black beard, medium height but muscular—and in his hands, an upraised baseball bat. *Hari's?* I wondered incongruously, as I edged down one step onto the stairs.

Rasheed Abdul was halfway across the backyard, his mouth twisted into an angry snarl. Looking around wildly for help, I saw it was that same black pickup truck, now parked under the pines. Not out for bayberries, after all. Where was my clairvoyance when I needed it?

"Who did you say you're looking for?" I'd try to play dumb. Already far down the beach, Scruffy came running back toward the foot of the stairs, barking at the stranger's voice.

"I know they were staying here, you whore! Do you think I'm some kind of fool? And now you've hidden them somewhere else. I've been searching for days—every motel, every rooming house. You'd better tell me, or . . ." He raised the baseball bat a little higher, all the while moving toward me, no longer running but advancing slowly and purposefully.

Not for a moment averting my gaze from his progress, I started down the stairs backward, not the easiest thing to do—second step, third step—but terror is a wonderful motivator. By the fourth step, Scruffy had climbed up behind me, still barking frantically, trying to push past me and get at the stranger who was making me afraid.

"Get back, Scruffy! Back! Back!" I ordered him.

Abdul made a swipe with the bat. I ducked, desperately hanging on to the railing of the narrow stairs. In a flash of fur, Scruffy squirmed under my arm, up to the head of the stairs. Abdul swung again, this time at the dog. Scruffy leaped away and circled around the man to nip at his heels. Abdul kept swinging.

"Scruffy! No, Scruffy!" The dog ignored my pleas to come away. I heard a fearful crack as the bat connected with Scruffy's head. I screamed and threw out my hand in an involuntary cursing gesture, little finger pointing outward. Scruffy was down, but I was thankful to hear that he was making little whimpering sounds.

I would have to lead Abdul away from Scruffy. I turned and climbed down toward the beach at a speed born of knowing those stairs by heart, not even looking back to see how close he might be. But I heard him following—his harsh breath, his curses, his hammering feet not moving as quickly as mine. "You will tell me where they are, or I will splatter your brains out!" he hollered after me.

If I could reach the beach, maybe I'd find a piece of driftwood to parry that bat. I practically jumped down the last few stairs. Surely Abdul would catch up to me any second.

When I heard a sharp cracking sound, I imagined it was the bat missing me and hitting wood, but when I turned around, I saw that the noise came from the rotting stairs, the ones Joe hadn't had time to fix. They'd given way under Abdul's weight, throwing him forward onto the beach. The splintered wood had torn his trousers and drawn blood from his leg. He'd fallen onto his knees, the bat landing a few feet away. He groaned and looked up. I snatched up two handfuls of sand and let him have them right in the face. He roared in anger, rubbing his blind eyes.

Grabbing the bat, I used it as a crutch to help me clamber up the slope where the stairs were broken. The part that Joe had repaired was wobbly now but still usable. Dangling from the broken handrail was my newly printed sign: BEWARE: THIS STAIRWAY IS DANGEROUS.

I would have thought that Scruffy was too heavy for me to pick up and hold in my arms while running into the house. He wasn't.

Gently I laid Scruffy down on the braided rug that is his favorite place in the kitchen. He was still unconscious but alive, a huge bump forming on top of his head. I locked the doors, slammed the windows shut and locked those, too, then called nine-one-one. While I was talking to the emergency operator, I wrapped ice cubes in a towel to lay on Scruffy's head.

Then I called Heather's new husband, Dick Devlin, at his animal hospital. "I need an ambulance," I screamed into his receptionist's ear. "Tell him it's Cass. Say that an intruder hit Scruffy on the head with a baseball bat and he's out cold."

"This isn't an ambulance service . . ." she began to explain.

"Who's that screaming?" I heard Dick's hearty voice in the background.

Obviously covering the mouthpiece with her hand, the receptionist must have begun to explain when he took the phone from her. "I'll be right there. I have something that passes for an ambulance. Keep him warm, in case of shock."

Right after I'd tucked a blanket around Scruffy, two police cruisers arrived, but the pickup truck had already sped away. I wondered how Abdul had managed to crawl up the slope with his injured leg and then drive with his eyes full of sand. Maybe he would have an accident. I tried not to wish for that too strongly. No telling what innocent soul he might crash into.

"He's gone," I said to the officers who arrived, but two of them ran down to the beach anyway. "Mind the broken stairs," I called after them. I'd just about given a description and name of the attacker to the two remaining officers—what the truck looked like, how he had come at me and my dog with a baseball bat—when Dick arrived.

After a quick examination—lifting Scruffy's eyelids, checking his heartbeat and temperature, examining the lump—Dick opened the back of his van, WEE ANGELS RESCUE WAGON emblazoned on its side, and pulled down a ramp. Then he rolled out a dog-size stretcher on wheels, and we lifted Scruffy onto it, fastening straps to hold him securely. I jumped in the front seat with Dick, and we roared away.

"You ought to have a siren so you wouldn't have to stop," I said while Dick was stuck at a red light. "Why don't you blast your horn and flash your lights. We're having a medical emergency here." There were tears running down my face. I wiped them away with my sleeve. "Will he be all right?"

"I won't kid you, Cass." Dick wove the van smoothly through commuter traffic, occasionally using a discreet beep of his horn. "It could be serious, and there isn't much I can do but wait to see if—when—he revives and how he behaves. His heart is strong, but we don't know yet if there's been any brain damage."

Black thoughts. As I sat in the hospital's waiting room, black thoughts about Abdul crowded in on me like a horde of killer bees. I batted them away, but they kept swarming back. Springing up from my chair, I shook my hands violently to rid myself of all negative vibrations. Then I struggled to fill my mind with the embracing white light and project those healing rays to Scruffy. This is hard to do when what you really want is to batter someone's brains out with his own baseball bat.

In the midst of my inner struggle, Heather arrived to console me. Dick had called her from his office. "You have a rather nutsy look in your eyes. Are you all right? Here, I brought you a Peaceful Heart candle. Be sure to light it when you get home." She handed me a thick blue-green candle with small starfish and some green things with tentacles embedded in the wax—rather strange-looking, I thought.

"Thank you, dear. It has your touch. But how can I be all right when Scruffy's practically been killed by that son-of-a-bitch husband of Rose's?"

"Tell me everything," Heather demanded, but she was already punching in one of the preprogrammed numbers on her cell phone. "We're at the hospital," she said without preamble when Phillipa answered. "No, not Jordan Hospital. The Wee Angels Animal Hospital. It's Scruffy. *What* are you saying? Well, I can't believe *that*, and Stone won't believe it, either. He's got better sense. Get over here in a hurry, will you?"

"You'll love this." Heather put a firm arm around my shoulders. "Rasheed Abdul is at the police station swearing out a complaint against you and your vicious dog."

I was speechless. And that's not something that happens to me very often.

"Your mouth is hanging open," Heather said. "I can just imagine what really occurred, but I guess this is Abdul's way of mounting what they call 'the best defense.' Phil will be here in a few minutes to fill us in on the improbable details. Meanwhile, why don't I just have a word with Dick. You stay here and try to relax. I'll tell him you're to be called the moment Scruffy stirs a paw."

Heather sprang up and headed for the trauma unit—and collided with Dick just coming through the other way. Dick's a big, comfortable-looking guy, lots of laugh lines, broad shoulders, and bushy hair. With his innocent eyes and warm, sincere manner, he inspires instant trust. He's a charismatic speaker, too, and in great demand as a fund-raiser. About fifteen years older than Heather, Dick's been her tower of strength—a whole new experience in husbands. "Hi, you beautiful creature," he said to his wife, catching her in a swift hug that nearly took her off her feet. Momentarily she seemed to teeter and lose track of what she was doing. Not a bad thing, I thought, smiling to myself.

"Scruffy's coming around." Dick sat next to me and took both my hands in his big comforting grip. "His breathing and heartbeat are nearly normal now, although his temp is a bit elevated.

He seems to be passing from a coma into a natural deep sleep. He's been transferred to one of our convalescent crates. When he wakes up he's going to have one hell of a dog headache. But I've given him some good meds to bring down the inflammation and lessen the pain. There's nothing you can do for now. Why don't you go home, have a quiet cup of tea or a shot of whiskey or something. I'll call you when Scruffy wakes up. I know you'll want to take him home right off, but the best thing would be to let him rest quietly here for a day or two so that I can keep an eye on him."

"Phil's on her way here," Heather said.

"Well, ring her up, sweetie, and tell her you're taking Cass home. Cass is in shock herself, you know."

Dick must have been right, because I don't remember a thing about being brought home. The next thing I knew, I was in my own kitchen and Heather was following her husband's prescription to the letter: hot, sweet tea with slugs of whiskey. Its warmth seemed to flow through my entire being. I began to feel better, but my eyes kept leaking.

Then Phil arrived with news of the preposterous complaint. "Abdul says he came to your house to inquire about his wife and their boy, not to disturb anyone, he knows there's a restraining order, but he just wanted to know if his beloved family is all right. His wife is liable to have these fits of hysteria, he said, accusing him of things that aren't true. He's never lifted a hand to her."

"Oh, yeah. Well, we have the photos to prove otherwise," I said.

"She walked into Hari's swing in their backyard, he says. Anyway, he got out of his truck at Cass's house and found her in the garden. He politely asked about Rose and Hari, and Cass seemed to go wild. She screamed and sicced the dog on him. Scruffy attacked, biting his ankles. And Abdul's got the teethmarks to show for it."

"Give me a break," I was yelling. "What about the baseball bat he was swinging at us?"

"Let's just relax ourselves and listen to the story, dear. We know he's lying," Heather soothed me. She lit the Peaceful Heart candle that she'd placed in the middle of the kitchen table. It smelled of seaweed. Maybe it would work—I should have more faith in Heather's magic. Even if her candles did look and smell funny, perhaps that was because they were truly potent, like milk of magnesia or iodine.

"He tried to protect himself from this ferocious animal," Phillipa continued, "but as he stumbled backward toward the edge of the slope. Cass ran at him while he was off balance and gave him a mighty push. He fell down the beach stairs, got a face full of sand, cut his leg, and sprained his ankle. Despite his injuries, he managed to crawl back up and drive away in his truck to Jordan Hospital, where he was treated in the emergency room for irritated eyes, a gashed thigh, a sprained ankle, and some scratches he claimed were dog bites."

"This is a complete fiction," I wailed. "Surely no one will believe him."

"Steady on, Cass," Phillipa said. "I'm just getting to the good part: Abdul's next stop in the Plymouth Police Station to lodge his complaint. Meanwhile, the officers that went to your house are filing their report and telling Stone about your version of the incident. My husband is no fool—not for one minute does he believe Abdul's fiction. He takes the man into an interrogation room to question him. Abdul says he knows nothing about Cass's call to nine-one-one, that he doesn't even have a baseball bat, nor does his son Hari. He demands that Scruffy be quarantined to determine if he has rabies."

"Quarantined!!" I screamed.

"Calm yourself. This will never happen," Heather assured me. "Dick will sign a paper certifying that Scruffy does not have rabies. This is Plymouth, after all, where there are two streets and a square named after some Devlin or another. Dick's word will be sufficient. How's that candle working?"

"Oh, great. Very magical influence. I've gone from totally insane to only mildly crazed. You don't think he'll come back, do you?"

"My guess is no," Phillipa said. "Abdul just lost it, and now he's covering up with this specious complaint against you. His real interest will be in winning even partial custody of Hari at the next hearing."

Whether I was having a clairvoyant quickie or just a paranoid flash, I knew exactly what would happen then. "If Abdul gets joint custody with unsupervised visits, he'll grab the kid and head to Mexico or someplace. Next stop, Saudi Arabia."

"Suppose we all attend that hearing," Heather said. "The circle united—surely we can work some good spell for Rose. Why, Fiona alone has a baleful glance that would stop a raging bull in mid-charge."

"All of us right in the front row." I liked the mental picture I was getting. "The Formidable Five."

Chapter Eight

I don't know whether Dick Devlin's meds or my healing spells ought to have gotten the most credit, but by the next afternoon, Scruffy had made one of those miraculous recoveries that are a canine specialty, with hardly a bump left on his poor little head. He was more than ready to be released. *Take me home and feed me, Toots. The food in this hospital is the lousiest stuff I ever ate, and, anyway, the broad in the next crate smelled so bad I lost my appetite. I couldn't even get a decent nap. They kept waking me up to stick me with pins. I think I caught kennel cough. Ack, ack, ack.* Scruffy was well enough to complain loudly all the way home.

Greedily, he slurped up the chicken soup I gave him, and after a short, stiff walk around the premises, fell on his L. L. Bean faux-sheepskin bolster dog bed with a sigh of deep contentment. *A dog's home is his castle.*

A few years ago, when we five had met in Fiona's women's studies program at the Black Hill Branch Library, we'd become interested in matriarchal societies, ancient times when wise women wielded their natural power in spiritual communities. Learning more about the holy days that predated modern religions led us to the Wiccan Sabbats we celebrated now, holidays aligned to the seasonal cycles of birth, growth, death. As Deidre said, "I like that it's down-to-earth—literally. Hearth and home, love and healing—with a little useful magic on the side. What could be wrong with that?"

Lammas was one of the four great Sabbats of the year, the first harvest. It was our custom not to invite visitors—major Sabbats were for major magic. Phillipa had heaped the long marble table in her state-of-the-art kitchen with fragrant breads, cheeses, nuts, pears, and apples. But the feast was for later, when the ceremony played out into a celebration. First we would give thanks for personal harvests, and do magic work for ourselves and absent friends. Personally, I was working for love and joy in the lives of my three children, a safe haven for Rose, my glorious marriage to Joe, healing for Fiona and Maeve, a solution to the mysteries of Manomet Manor, good faring to all the little creatures in Jenkins Park, *finis* to the Pilgrim Nuclear Power Plant... once I got started, there seemed no end of psychic pots to be stirred.

Fiona said that with every Sabbat we were getting stronger spiritually. She herself brought into our Lammas a burst of warmth, benevolent sunshine to embrace us all. In the full flow of her glamour, she cast aside her aches and looked taller and absolutely regal—in recognition of which, Deidre wove her an instant crown with a few purple blossom stalks of hosta growing outside the kitchen door.

Pleased to have Will coping with the four little Ryans for the evening, Deidre was sparkling with enthusiasm and had her bag full of tricks—crafty stuff, including those protective amulets bordering on voodoo. But I wouldn't dwell too much on that. I only wished I'd had one of those "freezing" amulets when Abdul showed up with his so-phallic baseball bat!

Heather came laden with bottles of wine she described as "an amusing muscatel made from frozen grapes and a rich, fruity merlot," and her own handiwork, a candle called Midsummer Faeries for Phillipa. It looked remarkably like the spirit of Titania herself, a curvy, pale green free-form thing filled with glittering leaves, gilded bits of wood, odd berries, and a few tiny fungi.

It was a warm, still night, buzzing with doomed insects eager to take a last bite out of summer. After liberal basting with my all-natural herbal No-Bugs-on-You potion, we ventured forth to celebrate the first harvest of the year in the Sterns' pine-screened yard. A sliver of new moon shone palely over the treetops as Phillipa consecrated the nine-foot circle. With her flair for the poetic phrase, she invoked the four powers, the four elements. Then she invited the goddess of grain, Ceres (one of her many names), as she represented the divine female in us all, to bless our circle with a rich harvest of the strength and wisdom.

With innocent aplomb, Phillipa's black cat, Zelda, wandered into the magic circle and settled herself for a nap near the pleasant little altar fire crackling at the center. Once an emaciated waif that Fiona found in a Dumpster, Zelda was now a sleek, muscular creature, well-nourished, I didn't doubt, on liver pâté, salmon sushi, and crème fraîche.

With Fiona slowed by arthritis, we couldn't dance our way to power that night, so we passed our energy around the circle hand to hand, faster and faster, until, at a sudden signal from Phillipa's athame, we let fly into the invisible world all our stated and unstated wishes. A collective sigh rose from us like a breath of the August night—from our hearts to the stars!

Well, you can only be filled with the higher spirit so long before you really have to pour the wine and get ribald! Phillipa's deeply wicked laugh started us off, as she sliced off parts of the loaves she'd baked in the man-shaped Lammas tradition.

"What should we wear, do you think, to the Abduls' custody hearing?" asked Deidre. "Although it's difficult to imagine that he'd have the balls to show up after he attacked Cass."

"Black is traditional for magic," Fiona said, "but, honestly, I get depressed when I see a gathering of Wiccans in bedraggled black dresses with fringe-things hanging from them and weird jewelry that looks like globs of dried blood." As she described the scorned outfits with a dramatic gesture, the myriad silver bangles she wore on her arms tinkled like little bells and her baggy coat-sweater of many colors fluttered around her hips.

Phillipa, who was, in fact, wearing a soft, swirling black outfit, raised an eloquent eyebrow. "It's my signature color, dearie. And I think it's quintessential magic, having the power to absorb all colors." She pulled a small cleaver out of the knife block and began to whack wedges off a large round of cheddar.

"Nevertheless, to me black is a noncolor," Fiona declared, looking down with satisfaction at her own multi-striped skirt.

"Yes, but with her dramatic style, Phil looks marvelous in black," I said. "And you, Fiona, seem to have been born to wear the rainbow." I was into one of my Libran balancing acts here. "Heather responds to rich earth tones, and Deidre blooms in spring colors. I think we just naturally reach for the colors that fuel our spirits. Let's wear what we always wear to court. A whole spectrum of power to affect a good outcome."

"What about you, Cass?" Deidre eyes held their familiar mischief. "Ms. Green Goddess?"

"I like blue, too," I declared defensively.

"Blue jeans, you mean," Phillipa said, cutting fragrant slices of a perfect apple pie.

Deidre leaned over to examine a slice more closely, nibbled a flake of the crust. "It takes some witchery to make pastry like this. What's your secret spell, Phil?"

"Same as the spell for getting into Carnegie Hall. *Practice, practice, practice.*"

"The trouble with making pies," Deidre said, "is that people eat them, and then what do you have to show for all that effort?"

"Deep appreciation," I said. "Okay, I'm going to check with Serena Dove to see if a date's been set for the hearing. Rose got a job, you know. Phil, did you tell them?"

Phillipa gave me a dark glance and a slice of pie. "Not yet.

Cass's new protégé is a lab technician who's been hired by Dr. DeBoer for Manomet Manor. They have some kind of a postage-stamp lab there for taking blood and urine samples, not really a full-time occupation, so Rose's going to be handling the pharmacy supplies as well. She's thrilled, of course, poor baby. She may have been better off keeping house for Abdul."

"Never," said Heather.

"A man like that should be shot," Fiona added, reaching for a wedge of cheddar. "This stuff is so lovely, isn't it?"

Nervous looks passed around the table with the merlot and muscatel. Fiona's pistol was a matter of some concern to us all.

"Actually, it may be handy to have Rose at the Manor," Fiona continued, oblivious to our unease. "Maeve and I have talked it over, and we've decided to do a bit of sleuthing on our own while we're there for our physical therapy. Rather liven up those dull exercises, don't you think? Only not a word to Brian, girls! He's a bit of a worrier, you know." Fiona gave each of us a sharp glance to underline her point. "Anyway, facing facts squarely, Maeve *is* in a wheelchair, and I'm not so spry myself these days, so it will be a comfort to know that Rose is just down the hall. Or wherever the lab closet is."

"I didn't hear any of that," Phillipa said. "Remember, I have to live with the Plymouth Detective Squad and their silly little rules about interference. More pie, anyone?"

"A funny thing happened on the way to dock the *Rainbow Warrior* for an overhaul," Joe said, his voice crackling; it was another weird connection. I wondered if he did this on purpose to avoid long explanations. No, static was more my style. Witches love to screw up phones.

"Okay, lay it on me. Another emergency?"

"Yeah, I guess you could say that. I had an urgent call to join the crew of the *MV Argus*. There's a burned-out car ferry that's become a floating toxic waste dump. Right now, it's bound for a scrapyard, and no one's been alerted to its danger. We're going to put some Greenpeace activists aboard to hang a banner, and a couple of experts in toxic contamination to take samples."

"Where?"

"Antwerp Harbor. I shouldn't be gone more than another couple of weeks."

"Oh, Joe," I said with a sigh. "Well, I imagine the Belgian jails are very pleasant. They probably serve hot chocolate for breakfast. Do you think you can make it back by Yule?"

"It's only August. Is everything okay with you?"

"Oh sure. I wouldn't want to worry you while you're so busy saving an Antwerp junkyard and all. I did have a little run-in with Rose's husband, Rasheed Abdul—nothing Scruffy and I couldn't handle. The bottom of the seaside stairs, though—that clumsy devil Abdul's gone and splintered them into matchsticks. Made a much worse repair job for you, I'm afraid."

"*Jesu Christos!* Are *you* all right? You'd better have Stone get you a restraining order. As soon as I get home, I'm going to have a word with this, whoever-he-is—Abdul?"

"Yes, Rasheed Abdul. I'm fine. Scruffy spent a night in the Wee Angels Animal Hospital. He's okay now, too. But you should see the other guy. Abdul's got a sprained ankle, a torn thigh, and some eye irritation from the sand I threw at him."

Joe uttered a long string of curses, all Greek to me.

After repeated cautions from him to me and from me to him, we got back to the sexy love talk. Then he had to run and catch a flight to Belgium, and I was left to contemplate a few more lonely weeks. Maybe I would just see how much trouble I could get into. It would serve Joe right!

Chapter Nine

Plymouth Courthouse is set on an impossibly steep hill that many applicants for a driver's license in Plymouth County have had cause to dread. It's a favorite proving ground for sadistic DMV road tests. Using my best visualization techniques to zero in on an empty parking place—a skill that Fiona assures us should come naturally to a witch—I parallel parked, then carefully set my emergency brake. If this had been my driving test, I would have passed it with flying colors.

Speaking of colors, as I got out of the Jeep, I caught sight of Fiona in a flowered outfit that made her look like an advancing rosebush. As she labored up the hill on Heather's arm, I hurried to offer another helping hand and was allowed to carry the green reticule. Hefting the thing surreptitiously, I tried to discern if there was a pistol in the bottom.

Fiona, in her pixilated way, noticed everything. "I left it home, Cass," she said. "In case they're searching handbags. You know how paranoid judges have become in these uncertain times. Especially family court judges. That's where the real nuts come out of the woodwork."

"Bit of a mixed metaphor, that." Phillipa strode up behind us. "How about 'rats come out of the woodwork' instead." She was wearing that swirling black outfit again and had added a black hat and a pentagram swinging on a silver chain.

"Gee, Phil, don't you think you're overstating the role a bit?" I asked. I wore my own pentagram inside my green shirt.

"She doesn't want to be mistaken for a mundane," Fiona said, her words coming in little puffs of labored breath.

"Not likely," said Heather, hauling Fiona up the courthouse stairs with Dianic grace. "But just watch how fast that pentagram disappears if she happens to meet her rabbi."

"Ours is a Reform temple." Phillipa's hand hovered over the pendant in an undecided fashion. "Shrimp cocktails at bar mitzvahs. Female rabbi. And she happens to be quite interested in the goddess myths. In the Jewish faith, there's a celebration of the new moon called Rosh Chodesh—"

"Hold it, ladies." A uniformed policeman stopped our progress just inside the doors. "Oh . . . hi there, Phil. If you'll just put your bags on that table, Dottie will have a quick look while you step through the detector. Going to sit in on the hit-and-run upstairs?"

"No, the custody hearing in family court, ten a.m.," Phil said. "Friend of ours."

"That so! Both parties are here, I believe. Have a good one."

Dottie, who looked as if she would be more at home dishing out American chop suey in a school cafeteria, was seated at a long folding table. She glanced into each of our handbags in a cursory manner, pausing only to read with interest the titles of several pamphlets in the green reticule. *When Bad Magic Happens to Good Witches* and *Materializing Magic Money* were two I could see from across the hall. Fiona winked at me, then said to Dottie, "I do so hate to get caught in a line somewhere like the bank with nothing to read, don't you?"

We found Serena chatting with Deidre in the hall. It was the first time I'd seen Serena in a suit, which was, appropriately, dove gray and nunnish. Her wiry hair stood out around her head; it seemed to be crackling with energy. *A woman of power,* I thought. *Good—the best kind.*

"Oh, here they are, Serena. I thought you gals were going to be here early." Deidre, the time-stretcher, glanced at the wall clock with prim annoyance.

"Where are Rose and Hari?" Even as I asked the question, I saw Abdul and another man deep in conversation near the long windows. I noted with satisfaction that a crutch was leaning against the wall beside Rose's husband. His dark gaze turned our way, studying the group gathered around Serena with ill-concealed menace. I glared back, wishing I knew the art of *malocchio*. And dared to use it.

"Hari's safe at home with the other mothers. In my opinion, he's too young for these proceedings, unless the judge feels differently. I sent Rose to the Ladies. *He* is right over there, talking to his attorney and glowering at us." Serena's tone left no doubt as to who "he" was. "It's really cruel the way adversaries have to face each other in this hall. There ought to be separate waiting areas."

"One for the sheep and one for the wolves?" Phillipa suggested. "And maybe a third for wolves in sheep's clothing." Noting with interest that Serena's look quenched even Phillipa, I introduced Heather and Fiona to St. Rita's doyenne.

"And where's Rose's attorney?" Heather asked, depositing Fiona and her reticule on a nearby bench.

"I've decided to handle this one myself," Serena said. "Perhaps I didn't mention that I have a license to practice law in Massachusetts."

"And that's not all, Stone told me you're also a nurse, a teacher, a nun, and a notary," said Phillipa.

Serena smiled at our awed expressions. How many degrees could one woman hold? "I'm a pretty good cook, too, if you like soup. I used to run a soup kitchen in South Boston."

"Rose is in good hands, obviously. I'll just pop in and see how she's doing," I said. "Phil, do you want to find us seats in the front row, if you can, and hold them?"

Leaning against the sink, Rose was patting her face with a wet paper towel. She was deathly pale except for two bright red spots flaming on her cheeks. When she saw me, she tried to smile, but it came out more like a wince. "Oh, what will he do? I can't bear it if the court gives him my boy," she moaned in her rasping voice.

I put my arms around her and hugged her close. How slender she was—it was like holding a fawn. Yet again I felt her inner strength, a core that would not bend under pressure. "It's going to be fine. Serena is a woman of many talents, and she'll look out for you and Hari. My friends and I are here for moral support."

She looked at me fearfully. "One of the girls at St. Rita's told me that she'd heard you're involved with Satanists."

Even though that kind of rumor isn't funny, I couldn't help laughing. "You didn't believe that, did you?"

"I told her you had saved me and Hari when we had nowhere to go. She asked me if you made me sign a book. In blood."

"I don't think you have any blood to spare, Rose. No, dear, we're not Satanists. Satan came along with Christianity, and our beliefs and practices go back much farther. We're a Wiccan circle, and the word *Wicca* means to bend and shape, which we interpret in a spiritual sense. Nothing devilish about it. Tell the girl to check with Reverend Peacedale at the Garden of Gethsemane Church. He'll give me an anti-Satan reference, I'm sure." My neighbor the pastor and I had reached an amicable détente on the subject of religion. Last year I'd even agreed to talk to his parishioners about the origin of Halloween.

Serena put her head in the door. "It's time, Rose." We went forth to battle.

As the hearing droned on, we watched the proceedings attentively, a formidable presence of five in the front row, casting the occasional mean look at Abdul. No one fidgeted except Deidre, who knitted madly, hardly glancing at the needles, on something that looked like a monster scarf. I was willing to bet it was a spell of some sort.

Abdul's attorney, Seth Bettencourt, was a well-known Plymouth divorce lawyer who exuded a beefy bonhomie. In my mind's eye, I glimpsed him playing golf with Judge Lax at the Shawmut Country Club. Clairvoyance is such a mixed blessing, always telling me more than I'm comfortable knowing.

Serena was a marvel, but there was no way around the fact that Judge Lax's questions were leading toward shared visitation rights. In hopes of discrediting Hari's father, Serena brought up the complaint I had filed with the police after Abdul's attack. She even mentioned Scruffy's injuries and had the veterinarian's report to confirm them. As the coup de grâce, she introduced the photographs of Rose with a black eye. Unfortunately, it had already been healing and looked more yellow than black. Bettencourt described it as the result of a sleepless night and careless makeup. He countered my police report with Abdul's complaint about me and read every lying word of it aloud. Judge Lax looked dispassionately at both parties, then called for a fifteen-minute recess. Out to take a leak and have a smoke. More than I wanted to know again.

Abdul strode out of the room, Bettencourt following hurriedly after him. While they were gone, Serena talked quietly and calmly to a distraught Rose, who was looking down at her clenched hands. We stayed in our seats, waiting for the proceedings to continue.

Fiona whispered to me, "If Rasheed would only get angry. Show his true nature to the judge. I do believe the five of us ought to be able to crack that smooth mask he wears. It's very thin, you know."

"Yeah, how?" I whispered back. Heather, on Fiona's other side, leaned over to listen. Phillipa, beside me, did the same, and Deidre stopped her furious knitting to hear what we were up to.

"It's a certain vibration. When enough women start it humming, a man gets very uncomfortable. If he can leave, he will do that. If he's forced to stay put, he may just lose his cool. Men cannot abide that vibration."

"Vibration? What on earth do you mean, Fiona? Is this something out of *Hazel's Book of Household Recipes* again?" Deidre whispered fiercely, referring to a moldy leather volume that

Fiona had picked up at a yard sale, full of arcane wisdom and Early American magic that had proved useful on more than one occasion.

"No, this is something that every woman can do. It's partly the authority of the mother. Partly our suppressed wisdom, what we know without words. And it's our hidden laughter, ready to erupt at any moment. Especially the laughter. Think of the expression 'she laughed up her sleeve.' Think of three women in a kitchen preparing dinner. Each busy at her task, they are smiling at some foolish business and humming. A man walks in. Stops. Finds some immediate reason to leave, to run away before that vibration shrinks him to nothing. It's not only to avoid tedious work that men stay out of kitchens. It's a secure man indeed who won't back away from his mother-in-law, his wife, and his grown daughter all together in the same room, no other male present. It's too unnerving."

"So, how exactly do we set that vibration going, Fiona?" Deidre asked the question on all our lips.

"Like I said, it's a humming thing."

"It will have to be a silent hum, or Judge Lax will have us thrown out of his courtroom," Phillipa said in a low tone.

"Yes, a humming thought will do it," Fiona continued. "You must concentrate on how ridiculous Abdul is with his posturing, how fearful he is to let a woman be free, how ineffectual his efforts are, and how small his penis must be."

Heather snickered. "Ah, that, too. Will this work, do you think?"

"What have we got to lose?" I said, half-converted. Fiona might be a bit eccentric, but she was magic, too. "As we know, thoughts are things."

Deidre began the quietest *sotto voce* hum to the tune of *I'm going to wash that man right out of my hair*—which got us all giggling.

Still smiling when the hearing resumed, we beamed the full measure of our humor and our scorn straight at Abdul. I don't know what the others were doing, but I found the ghost of hum within myself, like an inner tuning fork, and set it going. When we saw Abdul shift uncomfortably in his chair, we knew we were doing something right. I could almost feel the bench beneath us quiver and tremble. I thought of Abdul, the woman beater, falling on his knees in the broken stairway, rubbing at his eyes full of sand. The soundless laughter bubbled up in my soul, the disdain and derision.

In the middle of Serena's carefully worded implication that Hari's father intended to leave the country with the boy and return to Saudi Arabia, something in the balance of the room shifted. Abdul sprang up from his chair with clenched fists. Bettencourt pulled him back. Abdul shook his finger at us, then turned and whispered heatedly to his attorney. Loud enough for everyone to hear, he demanded, "The judge must clear the courtroom of these whores. Look at them. They are without modesty. They are distracting the judge from the truth. He is believing the lawyer's lies."

Judge Lax brought down his gavel, sounding a warning note. "Mr. Bettencourt, please restrain your client from any more outbursts of that nature, or I will have him forcibly restrained. Bailiff . . . ?"

On the bench, we linked little fingers invisibly and hummed on in silence, the smallest of smiles lifting the corners of our mouths as we studied Abdul with disparaging expressions. Serena looked up at us with a startled expression. Rose watched us for a moment, then glanced nervously at Abdul.

Sweat was beading on her husband's forehead. He crumpled the page of notes he had been holding. He jumped to his feet again so suddenly that his chair crashed to the floor. "I demand that these . . . *women* . . . be excluded from the hearing. They have no business here but to corrupt my wife. Women should not be allowed to leave their homes and solicit trouble. Women should not be attorneys. This woman speaking for my wife is an absurdity, like a monkey driving a car. She ought to be dragged into the street by her hair."

Bettencourt was a muscular man despite his thickened middle. He managed to pull Abdul back from the brink, righted the fallen chair, and sat his client down in it. The pencil in Abdul's fist broke in two, but whatever his attorney whispered into his ear convinced him to remain quiet from then on. The lawyer wiped his forehead with a large white handkerchief. He apologized profusely to the judge, to Serena, and to everyone else in the courtroom, which was nearly empty anyway, family court not being as great a draw as criminal proceedings. But the damage had been done. Judge Lax was not amused.

Citing the volatile nature that Hari's father had exhibited in his courtroom, the judge ruled that visitation would be restricted to two hours every other Sunday under the supervision of Hari's mother and whomever else she might choose to have present. He strongly advised Abdul to attend an anger management seminar and promised, if he did so, that the matter of custody could be revisited six months from the present date. He banged down his gavel once more and rose. I wondered if he'd felt some of Abdul's discomfort. We all stood respectfully while he swept out of the courtroom, headed for, I didn't doubt, a stiff drink and a comforting lunch.

Before any further confrontation could occur, Attorney Bettencourt briskly escorted his client out the door. Abdul would leave now, roar away in his black pickup, but he would be back, I thought. He would always be trouble.

"My God, what did you do to him, Cass." Serena had made a beeline for us as soon as the courtroom had cleared. "I could feel something very disturbing in the air. What *was* that?"

Rose followed her attorney in a bemused fashion, hope beginning to light up her face. "It's over, then. We won?" she whispered. "Whatever happened, I thank you for it. Rasheed lost his temper. Everyone saw that."

We all looked at Fiona, who smiled modestly. "I call it a humming. We hummed at Abdul—silently, of course. Men are so sensitive, poor dears."

"Wicked . . . but effective," Serena said. I sensed that she wanted to cross herself but thought it inappropriate to her present role.

"It's not wicked at all," I protested. "Just one more of those spirit gifts everyone possesses. But don't be alarmed. What happened to Abdul, he did to himself. 'Harm none' is our creed."

"I don't think Rasheed Abdul will see this morning's work as harmless," Serena said. "I would say extra precautions are in order, and I intend to take them at St. Rita's. Coming, Rose?" She took Rose's hand in her firm grip.

Led like a child, Rose smiled at me over her shoulder all the way out of the courtroom door.

"This calls for a celebration," Heather said. "Let's do lunch, my treat. There's a nice little restaurant just opened on the wharf. No liquor license, alas, but they will provide stemware. And I just happen to have a few bottles of Moselle in the trunk of my car. Perfect with seafood . . ."

After the successful conclusion of a new enterprise, a raucous lunch, and a long walk on the beach with Scruffy, I was fit for nothing except ladylike collapse. But first, to assuage my conscience, I'd check my computer for orders before retiring to my favorite reading chair with the new Tony Hillerman novel. Among the *Lose Weight While You Sleep*, *Make Big Money at Home*, and *Enlarge Your Penis* ads, plus a few genuine orders, an e-mail from Freddie came as a pleasing surprise.

From: witch freddie freddie13@hotmail.net
To: witch cass shiptonherbs@earthlink.net
Subject: help!

hi, cass. it's me at the library in orlando. this place is awesome. free email and all the fixings!

hope you're in HIGH SPIRITS and still grooving on the footloose greek dude. by the way, how's that hunk adam? in atlanta, right?

been working at epcot center and so far have not
screwed up any of the futurama, if you don't count making
the hologram of yr typical astronut dance around the moon
like he had a hotfoot. it's okay, though—no one caught on
it was me.☺

speaking of NUTS, i think i got here just in time. step-
dad is long gone, and who gives a s**t! but what a piece of
work mom got herself mixed up with this time. billy
coates, AKA billygoat. Don't have to be no psychic genius
to catch the vibes here. he's after the boys, the dirty pervert. but never fear, freddie is here.

but here's the thing, i do need some hex info. i mean, i
know you drummed it into me not to do a REAL hex in
case it should, like, boomerang back and lay the plague on
yours truly. but there must be some loophole when you really need to push a guy under a truck. so, what do you suggest, o wise one? from my vast wiccan studies you forced
me to do, i'm dredging up the word BANISHING. or was
it VANISHING? either way, i'd like to see the last of this
SOB.

you can write me here at the library, see address above.
i'll check back to see what you've come up with. not
exactly private, but if i get screwed, i can always frizzle the
bank of computers. ONLY KIDDING! HA HA ☺☺☺

hugs to all the witches. tummy scratches to Scruffy.
freddie.

P.S. RSVP ASAP!

Best to send her some simple ritual to satisfy that urge to hex,
I thought. That gal had so much psychic energy, Billy would be
fortunate indeed to escape in one piece. I recalled how Miss
Manson, a teacher who'd blamed Freddie for the crash of her
computers, had wound up in a car crash with a broken jaw. Poetic
justice of the poltergeist sort. Of course, Freddie was nearly out

of her teen years now, so we could hope that her personal poltergeist would fade away like an imaginary playmate. Those mischievous imps hardly ever survived into the young adulthood of their doppelgangers.

From: Cassandra Shipton shiptonherbs@earthlink.net
To: Winifred McGarity freddie13@hotmail.com
Subject: Harm None!

Hi, Freddie.
So glad to hear from you.! I'm sure you can find a POSITIVE way to rescue Jack and Jim. Concentrate only on happy outcomes for all, even for B.C., resulting in his traveling to points unknown. Banishing is best done at the waning of the moon. Appropriate herbs are Bay, Cinnamon, Rosemary, Sage etc. If all else fails, makes a good chicken rub. Am sending frankincense & myrrh, also one of Dee's amulets, by Priority mail. Colors are black, blue. Remember, threefold law, and THINK GOOD THOUGHTS.
BIG NEWS! Joe and I are getting married at Yule!! Plan to be here!!! (Handsome Adam will also attend.)
Love from me and the Circle. Scruffy sends sloppy kiss. Keep in touch.
Cass

I had Fiona to thank—again—this time for the book-cart brainstorm. The week following Abdul's downfall at the hearing, Fiona called and asked me to meet her at Black Hill Branch Library, where she was the chief librarian on the three days a week it was open. A cozy bungalow of the kind people used to order out of the Sears catalog (some assembly required) in the 1920s, the building had lost none of its charm in being converted to a library. It was owned by the Women's Cooperative for Folk Arts, who had a quilting room in the basement.

The interior was furnished like an old schoolhouse, a little worse for wear—a teacher's desk with a cushioned swivel chair, sturdy bookcases, readers' tables and chairs, and even the obsolete catalog file, all made of warm aged oak. The only crack in this time warp was the functional little PC on Fiona's desk, which hummed and buzzed alongside a Tiffany dragonfly lamp, a dish of butterscotch candies, and her Persian cat, Omar Khayyám. As our resident "finder," Fiona was as much at home researching in cyberspace as she was dowsing with a crystal pendulum over a map.

When I arrived, Omar welcomed me with his usual frosty, unblinking stare, then stalked off to police the crowded Periodicals Room, where a naive field mouse might occasionally creep in for shelter. Fiona, however, greeted me with a satisfied smile and a gleam of triumph in her eye, the sure sign she's made a 'find.' One could always gauge what kind of a day she was having by the number of pencils stuck in her coronet of braids. Today there were three, and it was barely past lunchtime. Obviously, some excitement was afoot.

"Oh, goodie, you're here. Just read this, Cass." She thrust a wrinkled interlibrary memo into my hands, then put the kettle on the hot plate and measured out real tea leaves into a fat brown teapot.

I read. The Friendship League Outreach to the Troubled, Sick and Mending was organizing a bookmobile to visit Jordan Hospital, Harbor View Rest Home, Indian Hill Hospice, Manomet Manor Rehabilitation Center, and Red Sails, the Retired Seaman's Home. Twice a week, volunteers would wheel a book cart from room to room at each establishment, offering new books to read and collecting the returns. I was beginning to see the light, but I waited for Fiona to unveil her inspiration.

"Cass, I know you've been taking to heart the string of untimelies at Manomet Manor, even lecturing Maeve and me about poking around while we're there to spend a few days on physical therapy. Now Rose's got herself a job at the Manor as lab technician and part-time pharmacist. Meanwhile, as usual, Stone is warning you to stay away. Honestly, wouldn't you think he'd learn just to relax, and let us clear a few of his cases?" The teakettle began to whistle, and Fiona got up to pour boiling water into the pot. She rattled around in a cupboard and came out with a tin of gingersnaps.

"It's very frustrating," I admitted.

"Yes, because once you get that investigating bee in your bonnet, it seems to keep on buzzing. Just part of your nature, dear. So when I read this, it occurred to me that you might like to volunteer to woman the book cart at the Manor." Fiona massaged her hip in an absentminded way. Remembering how sprightly she had appeared last year, dancing the circle with a youthful glamour, I felt a quiet sadness and wished with all my heart that I could find some healing magic for my ailing friend.

"What an outstanding idea! Fiona, you're a wonder." I had been chafing at being left out of the action. This was a perfect opportunity to scout around the Manor in a disarming way. Not even Stone could prevent me from being a volunteer. The visiting book lady! *Just my cup of tea*, I thought, sipping the fragrant green brew that Fiona had poured into Asian cups.

"Yes, well . . . I fancy I have some clout with the FLOTSAMs, as I like to call them, so I've already put your name right at the top of the volunteers list for Manomet. The libraries are stocking the bookmobile, and some Friendly will be driving it. Your job simply will be to meet the FLOTSAM bookmobile, load up your cart, and wheel it around to needy readers. Some bright new novels will be a nice change from daytime TV—*Jerry Springer* and *One Life to Live*. You'll have to keep records, of course, and pick up returns—we're not giving away the books. This will be a circulating lending library."

"It's perfect, Fiona. When can I start?"

"A FLOTSAM committee is meeting to give out assignments

next Tuesday. Just show up at the main library and give your name to Candy DeFrees. She'll have the assignment set up ahead of time. Here, have some gingersnaps."

Now all I had to do was to figure out what I was looking for.

The barely audible crunching of cookies didn't escape Omar's sharp little ears. He oozed through the doorway from the Periodicals Room and rubbed against Fiona's ankles in a proprietary way.

"Does Mommy's precious little pussy want a cookie?" she crooned at him.

Really, I hoped I wasn't that fatuous about Scruffy. He would be mortified.

Great minds, they say, run in the same ley lines. It wasn't two days later when Heather had *her* bright idea. "I have the most wonderful plan," she caroled into the phone. "Come for drinks! And a barbecue." I looked at the pile of orders I had printed out. What kind of a businesswoman was I? Shouldn't I really be packing and shipping my herbal products, for which I'd already been paid, and not carousing around with the Queen of the Vine?

"Sounds great," I said. "What time? Okay to bring Scruffy?"

"Early, so that we can get a jolly start. Of course bring Scruffy, only be warned that I don't allow doggies to have preserved garbage like hot dogs and sausages, or any people food, for that matter. We will, however, grill a few smelts for the pups as a special treat, and because Dick begged and pleaded. We humans will have swordfish. I feel that the swordfish leads a happy, productive life in the ocean before it becomes my dinner, not like some indecently crated veal. Honestly, one of these days I really will become a total vegetarian!"

"Then you'll expect the dogs to be vegetarians, too, and that's not fair to carnivores. Also, whenever you're a guest, people will feel called upon to serve you a boring vegetable lasagna. I can't believe that Lucrezia does barbecue," I said.

"Oh, Lucrezia and Caesare have some urgent business in Boston. 'A *commissione*,' she called it. She said they'd be back tomorrow. I said, 'Take the whole weekend.' Dick will man the grill, like a quintessential suburban husband. But don't worry. Lu left several kinds of Italian picnic food—macaroni with shrimp, green-bean salad, eggplant relish, and Goddess-knows-what-else to keep us nourished until she returns. Phillipa would be entranced with her recipes. I wish I could invite them, too, but Stone might think my great new plan is interfering."

As Heather burbled on, I had the strangest mental picture of Lucrezia and her brother, crouched down in Heather's Mercedes, waiting for someone to emerge from a popular North End restaurant onto the dark street. Luciano's Villa. The sign flashed plainly across my inner vision, then disappeared just as quickly. But years of putting up with this strange talent had taught me to grab the moment and describe it to myself in words before it slid out of my brain into oblivion.

"Did Lucrezia and Caesare go by train?" I asked.

"No need of that. We have acres of cars here now that I have Dick. I loaned them the dog car." Heather's "dog car," of course, was the Mercedes.

"Well, it's nice to know they're having a little holiday. And they wouldn't need to pack much for just a night or two. Especially as Lucrezia always seems to wear the same black dress."

"Yes, you'd think so, but they went off dragging quite a large leather case. I said, 'Wow, Lucrezia, what's that, the Malatesta family memoirs?' "

"And she said?"

A short pause, then Heather said, "You're after something. 'Bringing presents for her nieces and nephew,' she said. What's up?"

"We'll talk later. Scruffy and I have to get gussied up for dinner now. Looking forward to it!"

It was a mellow August evening, the trees heavy with their dark green burden, the air scented with sweet over-ripeness. Dick had the gas grill fired up on the patio, a flagstone floor expansive enough for a Gatsby party. His mane of hair was tied

back in a ponytail, and he wore a chef's apron with the legend
GRILL OF MY DREAMS, I LOVE YOU. Waving a basting brush like a
baton, he whistled a fanfare.

"Greetings, Cass." With his hearty kiss on my cheek, I caught
a whiff of garlic and antiseptic. "I see that your loyal companion's
looking quite recovered from his encounter with that son of a
bitch." Laying down the basting brush, he checked Scruffy over
with a professional air, feeling his head where the bump had
been, lifting his eyelids.

Hey, back off, big guy. Scruffy twisted his head away and trotted
over to check out the fish steaks marinating near the grill.

Assorted dogs were woofing plaintively in their kitchen-yard
enclosure. Heather nipped into the fenced area and brought out
Honeycomb, groomed and shining. "Good girl, sit and stay." The
grinning dog barely poised on her rump, which was ready to wiggle into action at any moment in the way of golden retrievers.

Heather gave me a sisterly hug and Scruffy a brisk pat. Filling
glasses with white wine from an open bottle on the table, she
handed me one properly by the stem. More bottles were cooling
in a bucket of ice. "Isn't she a doll?"

*Hey, get a load of the blonde. Maybe she's not fixed. The evening's
looking up.* Scuffy, who'd been brushed and adorned with a jaunty
red scarf he wore most reluctantly, was now in high good humor
to be sniffing up this delectable female. She turned her head modestly away from his gaze and laid her ears a little flatter against
her head. *What a babe!*

The wine was a perfect Soave, deliciously refreshing. I helped
myself from the antipasto tray on the long patio table and asked,
"So what's the deal? I'm dying to know . . ."

Heather glanced back at Dick; he seemed engrossed in slather-
ing French bread with oil and herbs. "Think about this: Honey-
comb, this good-natured darling, was once registered as a Therapy
Dog with a Massachusetts group called BONES, an acronym for
Building Opportunities for Nurturing and Emotional Support.
You're not giving those dogs *cheese*, are you?"

I'd been nabbed in the act of holding a small wedge of provolone in each hand for Honeycomb and Scruffy. Heather was very strict about feeding dogs from the table. I changed the subject. "How did a highly trained dog like Honeycomb wind up at Animal Lovers shelter?"

"Dogs thrive best on an unvaried diet, Cass. It's not a kindness to ruin their appetites with tidbits." The dogs, however, were licking their chops and gazing at me fondly. "It was just one of those grim chain of events in some dogs' lives. Her first owner, the trainer, contracted AIDS and passed away. His sister was glad to give Honeycomb a home, but then her husband was transferred to South America for a two-year stint, and carting a dog around became unfeasible. Honeycomb was supposed to live with a couple of dear old ladies who sell worm farms in Kingston."

"Worm farms?"

"Three or four crates stocked with starter worms for seventy-five dollars a pop. Worms are environment-friendly. People raise them to aerate their gardens. They're voracious eaters, but they live on any old kitchen scraps, chopped real small, even soaked pizza-delivery boxes. Anyway, right after her family left for South America, Honeycomb stayed with a neighbor who was supposed to deliver her to the worm ladies."

The swordfish hit the grill and smelled heavenly. Heather went into the house for the cold dishes, and I followed to help and hear the rest of Honeycomb's story. While Heather and I loaded up trays and returned laden with garlicky goodies, she continued: "Before the neighbor could get to Kingston, however, one of the worm ladies had a heart attack—a mild one, but taking on a new dog didn't seem to fit into their plans after all. Meanwhile, Honeycomb took off in search of her family. Fortunately, the kid who found her, starving and shivering with fear, brought her to me. She still had her tags, so I called around, reached the family in South America, and got the whole story." We laid the serving dishes on the table. A splendid feast!

Dick had finished the swordfish and was grilling a mess of

smelts for the salivating canines behind the wire fence, plus the ones at my feet. While he was busy flipping fish, Heather said in a much lower tone, "Don't you think I'll be able to pay a few visits to Manomet Manor with my trained Therapy Dog? Have a look around, you know? You could come with me, if you like. But don't say anything to Dick about our real agenda." Expertly opening another bottle of wine, Heather refilled our glasses. "Here's to sleuthing!"

"A fine idea, and I thank you, but I've already volunteered to be the book-cart lady a couple of days a week. Do you realize that most of us are now going to be tiptoeing around there looking for malfeasance? Except for Dee and Phil, of course. Poor Dee . . . she has her hands full with all those kids."

"Well, Phil had to go and marry the law, and Dee—let's face it—is frighteningly fertile. If she isn't turning out dolls like a machine, she's making babies. But Dee's a very resourceful gal. What do you want to bet that she thinks of something? Geez . . . cool it, here comes the chef," Heather whispered, with a brilliant smile for Dick.

Scruffy and Honeycomb were lying on the patio, each with a smelt held neatly upright between paws. The treats didn't last long, but the nice fishy oil lingered to be licked off lips and paws appreciatively from time to time.

As we drove away later, Scruffy leaned out as far as the half-open window of the Jeep would allow, looking back at Honeycomb, the wind riffling his smelt-stained red scarf. Memories! *Swell party, Toots.*

Chapter Ten

On Sunday, keeping in mind that it was three hours earlier in San Francisco, I waited until past noon to call Cathy, but still she sounded groggy. Clearly, I'd woken her up. The life of the theater has its own protocols. "How's the play going?" I asked.

"It's been a disaster," my daughter said in a low, tragic tone, nearly a whisper, yet projected clearly from coast to coast. "Between the collapsing scenery, the disappearing props, the missed cues, and the freakish lighting, I have never experienced so many screwups since I did a stint in that Scottish play last year."

"You mean *Macbeth?*"

"*Mother!* It's bad luck even to say the name."

"Really? I wonder that they keep producing it, then. So, is O'Neill closing?"

"No, we're still going strong. A couple of solid reviews, and even a flattering mention of me, 'Catherine Hauser brings a bright new flame to the brooding darkness of O'Neill's vision . . .' "

"Wonderful, darling! Please fax me a copy so that I can show it off to my friends."

She sighed. "Ah, yes, the white witches' sewing circle. I'll see if I have a copy around here somewhere. How are you and Rose getting on?"

"Rose isn't with me at the moment."

"Oh, Mother . . . and here I thought you'd watch out for the poor thing. You've always seemed to have such a penchant for taking in strays."

Defending my dereliction with the news of Rose's progress, I explained that my Wiccan friend's husband, the detective, had helped Rose get a restraining order and find sanctuary at St. Rita's. I made a humorous anecdote of Abdul losing his cool and shooting off his mouth at the custody hearing—but I didn't mention our efforts to unsettle him in the courtroom, nor Abdul's earlier attack on me. It has always been my first instinct not to worry the children with my pursuits and problems. Maybe that was not such a good idea—ignorance now, shock later. "And Rose has landed a good job at a local medical facility," I added. "She's a sweet thing, and I'm glad she's doing so well."

I could hear Cathy yawn. "I must give her a call sometime. Speaking of damsels in distress, what have you done about Becky, Mother?"

Here comes the guilt trip. "Well, we had lunch, dear, and a nice chat. All marriages go through these difficult patches, you know. I wouldn't worry just yet." Even as I laid out the appropriate platitudes, I felt a twist in my stomach that said it was high time I got back to my oldest daughter to see what, if anything, she was going to do about the philandering Ron, instead of just obsessing about Rose and Manomet Manor.

Before we hung up, I sent up a trial balloon. "Cathy, darling, I have some good news of my own. Joe and I are getting married around Christmastime. Do you think that you and Irene might be able to come east for the ceremony? It would mean so much! I'll help with the tickets, if that's a problem."

"It's hard to tell, at this point, if we'll have the time. I mean, if the play's still running and all. Let me talk to Irene and get back to you. But, cheers, Mother! Wonderful news! Break a leg, and all that."

My wedding! Just the news that Becky had been waiting to hear, and a perfect reason for me to call and then gently probe into her personal life. But the problem was, I couldn't find her. For two days I reached only Ron's disembodied voice on the answering machine, even at nine at night, which was as late as I would allow myself to call anyone who might be taking a relaxing bath or making love. Despite my increasingly pressing messages, Becky never called back. Much as I avoided calling her at work, since I seemed to have a knack for interrupting vital conferences, on Tuesday I finally did ring Lowell, FitzGerald & Lowell.

"Rebecca Lowell, please. This is Cassandra Shipton calling."

"Becky's mom? Hi, this is Sherry, the receptionist. I'll put you through to her secretary, Beverly . . . well, she used to be Ms. Lowell's secretary. Please hold."

After a short interval of soft rock, a woman's voice answered, "Robert Holland's office."

"Oh . . . there must be some mistake. I'm calling Rebecca Lowell. This is Cassandra Shipton."

"Mrs. Shipton? Ms. Lowell's mother? Was Ms. Lowell supposed to be here today? I'm sure you must know she's left the firm. This is Beverly Myers, her former secretary. I've been reassigned to Mr. Holland."

"I see. Yes, of course. Thank you so much." I hung up in total confusion, too embarrassed to ask more questions.

If Becky had left Lowell's, why hadn't she told me? Had she left home, too? Where in the world could she be? I called her home number and left a new message. "This is very urgent, Becky. Call me at once! If I don't hear from you by eight, I'll assume something terrible has happened and call the police." That should do it. There was nothing Ron avoided more assiduously than the kind of neighborhood gossip occasioned by the arrival of a patrol car to inspect the premises.

The rest of the afternoon I stomped around the house, banging together herbal orders for tomorrow's mail. I could have just jumped in the car and headed up to Boston, but then I might have missed my daughter's call. Or I might arrive at her house to find her angry with me for my reasonable worries. It wasn't as if Becky told me much about her life—she hadn't even shared news of her pregnancy nor her sadness in miscarrying.

Scruffy watched me with some dismay, occasionally rolling his orange sponge ball between my pacing feet to check my reflexes. *Fancy a game, Toots? How about a walk on the beach?* He wagged his tail invitingly and trotted over to the hook by the door to nose his leash. Then he looked back at me with that canine equivalent of a winning smile, which sat so oddly on his bushy-browed face, it always made me giggle.

"Not now, Scruffy, that's a good boy. I'm waiting for a phone call. You go for a walk by yourself." Opening the kitchen door, I shooed him out. Glumly, he dropped the orange ball on the porch where Joe had installed a new screen door with a pet flap. Looking out from the kitchen window, I could see Scruffy standing half in and half out of the flap, taking in the neighborhood news with alert ears and a sensitive nose. At that moment, a squirrel raced across the yard toward the clump of birch trees, and Scruffy dashed down the porch stairs in hot pursuit. Now there was a real game! He'd never yet caught one of those wily fellows, but he hadn't given up, either.

Scruffy was back from his stroll and we'd both had supper by the time my message finally was answered. But it was Ron, not Becky, who called, his voice sounding thick and loud, as if he'd been drinking his dinner. "Jesus, Cass, sorry we didn't get back to you right away."

"Hey, Ron, what's going on? I haven't been able to reach either of you at home, and now when I called your firm this morning, I was told that Becky's not working there anymore."

"Nothing to get frantic about, my dear. Becky's taking herself a little vacation, that's all. She's been working those sixty-hour weeks—you know how demanding the firm can be for associates. It just got to be too much for her, and she called it quits. Up to her, that's what I said. If she wanted to make partner, she should stick her nose to the grindstone and stop whining. If that wasn't her first priority, okay by me. Stay home and read novels, for all I care. *Entirely* up to her."

"How reassuring, Ron. Since you're not only a partner but a Lowell in a Lowell firm, couldn't you have simply eased up on your wife's schedule a bit before she reached the breaking point? And where is she exactly? I mean, where is she right this minute? As I told you on the phone, if I can't reach her, I'm calling the police."

"Jesus, Cass. What do you think, that I've buried her in the cellar? She's a big girl, and she's gone off on her own. But she didn't do me the courtesy of telling me where to find her. Just left me this goddamn note."

"What does the note say?"

"That's private, Cass. You've never been a prying sort of mother-in-law, so don't start now."

"Read me the note, Ron."

"No, Cass, I won't. But I will tell you Becky says she's perfectly fine. Needed a little space to think things over, that's all, and she'll be back in a few days. It's enough for me, so it should be enough for you. We don't live in each other's back pocket, you know. I like to think ours is an open marriage. But if anything were really wrong, don't you think I'd call you first? Trust me."

No sense my telling him that I didn't trust him because Becky couldn't, and the open marriage was all on his side. Whatever nasty thing I said now might rise up to haunt me later. I'd learned the risks of taking sides in a marital quarrel. When and if the warring couple decided on a truce, it was the well-meaning sympathizer who got trashed. So I kept it simple and firm: "If you hear from Becky, please tell her to call me at once. I'll give this two days, and if I haven't heard from my daughter by then, I'm going to report her as a missing person."

"Jesus, Cass—"

Gently I hung up the phone, then punched in Fiona's number, my hot line for whatever was missing. Now that she'd taken to carrying a cell phone in the reticule from which she was never parted, she answered immediately. "Cass, dear. You're sounding a wee bit stressed."

"*Stressed* doesn't begin to describe it. Try *crazed*, or *demented*. I can't find Becky!" I wailed on Fiona's imagined shoulder. "She's left the firm and left home, and Ron doesn't seem to know where she is—or care. Oh, I wish she would have confided in me. Do you think you could dowse for me? I need to know where she is, and if she's all right."

"Of course I will. Give me a half hour, and I'll call you back. Meanwhile, you have yourself a nice cup of that calming tea mix of yours. Make it plenty sweet."

I took my tea prescription, with extra honey stirred in, while sitting on the porch and watching the moon rise full and magnificent over the ocean, throwing its road of light across the water directly to my shore with its broken stairway. Whatever expression you see on the full moon's face, whether sad or merry, foretells your fate in the month ahead, according to the old beliefs. But this moon seemed to me to be completely enigmatic—September would be a month of unsolved mysteries perhaps.

Traveling on moonbeams, I jumped when the phone rang. "Now, dear, I'm perfectly sure she's all right," Fiona began. "I find her on the Cape, and why not? It's an ideal retreat this time of year. May I suggest that you try your own vision thing? I never understand why you're so reluctant to do that. As the Marines say, see all that you can see."

"*Be.* It's *be all you can be,* Fiona. I'm always afraid of what will materialize, you know that. So many terrible things out there. Okay. Thanks from the bottom of my heart, and I'll give it a try. The Cape seems a nice safe place, doesn't it?"

Around ten, I took Scruffy for a walk in the bright moonlight, around my herb-garden paths and up to the pines near the main road. *Boring, boring. When are we going to run on the beach?* Scruffy trudged along, complaining and marking one or two of his favorite trees. "Not until Joe comes home and fixes those broken stairs," I explained. *It's always something spoiling my fun. The least you could do is throw a stick.* I picked up a smooth little branch and gave it a toss back toward the house.

That night, before I went to sleep, I concentrated on an answer to my questions about Becky. Perhaps I could prod my unconscious a bit, for, truly, my clairvoyant skills are not under my control. I slept fitfully, with dreams that were insistent but not illuminating.

It was past eleven the next morning, as I was gazing at the computer, thinking I should turn it on and check my orders, when an image began to form in my mind of Becky. I actually saw her on the dark monitor, as if I were scrying in a crystal ball. She was at the wheel of her Volvo driving over a bridge. Her mouth was set in that determined line I knew so well, but her brow was calm. A moment later, the vision faded.

I had my hand on the phone when it rang again. "Hi, Mom."

"Oh, Becky, I've been *so* worried about you. I called your office, and last night I talked with Ron. Where are you, honey?"

"Oh, sorry, Mom. I was just in no mood for a heart-to-heart. I've been in Truro for a few days, so lovely, walking the dunes and all. The peace of it quite restored my soul, as the psalm goes. I had to get away, you know. Long story. I found something— credit card receipts in Ron's desk at work. Couldn't stay another minute at dear old Lowell, FitzGerald, & Lowell. No more Mrs. Nice Wife, slaving away in the background, like a donkey turning a mill wheel. Besides, I've had another job offer that interests me. But I'd rather tell you about all that in person. So I thought I'd come by and stay with you for a while, if that's okay."

"Wonderful, dear. Are you on your way now? I'll get your room ready."

"I'm in Bourne. Less than an hour. And, Mom?"

"Yes?"

"Thanks."

The sunshine of my relief was somewhat dampened by a few niggardly questions. Wonderful to know that Becky was healthy and safe! And she'd sounded quite levelheaded. But how long was she planning to stay? Would she be here when Joe came home? A slight crimp in my new sexual freedom, confining love-making to extremely quiet romps in the bedroom. And how would she react to my Wiccan activities? I looked around the kitchen. Perhaps it was time to take down the bird-feathered witch's ladder that Deidre had made for me and put away Heather's weird woman candle with the fingers in it. Well, not real fingers, but a rather lifelike facsimile in the horned sign that Lucrezia had told her meant "good luck." I sighed. No, this was my style, my faith, my love affair, and my daughter must take me as I am.

"Come on, Scruffy. Let's get ready for Becky." I wished I could shine up her life as easily as I buffed the bureau top in the rose guest room, which I always thought of as "Becky's room" anyway. How many times I had felt sorry for myself because my children so rarely visited, and now here was my eldest daughter coming to me for help in a crisis and I was balking. Embarrassed by my own vacillation, I whipped a mop under the bed and around the braided rugs, then shook it vigorously out the window. After plumping up the pillows and duvet, I gave the room a shot of lavender fragrance—so uplifting!

Gasp! Ick! You're gassing me. Scruffy sneezed mightily. With their sensitive olfactory equipment, dogs don't care much for room sprays. He shook his head and leaped up on the flower-sprigged duvet, settling down for a pleasant nap. *Comfy den place!*

"Get off there, you horse." I waved my mop at him. "We have company coming. You can nap in the blue guest room—that's for boys." *Whoa! Who you calling 'horse.' Don't shake that mean old scare-dog at me!* Leaping off with alacrity, Scruffy slunk off with one re-proachful, backward glance. A moment later I heard him jumping up on one of the twin beds next door.

The blue guest room had been Scruffy's favorite retreat ever since he'd frequently shared it with Tip, a Native American boy whom I'd once fantasized about adopting. Tip's mother had deserted him, and his father was a drunk, but always Tip had been called back to them whenever they needed him. This summer, however, Tip was living with his uncle in Wiscasset, working at a fast-food place that wasn't too fussy about his age. Big blond John Thomas, who looked nothing like a Native American and liked it that way, was a master pipefitter at the shipyard, unattached and generous. J.T. had invested in a triple-decker, lived in the first-floor apartment himself, and had plenty of room and odd jobs for his nephew. If Tip decided to stay on after Labor Day and go to school down east, his father would hardly care, but I would miss the brightness of his presence—always helpful, willing, and cheerful. We'd been through some adventures together.

Maybe Cathy was right about my penchant for taking in strays. The year after Tip, it had been Freddie, my "apprentice," with her black spiked hair, sooty eyes, and miniscule skirts, who took over part of my life. I hoped I'd helped her to control her runaway psychokinetic energy. I wondered how she was getting along in protecting Jack and Jim from the "billygoat." Banishing can be a fairly tricky business. I missed her computer wizardry in running my on-line herbal business, but more than that, I missed her irrepressible spirit.

Recently, Rose and Hari had appeared, dumped on me by Cathy. Yet somehow, that reaching out to protect and nourish always seemed to be part of my karmic heritage. Perhaps it went along with being a clairvoyant. We always saw too much, knew more than we wanted to, and felt destined to help.

Now Becky, my own flesh and blood, needed something I could give. So never mind the intricate dynamics of my new life. I would do all I could for her; she could stay as long as she wished.

"Let's go, Scruffy. We need to cut a nice bouquet for Becky's room." Immediately he bounced out of the blue guest room and stood ready to accompany me. Dogs are never too comfortable to share a trip outdoors, where any adventure may happen. A cool breeze was coming from the west, bringing with it the barest hint of fall. Two or three leaves on the birch tree had turned yellow, and I could see one blazing branch of maple at the border of Jenkins Park. Scanning the sky for signs of rain, I began to cut a few sprigs here and there: sage for wisdom, mint for cheerfulness, a few late roses for color and beauty.

Scruffy, who had run off to chase a squirrel in the park, finally trotted back, tongue lolling. *Water, I need water. You should have seen the size of that ratty bugger. I almost got him, too.* We went indoors, where I found a fat white vase, like a little Buddha, in which to arrange the bouquet for the guest room's night table.

Maybe Becky would be hungry. Surely she wouldn't stop on the road for lunch on the way to her mother's house? Soon I was sautéing vegetables and adding broth and noodles for "emergency soup." Sandwiches! I'd hardly started on those when I heard a light honk in the front yard. Scruffy, who had been lying at my feet in wait for whatever scraps might fall his way, bounded to the kitchen window, barking excitedly, scaring away a couple of finches who'd been pecking at the bird feeder.

Becky had already reached the porch stairs when I met her, taking the satchel from her hand, leaving the garment bag that was slung over her shoulder and trying to throw my arms around both. Scruffy offered her the semi-enthusiastic greeting he reserves for siblings.

Between hugs, smiles, and exclamations, I studied my daughter, as mothers do after a separation. The last time we'd met for lunch, she'd been wearing her impeccable law office "uniform," navy blue suit and pumps. Now in jeans, an untucked black T-shirt, and ankle-high leather boots, she showed a little weight gain, the roundness in her face even more apparent with her hair tucked haphazardly behind her ears. Although she'd taken a slight tan that gave her face a becoming glow of health, her dark blue eyes still looked tired. "You look wonderful," I said, just as always.

"No I don't. I looked tired and scruffy. Oops. Apologies to the pooch." She offered the dog a desultory pat on the head. "Well-named, isn't he? Is that soup I smell? Mmmm, sandwiches, too, I see. I'm starved—and thirsty! After that long ride, I could use a drink."

I opened a special bottle that I'd been keeping chilled for Joe's return, some good German wine that had been a gift from Heather. During lunch on the porch, so pleasant now that it had been painted and refurbished with white wicker furniture and blue cushions, I asked not one of the many burning questions on my mind about Ron. She would get to that in her own good time. Instead I chattered on about my own last visit to Truro and how bizarre Provincetown had become. "Cathy and Irene will love it," Becky commented. "The funkiness, the freedom, the drama . . ."

Becky ate and drank quite a lot and gazed silently at the ever changing vista of the ocean. "Truro was a treat after a summer of slaving in Boston," she said one time. Then, "What's *really* new with you?"

I did have big news. Marrying news. But I thought I'd wait on that. "Oh you know—same old, same old. Cathy sent this little abused wife to me. Rose Fiorella, she was when they were in school. Maybe you knew her? She's married to Rasheed Abdul, who wants to take her and their son Hari back to Saudi Arabia to live. He's an abusive bastard, but Rose is in a good safe place now. St. Rita's, it's called. Run by an ex-nun, Serena Dove."

"Small world," Becky said. "I know them both. Rose was a slender waif with the most perfect skin when all the rest of us were getting zits. Pink cheeks. Clouds of dark hair."

"Yes, she reminded me of Rose Red from the fairy tale."

"And Cathy could have passed for Snow White when they hung around together. No wonder they were friends—they stepped out of the same fantasy world. What the hell was Rose thinking of, marrying a Saudi?"

"Prince Charming, maybe. Dark, mysterious, masterful. Maybe he was like that once, but I've run into him lately, and he's more the Bluebeard type now. And you say you've heard of Serena Dove, too?"

"Oh, yes. She was fairly well-known in Boston as an advocate for abused women. Rather high up among the charitable sisters until she got into trouble with the Church and sort of disappeared from the scene. So she's in Plymouth?"

"Yes, she's running a battered women's shelter called St. Rita's, but only because it used to be a convent. Privately funded now. What sort of trouble? Birth control?"

"Of course. When you're working with disadvantaged, abused women, it becomes obvious that one of the dangers they need to be protected from is unwanted pregnancies. Any more in that bottle?"

I poured the last of the wine into Becky's glass. Her face was flushed and her eyes a bit watery. *Time to get her settled in her room*, I thought. We could talk about her life later, when she was ready.

But just then she said, "I've been offered an interesting job I might take, now that I've left L. F. & L. Not much money but, I hope, more satisfaction than I got out of saving corporations from environmental responsibility. Katz and Kinder is looking for an associate in family law—divorce, custody. They also do civil rights, social security, and medical malpractice. But a decent reputation, not ambulance chasers." She drained her glass and shut her eyes, leaning back in the chair.

"Let's take your stuff upstairs. Just leave the dishes, I'll tend to them later," I suggested. "Do you have any experience in family law?"

She got up and walked wearily into the kitchen, where her bags were still stashed near the stairs. I picked up the heavier garment bag.

"Just a few months internship. Maybe you remember? With Deborah Perlmutter? Then I went to work in the senator's office and met Ron," she said as she trudged upstairs. Dropping her satchel in the guest room, she fell on the bed with a deep sigh. I hung her garment bag over the door.

"You rest a while. That was a long drive." I kissed her on the cheek and pulled the duvet over her.

Scruffy was sitting in the hall, watching us. *Need a warm dog to keep the girl company?*

"No, she doesn't. Downstairs, mutt!" I decreed.

"Might come in handy," Becky's sleepy voice continued. "Divorce law." She rolled over with her face toward the wall. I tiptoed out, put a hand on Scruffy's collar and guided him downstairs with me. *Divorce*—the word had been said.

Chapter Eleven

That night we went out for supper, a cozy oyster bar and restaurant called The Walrus and the Carpenter, where you could select your own lively lobster swimming in a tank and have it executed for your dinner, which I was too squeamish to do. We both ordered stuffed filets of sole with lobster sauce, however—which we hadn't had to personally condemn to the boiling pot.

When the waitress had opened and served the wine, Becky took one sip and began to relate everything about Ron's presumed infidelities as if the Pouilly-Fuissé were truth serum. After the miscarriage, he'd cooled toward her sexually, but she had thought that would pass. But then a few small, telling details had made her suspicious that he was seeing someone else. She'd searched his desk at work and found credit card receipts for lingerie and flowers that had never been gifts to her. Leaving the evidence strewn across the top of his daily diary, she'd typed a letter of resignation to the head honcho, Ron's uncle, Justin G. Lowell, that very day. After her stint on an exciting political campaign, the slavery at Lowell, FitzGerald & Lowell had seemed especially dull and unrewarding, so shaking off their archival dust was no loss at all. Then she'd packed and left Boston before Ron had a chance to befuddle her with denials, explanations, and promises.

By the time we got to the chocolate mousse, she was talking about divorce. With great restraint, I murmured sympathetically and listened. But a mother doesn't really have to voice her opinion to a daughter—it's been internalized already. "You're thinking I have to be quite sure that it's better to live alone than to live with Ron," she said.

"Yes, because that's what may happen. It's not easy being on your own, and you can't count on finding someone else to share your life." That seemed a gloomy prediction, however true. "Of course, if all else fails, there's always magic."

"Oh, God . . . don't trot out the love charms just yet, Mom. I think I might enjoy being a free woman for a while." She reached across the small table to take the check out of my hand, and we had a good little tug-of-war that tipped the fat little candle-in-a-jar at the back of the table. The linen napkin in the bread basket caught the flame and began to burn along the edge. A woman at the next table laughed a bit wildly at this unusual entertainment.

As we sprang up from our chairs, batting ineffectually at the flame dancing around the bread, the waiter hurried over to cover the conflagration with a large silver casserole cover he'd grabbed on the way. "Happens all the time," he said coolly. Looking down, I saw that I no longer had hold of the check, and Becky was fishing for her charge card.

"I don't know where you got that hardheadedness," I said.

She grinned. "You don't?"

After Becky had been with me for three days, we'd pretty well exhausted Plymouth's entertainment possibilities, and I could see she was getting restless and depressed. I persuaded her to call Ron, just to let him know she was okay and where she was. I guess I was hoping that underneath his cool manner he still cared and worried.

After that first short exchange, he called her back several times on her cell phone. Once she headed for the beach to talk to him, and I had to warn her off—the stairs were still broken and treacherous. Instead, she settled into an old Adirondack chair in the herb garden. From the kitchen window, I could see her talking a long time with her head leaning on the tiny black instrument, and even smiling occasionally. Becky would be going home soon. She'd try again. But in my experience, once a man has taken to chasing other women, he seldom gives it up, no matter how sincerely he promises to reform. Too bad there wasn't a Cheaters Anonymous Ron could join. Might backfire, though, if both sexes with roving eyes attended meetings.

At least there were no children . . . yet.

Turning away from the scene of Becky embracing her fate in the herb garden, my eyes focused on the postcard propped on my kitchen windowsill. *Wiscasset Harbor.* I turned it over and, for the umpteenth time, read the short message hand-printed on the back.

> *Hi, Ms. Shipton. Uncle John says okay for me to stay, and Pa don't mind. Starting 8th grade in Sept. Track & clarinet. Miss you and Scruff. Joe, too. Will be home for Xmas, in case Joe needs help with repairs. Love, Tip.*

He'd forgotten to add his new address, but I'd ferreted that out from his father and sent a short letter with some innocent news of our lives and an invitation to Joe's and my wedding at Yule. Because, after all, Tip was part of my family. As Fiona has said, everyone has a spiritual family as well as a biological one. They are the people to whom we are drawn, who reach out to us, who have something to teach us, whom we must care for when they appear in our lives. And it seemed as if my family would never stop growing. The heart always has room for one more.

On Saturday, when Joe arrived in another rented Chevy. I rushed out to the porch to meet him. "Becky's here," I warned him as he dropped his duffel bag, pitched his Greek cap onto the chair, and swept me into his sturdy arms. "Looking out the kitchen window with the barking dog."

"I never know what I'm going to find when I come home. Could be so much worse," he murmured into my hair, letting me stand back on my feet in a semblance of dignity. "What, no bombs? No runaway kids? No Saudis with baseball bats?"

"Oh, like your life is always smooth sailing. Becky's been on vacation in Truro and here for a few days. She's going back to Boston tomorrow night to start a new job, Katz and Kinder, family law. And you, how long are you home for this time?" Always my first question. I wished I could be more casual.

"I've been promised at least two weeks' leave. I'm planning on fixing those damned stairs once and for all, and anything else you need."

I laughed. "I think I can occupy your time in a meaningful way. But come on, say hello to Becky. Maybe we'll all go out to dinner tonight. Some new place—Becky and I set fire to the last restaurant we were in. Speaking of which, I hear you sailors always have money to burn when you're on shore. Is that true?"

"Not only am I loaded with back pay, I also have five pounds of Belgian chocolates to share."

"I thought that duffel bag looked unusually lumpy."

"And that's not all." He pulled me close to him again. Becky opened the window to the porch. "Hey, you two. Aren't you ever going to break it up? This dog of yours is going ape."

He's back . . . he's back . . . hey, Toots, this girl won't let me out there.

With our affluent sailor footing the bill, we dined at a posh place in the Harbor area called Winston's New England Nuovo— traditional fare updated with cutting-edge culinary innovation. The head chef was fond of tall presentations that looked like miniature Indian tepees, which he set on plates decorated with swirls of sauce too thin to taste. In general, though, the food was first-class if you avoided extremes in fusion like Succotash with Black Truffle Oil and Parmesan Curls.

But when Phillipa craved inspiration, she and Stone dined at Winston's, as did celebrity chefs on tour in Massachusetts. Once when Phillipa and Stone were on their way into Winston's, Heather had been outside the front door picketing the place for serving Provimi veal. "Waving placards with disgusting photos of crated calves," Phillipa had complained to me the next day.

"It's better than breaking into labs and freeing the rabbits," I said, remembering some of Heather's earlier animal-rights' exploits.

Joe slipped something to the maître d', and he obliged with a table overlooking Plymouth Harbor. An early September moon, just past full, was rising over the waves, casting an inviting path of light in our direction. *Now there's real magic*, I thought. In honor of love and hope and the moon goddess, I was glad I'd worn my best moss green dress, draped with the exotic embroidered shawl that was one of Joe's first gifts to me. Becky wore a smart, slimming knit in her favorite navy with a wide white collar and cuffs, and Joe was as dressed up as he ever got in a black blazer and gray silk knit turtleneck. I'd never seen him wear a tie except to church in Athens.

Not having to look my dinner in the eye before it died for me, I ordered the Lobster & Clambake, which was a no-work, no-shells version garnished with edible seaweed and tiny ears of pickled corn. Becky did the same. Joe ordered the Farmhouse Chop Marsala, which came with Fiddlehead Stir-fry and Cilantro Mashed Potatoes. We were just digging into this lavish repast, washed down with a light Beaujolais that went admirably with just about anything, when I glanced across the room and spotted Dr. DeBoer and a lady companion who wasn't the sinister nurse of my vision.

"Hssssst," I said. "Don't look now, but Dr. DeBoer is here. With a woman. Over there under the Squanto mural on the far wall."

"How will I know if I can't look?" Joe said.

"Who's Dr. DeBoer?" Becky asked. She was picking off the seaweed and setting it to one side of her plate.

"Well, just be casual about it," I said. Joe glanced back as if looking for the waiter. This worked too well. Our waiter caught Joe's questioning look and hurried over. Not to waste the moment, Joe ordered another bottle of the red.

"Dr. DeBoer," I explained to Becky after the waiter had scurried off, "is the director of Manomet Manor. It's a rehabilitation center that's come to our attention for its curious death rate. It seems as if too many patients go in there for physical therapy and come out feet first."

"Oh my God," Becky said with a stern look at me. "Tell me you and your friends are *not* getting into another crime-solving escapade."

"Sure, tell her," Joe said.

"Detective Stern hasn't been able to find any evidence of wrongdoing," I evaded.

"But you have? Another vision thing?" Becky's tone was accusatory.

"I can't help it, honey. A vision just happens, and what do you want me to do? Shut my eyes while innocent patients get flatlined? It's like an epidemic of respiratory and heart failures."

"Why are people still convalescing at this House of Usher then?" Becky demanded with her best courtroom manner—a bit too loudly.

"Shhhhh. I think he's with his wife."

"Another vision?" Becky asked.

"I think they're into the Indian Pudding with Pomegranate Sauce. Not talking, looking vacantly over each other's shoulder. Like two cows grazing in a field. Let's never get like that, Joe." His knee was leaning comfortably against mine. Under cover of the blue-and-white checkered tablecloth, he took my hand and held it warmly.

"Did you tell Becky yet?" he asked.

"Tell me what! That you're getting married, I hope?"

"Yes, honey, we are. We're planning a Yule . . . that is, a winter solstice wedding. I've already told Cathy, and I've just been waiting for the right moment to tell you. You will celebrate with us?"

"Of course. Ron will be beside himself."

I may have raised an eyebrow. She said, "Well, I'm going to give him another chance, but not L. F. & L. I've decided to take that new job at Katz and Kinder."

"Oh, goodie," I said. "Maybe you'll be able to squeeze in a little pro bono work for St. Rita's. I think Serena Dove is probably stretched a bit thin there."

"Gee, Mom . . . first let me get my briefcase unpacked, will you?"

"All this calls for a toast, I think," Joe said, refilling our glasses from the new bottle. We toasted—to Becky's new job, our wedding, happiness and success for one and all.

"Do you think he's good-looking?" I asked.

"Who? Joe?"

"No, we already know Joe's devastating. Dr. DeBoer."

"I never cared for that big florid look. But some women would think so. Especially *older* women. Is that a diamond pinkie ring he's wearing?"

"You're making me mighty curious," Joe said. His back faced the Squanto mural while Becky and I had a clear view of the DeBoer table. "What's his wife look like?"

"An aging opera star," Becky said. "Wagner."

"Same type," I said. "Could be first cousins, they look so much alike. Brunhilde and Siegfried."

At that moment, Dr. DeBoer looked full at me, catching me studying him intently. Immediately, I looked away, back to my companions, and adjusted the shawl around my shoulders. "Uh, oh. I hope he doesn't remember me."

"Remember you from where?" Joe wanted to know.

I may have blushed. "Oh, you know. When he happens to see me again."

"Which would be when?"

"Which would be tomorrow when I'm going to be pushing a book cart around the Manor. I'm a library volunteer."

"*Jesu Christos!*"

"Oh, Mom!"

"Hey, don't worry, I won't be alone. Heather's made arrangements to drop in with Honeycomb. Honeycomb is a licensed Therapy Dog. A golden, you know. After all, it's not as if I'm doing anything wrong. Just livening up his patients' dull days with a few scintillating bestsellers. He probably won't even recognize me when I'm not dressed up. It's my intention to keep a low profile."

"Ha ha," Becky said. "When did you ever do that? Remember when you accidentally got trapped into an interview for *America's Fugitive Files*? Or how about getting kidnapped by a crazed kid-killer? And then there was the time—"

"Okay, okay," I said. "Maybe it's my karma."

The waiter had laid the check on Dr. DeBoer's table. The doctor was studying it. His wife was looking through her purse, taking out a small compact and peering into it. I guess her face looked all right, because she put the compact back without retouching the paint. Dr. DeBoer put a credit card into the little leather book, and the waiter took it away. He leaned over and spoke to his wife. She looked over at me and shook her head. The waiter brought the credit card receipt, the doctor wrote on it, probably adding a tip, and the couple rose from their chairs to leave. I busied myself spearing a slippery baby corn.

"He's looking back at you, Mom," Becky said. "Kind of an artless face, a bit jovial with those red cheeks. What is it, exactly, that you're suspicious of?"

"Murder." I said. "But I don't think Dr. DeBoer is involved. It's some nurse I haven't met yet. Down-slanted eyes. And maybe a guy she's involved with sexually."

"Your visions are getting racier all the time," Joe said.

"Sex and violence," I agreed. "Works for me."

Chapter Twelve

"Now, this is perfectly easy, dear." As she loaded up the cart with romance novels, spy stories, gory thrillers, and self-help health books of various persuasions, the FLOTSAM lady explained how the bookmobile's records were to be kept. Grace Coots was a thin, plain woman with short-cropped gray hair who looked as if she'd just stepped out of a BBC mystery, tweed skirt and all. "*Miss* Coots," she'd insisted. "You're expected, of course, but just check in at the admitting desk anyway. She'll direct you to the floors we're going to service. We'll be especially welcome to the long-termers, you know—the not-so-patient patients. Only we're not to call them 'patients.' The director prefers 'clients.' We're a little late, so you'll have to work fast. They'll be serving lunch in an hour or so."

"But it's only nine-thirty," I protested.

"The Manor's on a tight schedule. Breakfast at seven, lunch at eleven, and dinner at four-thirty. The staff have their hands full right now, due to a continual exodus of nonmedical help—aides, cleaners, kitchen help, even the chef. Their wages are standard, so I don't know what's the problem. The new hires are mostly émigrés. Do you happen to speak Spanish, dear?"

"I'm afraid not." I straightened a heap of historical romances that threatened to topple over, possibly from the weight of all those exposed bosoms.

"Oh, too bad, dear. Well, maybe you can sign, if you need anything. I'll be back for the cart at eleven sharp. Good luck, dear, and thank you!" Miss Coots's smile came and went like a flash of neon. She checked the time. I synchronized my watch against hers, and waved a cheery good-bye as she sped off to her next rendezvous.

Into the fray!

Not as depressing as I feared, I thought, as I peeked in the first few rooms with my diffident offer of books. There was a faint underlying odor of disinfectant and the wheaty aroma of whatever had been served for breakfast, but no serious illness smells. Walls were painted blossom pink, which in color therapy is thought to tranquilize the most agitated psyche. It's been recommended for prisons, but somehow the idea never caught on. Perhaps in this case it was a tad too calming. Few so-called clients showed an interest in my book cart—most appeared to be TV zombies or still sleeping. But as I popped into the last room on the right, I encountered one lively old doll who seemed to be waiting for me.

"Oh, goodie—the Book Lady. I heard you were coming today. Please roll that contraption right over here, miss. The books they have here are an anemic lot. I can't tell you how delighted I am that our so-called library is going to have a transfusion. I'm Euphemia Wilson, and this here is Sleeping Beauty, otherwise known as Mary Cork." She gestured toward the blanket-shrouded form in the other bed. "Mary's not quite right in the head. Sleeps all day; have to wake her up to eat." Euphemia's snow white curls were tied up with a blue satin ribbon, like a little girl's. Her eyes were bright and quick as a bird's. "Stays up all night moaning. You get used to it, though. Got any Stephen Kings there? I love Stephen King, don't you? *Misery* was my favorite. She fixed that writer, didn't she? The movie was good, too."

I confessed I wasn't familiar with *Misery*. After scanning the top of the cart and not finding any Kings, I crouched down to read the jackets on the bottom. "Oh, good, Mrs. Wilson. We're in luck—if you haven't read *The Girl Who Loved Tom Gordon.*"

"Maybe I'll just have a look myself." Euphemia lurched painfully into her walker and inched toward me. I moved the cart as close as I could through a maze of tables on wheels, IV stands, and assorted chairs. "That Gordon book looks kinda thin. Probably won't last the night. I'd better take a few more. Would you pass me that James Patterson one, too."

"*When the Wind Blows,*" I said. "You can take up to six books, you know, and keep them for two weeks."

"Gracious me, miss, I'll have all six read before this week is out. When you coming back? I'll take a couple of Patricia Cornwells, too, if you've got them." The little woman peered over the racks and pulled out a few more thrillers. I piled them neatly on her night table, noting their numbers in the little record book Grace Coots had given me.

"Call me Cass. I'll be here every Tuesday and Thursday. And I'll make sure you have plenty of books to read. You're my best customer so far."

"That so! Well, there's a lot of deadheads in this wing."

"Any special requests?"

"I missed *Gerald's Game.* I'd sure like to read that one."

"What about the Miss Marple mysteries. Do you like those?"

"You got to be kidding," Euphemia said. "Don't you watch the news, Cassie? It's a sad, mad, bad world out there. Which reminds me. I like true-crime books, too. How about that case— oh, I can't remember the name—guy fed his wife into a wood chipper . . ."

As Euphemia struggled to recall the bloodcurdling details, I heard a familiar commotion down the hall. Looking out the door, I was not surprised to see Heather talking to someone at the nurses' station, accompanied by Honeycomb, who was on a golden retriever's version of *sit-stay,* wiggling across the floor, tail wagging against a metal cart loaded with dishes. The nurse was pointing in the other direction, toward a sunny sitting area with long windows that I'd glimpsed earlier. Overlooking the back garden and a wall of arborvitae that screened from view another big old mansion, now a funeral home, the sunroom attracted some of the more ambulatory clients. I hoped they would have a firm grip on their walkers when Honeycomb burst in with her enthusiastic canine therapy.

After I finished dispensing books to all those who wanted them in the units to which I'd been directed, I rearranged my bookmobile cart and strolled toward the sunroom, just to connect up with Heather. She waved at me and beamed. "It's going really well," she said. "How're you doing?"

Honeycomb was scampering from client to client, bringing smiles and getting hugs and pats. But just then one cadaverous old man stumped in with his walker, saw Honeycomb, and turned ashen, pressing himself against the wall. "Not supposed to be no dogs," he muttered. "Dirty things, full of germs. I don't want no dog licking me."

"Oh, I'm so sorry," said Heather. "She is a rather rambunctious creature, isn't she? Perhaps I ought to help you back to your room. Cass, you keep an eye on Honeycomb for a sec." With a line of soothing chitchat, Heather eased the terrified man back out the door and down the hall.

"Oh, thanks a lot," I called after her.

One of the more flighty-looking clients began to laugh and clap and hiccup. Another banged her cane against the floor to attract the dog's attention. Honeycomb obliged, racing over to dispense a doggie grin, a cold nose, and a sympathetic expression.

"Now what exactly is going on in here?" A tall, full-bosomed nurse stood in the sunroom's double doors, holding a clipboard in the crook of her arm as if it were a baby.

Despite the vicissitudes of her early life, Honeycomb had never met a person she didn't like. She responded to the crisp voice as if it were an invitation to a romp. Trotting over eagerly to greet this new friend, she jumped up, paws on the woman's chest, and bestowed lavish kisses all over her face. With a grimace and a quick movement of her foot, the nurse stamped on Honeycomb's back paw. Immediately, the dog jumped down and backed away with a sharp yelp, her baffled expression speaking for her. *Ouch! Hey, what happened? This is not a fun game.*

I had seen this nurse before.

"I'm asking you, what is going on in here?" she insisted, fixing me with a cool stare from her down-slanting eyes.

"I'm Cassandra Shipton, the bookmobile lady." I started to offer my hand, but thought better of it. "And this furry girl is Honeycomb, a registered Therapy Dog paying a visit to the Manor today. Heather Devlin is her guardian, but Heather's just stepped out for a moment."

"Has she indeed? And did the director authorize this 'visit'? I certainly have heard nothing about dogs being allowed to run loose among the disabled clients in *my* unit."

"You'll have to ask Mrs. Devlin about that. I'm only here for the books." It was every witch for herself with this babe, I'd decided. "The clients seem to have enjoyed Honeycomb's visit. From what I could see, although I only just got here. Except for one fellow who's not keen on dogs—Heather's helping him back into his room."

The clients, cowards all, were looking off out the windows or at the hands in their laps as if someone had turned of their good-time switch and "dog" was some foreign concept about which they knew nothing.

"That would be Mr. Donovan. Deathly afraid of animals. Really, this is too much!"

At that delicate moment, Heather reappeared, beaming. "Oh, you must be Faye Kane. You were off the floor when I arrived, but I explained my mission to the other nurse. Debbie Abrams. I hope you've been enjoying your little visitor. The patients certainly have had a ball with Honeycomb."

Said patients were still playing dumb. The woman who had laughed and clapped now appeared to be napping, head fallen forward onto her chest, softly snoring.

"Clients. We call them clients. I was just inquiring of this new book person who authorized a Therapy Dog for my unit. Nothing like this is supposed to happen without my express permission. In fact," she said, turning toward me, "I should be informed in advance when the FLOTSAM people are expected."

Feeling the chill wind of Nurse Kane's demeanor, Heather's smile faded. "If you'll just check with the director's office, I think you'll find that Dr. DeBoer was very gracious when I suggested bringing in a Therapy Dog. He said he had a dog himself and thought a visit from a friendly fellow might perk up the patients. I mean, clients. It was his suggestion that we confine our visit to the sunroom for openers."

"I find it quite surprising that Dr. DeBoer didn't inform me. I wonder if he had made a firm appointment for this experiment or did you just decide to show up? Dr. DeBoer's dog is a Pomeranian with very good manners—not a big horse like this."

It was clear to Honeycomb, that this paw-stomping person was not speaking pleasantly to Heather and might even pose a threat. The dog positioned her body between the two women, who were glaring frostily at one another.

"Next time I venture onto your floor, I'll be sure to bring a signed note from your boss," Heather said in the snobby voice she could summon at will: Lady of the Manor to pushy peasant.

"Not after I talk to him, you won't," Kane snapped.

"Come on, Heather, let's go," I said. "It's nearly eleven, and I have to meet Miss Coots in the parking lot. Believe it or not, the lunch carts will be rolling pretty soon, and we'll want to give them a clear field."

I'm not sure exactly what happened next. Perhaps Kane shifted her clipboard in some way that Honeycomb took to be a threat. Or possibly she lifted a hand to push back her blond hair, which was shoulder-length and quite well cut. Whatever the menacing move was, Honeycomb leaped straight up and, with her whole body, gave Kane a mighty shove that sent her sprawling across the tile floor. To the dog's credit, no teeth or claws touched the woman. Just the sheer weight of worried dog. I suspected this might be the end of Honeycomb's career as a Therapy Dog, but a golden retriever's retirement can be sweet in a mansion with a lavish pool and many wooded acres.

"Oh, Great Goddess! Here, let me help."

Grinning and giggling, the clients behaved as if Kane's encounter with the floor had been an entertainment arranged for their benefit.

"Get that stupid dog the fuck out of here before I call the cops." Kane picked herself up with a quick, graceful motion, ignoring the hand I was extending and glaring at her clients.

Meanwhile, Heather had clipped a leash to Honeycomb's collar. "Heel, Honeycomb. That's a good girl. I know it wasn't your fault." Far from being abashed, the golden was wagging her tail and panting with delight.

With a wave to the clients, and a gesture toward the nurse that I didn't like—her pointed little finger being much in evidence—Heather strode out the sunroom door with Honeycomb in tow, leaving me to scurry after her, pushing the bookmobile cart pell-mell through the reception area.

Miss Coots was waiting for me. "Well done! You're right on time, dear. What's that dog doing in the parking lot?"

"Honeycomb's a registered Therapy Dog who's been visiting the clients." I handed her the circulation notebook, and the two of us rolled the cart back in the FLOTSAM van.

"Splendid idea, splendid. I'm sure the League will hear great reports of this morning's work. See you Thursday, then? Same time, same place." With another of her lightning on/off smiles, Miss Coots hopped into the driver's seat and sped off.

"I need a drink, a very strong drink." Heather tucked Honeycomb into her Mercedes, its half-open back windows nearly opaque with dog drool.

I glanced at my watch. Eleven-fifteen. Still, the sun must be over the yardarm somewhere in the world, and it had been a very trying morning. "Good idea. My place is closer. Why don't we fix some Bloody Marys with a bite of lunch while Honeycomb larks about with Scruffy."

"Sounds like a plan to me."

Scruffy was thrilled. Although Heather's canine crew were religiously spayed and neutered, the golden was new to the Devlin menagerie and had not yet been fixed. *Geez, it's her again. She smells really good. Let's keep her.* Honeycomb stood patiently while Scruffy checked her out from one end to the other, a smug expression on her face. She knew her power. Given a few minutes outside, she'd have all Scruffy's prize possessions—the new green sponge ball, the good tug-of-war stick, the grimy beef shinbone—heaped in front of her.

"Play nice," I said, letting the dogs out the back porch door. The light east wind had refreshed the garden, perking up the heavy, purple-flowered heads of oregano, spikes of rosemary, and curly bunches of parsley. I picked a few sprigs for a kitchen bouquet. Energized seagulls were screaming over a school of fish rippling the waves. I loved summer, but the first stirrings of September always filled me with a new spirit of enterprise and adventure.

"What did you think of Manomet Manor?" I asked Heather, who was already mixing a pitcher of drinks, her hand heavy on the vodka and Tabasco. I slapped my trusty old cast-iron skillet onto the stove, poured in some oil, and turned on the heat.

"Faye Kane is a nasty piece of work, isn't she? Not your regular Florence Nightingale. I pity the clients in her unit."

"She's the one, you know. I've seen her. Up to no good in my vision. Sort of a sex-and-violence thing. There's a guy, too, but I didn't find him there this morning." I chopped onions, peppers, boiled potatoes, and chunks of ham, distributing them over the sizzling oil, filling the kitchen with a robust Mediterranean aroma. In the midst of such goodness, it was hard to imagine that anything and anyone in the world could be evil and unhealthy. "It's up to us now, " I said, viciously mincing parsley and oregano for the frittata.

"I'm not surprised. Some smoldering lava is flowing under Kane's frosty crust, I don't doubt. The Hawaiian fire goddess Pele incarnate." Heather filled two water goblets with the potent pick-me-up and added swizzles of celery. "Here's to fighting fire with fire," she toasted, clinking goblet to goblet, then taking a long, satisfied drink. "What a bitch!"

"Hi, Heather. How'd it go, girls?" Joe, who'd been working on the broken beach stairs, appeared in the kitchen door, perhaps drawn by the comforting aroma of oregano, herb of his youth. "Scruffy's having a hell of a time cavorting around with that golden."

We related the gist of the morning's mishaps while he laughed and sipped a glass of Heather's heady drink. Later, however, after Heather had gone, he scolded me again for getting involved in yet another investigation. "Are you sure about this nurse? If she's as sinister as you believe, I wish you'd stay far away from her."

"All I'm doing is wheeling the book cart around to needy readers and keeping my eyes open. It's Fiona I'm worried about. After all, there's absolutely nothing Faye Kane can do to me." In retrospect, that statement is a perfect example of the quirky blind side to clairvoyance.

By the following Tuesday, my third FLOTSAM excursion, Joe had been summoned to join the *Rainbow Warrior* on the coast of Spain. The Greenpeace flagship would be leading a flotilla of 150 local fishing ships off the Galacian port town of Coruna. The protest sought to bring attention to preventing catastrophes such as the *Prestige* oil tanker disaster from ever happening again. I didn't need to be a clairvoyant to know that this new mission was a whole lot more exciting than hammering together beach stairs. The glint in Joe's eyes and the spring in his step as he packed his duffel bag gave the whole show away.

"Would it be too much to ask that you stay on the ship and out of harm's way this time? No jumping into the oil-drenched waves or getting yourself arrested for picketing the EU Maritime Conference."

"Don't you worry, sweetheart. I wouldn't care to spend any time in a Spanish jail."

"So, what will you be doing, exactly?"

"Running the engine. Keeping the electrical system ship-shape. And anything else that's needed. It's a flexible work situation."

"I bet. But just don't step up to volunteer when they need someone to hang off the side of an oil tanker with a banner, okay?"

"I'll promise, if you promise. No tackling the nurses at Manomet Manor while I'm away. I don't think I'll be gone more than two weeks."

"At least the beach stairs won't threaten to collapse under me and Scruffy anymore," I said. "What a great job you did!"

Joe pulled me into his arms and softly bit the lobe of my ear, whispering, "Are you changing the subject? Let me ask you the same question: what will *you* be doing, exactly?"

I leaned against him in the manner most calculated to distract him. "My little volunteer job for FLOTSAM. Making plans for Mabon, the equinox. I'm the hostess this time. Filling herbal orders. Nothing that needs to concern you. Want me to pack you a lunch for the road?"

"I don't have to leave quite yet," Joe said, "and I have a far better idea of how to spend the time."

He was right.

Chapter Thirteen

I was getting used to Joe's frequent absences. I even saved up things to do that were better done when he wasn't around. My many years as "head of household" had fostered in me a certain independence that strained against a double-harness. Perhaps I'd feel more comfortable with sharing every aspect of my life once we got married. At any rate, I was alone again and spent long hours at the computer, reorganizing my on-line catalog and adding new products: Spiritual Inspiration Tea, Peppermint Foot Cream, Peaceful Home Incense, and a Ghosts Begone Kit.

What a delightful break from staring glassy-eyed at the monitor to see an e-mail from Freddie pop up!

From: witch freddie freddie13@hotmail.net
To: witch cass shiptonherbs@earthlink.net
Subject: right on!

    hi, cass. it's me at the library again. got yr note, thanks. positive banishing thing worked out okay but not as expected, too good for that SOB.
    would you believe it, billygoat wins big bucks some f***ing football game? so he splits in mom's chevy. gets

brother jim to go along with phony promises. but the chevy runs out of gas (leak in gas line tch tch ☺) and jim calls home from gas station.

cops give billygoat rough time—big surprise, prior dirty old man arrests, slimeball never convicted. but mom won't press charges. jim and chevy get back home safe anyway. i think we've seen the last of that pervert, if he knows what's good for him.

i would rather he falls into a pit of snakes than win stupid bet, but am grateful to god(dess) and you for help anyway.

better not write back here as, now that the SOB is zapped, i'm getting itchy to move on

more later,

love,

f

How I wished that Freddie would come back to New England where I could keep my eye on her! A vivid picture of my lively friend sprang to mind, and I used its energy to send out my best words of power to help Freddie find her perfect home and rightful place in the world. I was gratified that her positive spell had brought about such a desirable conclusion. Well, *perhaps* it was positive—there *was* a question about that fortuitous gas leak.

Feeling frustrated that I couldn't fire back to Freddie a cautionary e-mail full of reasonable, mature advice (which she would have ignored or misinterpreted anyway), I went down to the beach with Scruffy, to clear my head. While I was admiring the new stairs and checking out the place where the fire would be lit for Mabon, Phillipa called on my cell phone.

A brisk south wind was roiling the waves "I'm having a hard time hearing you, Phil." I was marveling that I had even brought my cell phone to the beach, so unlike me. I much prefer to be unreachable when I'm communicating with the ocean.

"Pigs stink," she yelled in my ear. "We need to confer about Iggy Pryde. He's planning to run for selectman."

"Let me call you back from the house. The ocean is drowning you out. I thought you said that ignorant ass Iggy Pryde is running for selectman."

Back in my snug kitchen, I put on the kettle and spooned my Wise Woman tea into a small teapot before returning Phillipa's call. I'd need my strength and wits for this new emergency.

"You haven't heard from Heather today?" Phil asked. "Every time the wind's in the southwest, they're getting that disgusting odor from Pryde's Pig Farm. And it's worse for the Kellihers—they're closer. That whole ritzy neighborhood's complaining about the stink. It never used to be like that when Iggy's mother was alive. Just a small contained operation, no close neighbors. But now, of course, there's been some development, and it's even worse for those people. The farm's about forty or so acres, very secluded in the trees. You never even knew it was there. But Iggy's expanded his livestock. Probably a couple of hundred pigs now—no one knows for sure, because he's a genius at keeping out inspectors. He collects practically all the garbage from Plymouth restaurants and supermarkets for his pigs to rummage in. Plus he's got horses, cows, dogs, and a fleet of rusted trucks with chickens roosting in them. The stench has to be pretty strong to drift all the way to the Morgan place."

The teakettle was whistling. I poured boiling water over the fragrant tea leaves, took a china cup down from the shelf, and settled down for a conference.

"Did I hear you say Iggy is running for selectman? I can't believe that."

"I just found out about it. I thought Dr. Fitts was running for that empty seat, but then he dropped dead—you remember. Jogging. Makes you think, doesn't it? Next thing, Stone comes home last night and tells me that by some chicanery or payoff, it's Ignatius Pryde's name on the ballot. I was so upset, I scorched a very delicate lemon curd."

"Should we say a little spell for the wind to shift?" I asked.

"Yeah, but let's make it a huff-puff-and-blow-down-the-pig-house gale."

"No way. I wouldn't want to get that back," I warned.

"Heather says it's truly terrible today over at the Kellihers'. Not to mention she and Dick can't sit out on their own patio. But being Heather, naturally her concern is for the Kelliher cats. Delicate olfactory sensibilities, she says. And it's thirteen cats, to be precise. Can you believe that? I can barely abide my little Zelda's litter box, but of course the Kelliher cats are outdoor animals, practically feral. Ever seen them sunning themselves on that nice flat ranch house roof?"

"It's laughable, Phil. Who would vote for that puffed-up pig farmer?" I sipped my tea and gazed out the open kitchen window. A breeze laden with September herbs and salt water drifted in, stirring the white curtains.

"Stone says Pryde's canvassing the older residents, the ones whose families have lived here for generations. His slogan is 'Pryde Protects Our God-Given Property Rights.' Apparently, he believes that he holds the Pig Farm by Divine Right, and the same applies to all the other old farms. Next week he's hosting a giant pig roast to rout out the votes. You know, one of those gross cookouts with a whole pig the size of a water buffalo turning to mahogany on a spit over coals."

"Great Goddess . . . on the pig farm?"

"No, he doesn't let anyone in there. Runs them off with a pitchfork. Rumor has it that more than pig swill is being dumped on his farm, but no one has the proof—yet. Iggy wrangled special permission to roast that pig in Myles Standish State Park. The firemen are his guests of honor, of course. Will and Deidre will probably be there with the kiddies."

"Well, my dear, if everyone is off at the roast, won't that leave a clear field for snooping?" As soon as the words were out of my mouth, I was sorry I'd said that.

There was a long pause, and then, in tones of great reluctance:

"I can't, dammit. In the interest of marital harmony, you know. But maybe you and Heather?"

"How about if we work a spell at Mabon to clean up the place 'for the good of all and it harm none.' " I countered. "I bet *Hazel's Book of Household Recipes* has some powerful cleansing formula. Remember how successful her Recipe for Bringing Home was? Let me check with Fiona before we go trespassing around in pig manure."

"We'll get to the spellwork later. Meanwhile, let's find out what we're dealing with. An innocent look around, as if the car took a wrong turn by mistake?"

"Oh, sure. And maybe you'd like us to take a few soil samples while we're there?"

"*Would* you? That would be great! I'll call Heather. And Deidre. She can be our lookout at the pig roast. Warn us if Iggy or his girlfriend head home."

Any environmental cause was dear to Heather's heart, and undoubtedly I would be talked into accompanying her. We'd been on missions like this before, and I have to admit, we're a great team. At least, I could be grateful that Joe was in Spain tilting at multinational shipping interests while I was looking into a little neighborly pollution.

Before Operation Chitlins (as Deidre dubbed it) could get under way, however, there was another development at Manomet Manor.

"What happened to Mary?" I handed Euphemia Wilson the copy of *Gerald's Game* she'd been "dying to read." Her roommate's bed, where I was accustomed to see Mary Cork's somnolent form emitting occasional snorts and snores, was empty and taut with the pristine whiteness that bodes ill news of a recent occupant in a medical facility.

" 'Shuffled off this mortal coil,' " Euphemia murmured. Her white curls were tied back with a lilac ribbon today; it matched the faint smudges under her eyes. "Funny thing is, I used to curse her for waking me up nights with her moaning and groaning and cries for the nurse, and now I can't sleep at all. Could you fix me up with a few extra books?"

My heart was beating in fast-time, but I kept on smiling reassuringly. "Sure. I was thinking of you when I loaded on Stephen King's *The Stand* and Patricia Cornwell's Jack the Ripper book."

"Oh, goodie. One thing you got to say for that King, he writes a really big book." Euphemia was hefting *The Stand* with a satisfied expression.

"I never knew exactly what was wrong with Mary," I said.

"Had one of those back operations that's supposed to cure the pain and have you up and around in no time. 'Course that never happens. Mary still couldn't tend to herself, and she was in pain most of the time. Her doctor kept ordering physical therapy, and Medicare paid for it. Didn't work, though. Most nights she was hollering for her medication before it was due. The other morning, about two it was, Mary went into one of her screaming tirades and was banging on her table with a bedpan. Nurse Kane shows up. 'There, there, Mary, that's a good girl,' she says 'I'm going to fix you up with a nice IV,' and sure enough, as soon as the nurse stuck her, Mary fell right to sleep."

"When did she actually die, do you suppose?" I asked.

"Who knows? Next morning when one of those Spanish aides came in with the breakfast trays, she found Mary dead as a doornail. Respiratory and heart failure, Dr. DeBoer said. Could happen to anyone any time." Euphemia appeared undaunted by the grim realities.

"Did Nurse Kane know you were awake?"

"Oh, dear, no. I kept my eyes tight shut so's she wouldn't make me take another sleeping pill. I'd just got to a good part in *All That Remains*, and I wanted to read a few more pages after the nurse went back to her station."

"You probably don't know if Nurse Kane was alone, then?" I

straightened the teetering pile of books on Euphemia's night table. Then I filled her water glass and picked up the now empty water pitcher. Good to have a reason to hang around longer.

"I only peeked one time, when the nurse's back was toward me while she fussed with Mary. For a minute there, I thought I glimpsed someone right outside the door, but then I shut my eyes again, so I don't really know. Poor Mary Cork. Blessing in disguise, though. Bordering senile, you know."

"I'll just fill this pitcher." There was a filtered water station by the little snack area two doors down the hall. "What about Mary's family? Do you know if they've been notified? Will there be a wake?"

"All she had was a niece in Quincy. Cathy McIntee. She came by on Saturday afternoon, had a last look. Dr. DeBoer helped her with the arrangements. Cremation, the niece wanted, so that's already been taken care of. The ashes will be sent to her for distribution in some flower garden. And masses said for the repose of Mary's soul."

"Are you sure you don't remember who was in the doorway when Nurse Kane gave Mary that IV?"

"Must have been someone on the night staff. White coat and all," Euphemia said.

"Man or woman?"

Euphemia considered, cocking her head to one side like a chickadee. "I really couldn't quite make him out, Cassie. If I had to guess, I'd say a man. Not a big fella, though."

I ducked out and filled the pitcher. Then I peeked in the snack refrigerator. Jell-Os, yogurts, and, in the freezer, Hoodsies. I helped myself to a Hoodsie and brought it back for Euphemia. "I hope you like strawberry."

"My favorite. Thanks, Cassie." She wrestled for a moment with the little wooden spoon. "They're a wee bit shorthanded here, and a lot of new people—Spanish-speaking, most of them. I've been learning some of the lingo myself. *Agua. Manta.* That's 'blanket.' *Socorro.*"

"Spanish is good. You take care of yourself, Euphemia." I'd grown fond of my little library patron with her keenness for horror stories, and now I was worried about her. But I reasoned that even a murdering nurse wouldn't be so brazen and careless as to finish off her latest victim's roommate. "I'll see you on Thursday. Anything special?"

"Robin Cook. I read *Seizure* and *Shock* already. Anything else, though. *Via con Dios*," Euphemia said.

"It all went down too fast," Phillipa said. "Once DeBoer signed that death certificate, there was no call to perform an autopsy. Don't you think I've talked to Stone about this? There's just no basis for an investigation."

Mabon was still a week away. Having gathered at Fiona's for an early conference, we were sipping the incredible single-malt Scotch whiskey that our hostess had brought to light from her mysterious liquor cabinet, dusting off the bottle's McCallan label with the sleeve of her coat-sweater. Phillipa passed a plate of her cayenne-cheddar crisps for nibbling. The combination perfectly suited the waning Fire Moon of September.

"Is there some way Dr. DeBoer could be persuaded to call in the medical examiner next time?" asked Deidre. "I suppose, though, he wouldn't want to know the truth. A murder or two on the premises might cut into his profits."

"He may be involved himself," Heather suggested.

"It's some other guy . . . uptilted nose," I said. "I haven't got his name yet. But I do have Faye Kane in my sights, so to speak It's definitely she I saw in my vision. And Euphemia confirms that there was a man in the doorway when Kane administered that fatal IV. I have to admit I'm really worried about my little friend. She's entirely too sharp to be safe."

"Okay, there are two things we have to do," Phillipa said. "Throw some protection around Cass's dear old gal and find a safe way for Heather and Cass to get into Pryde's Pig Farm next weekend, while Iggy's at Myles Standish Park turning the spitted pig."

"What are we looking for at the Pryde place, exactly?" Heather asked. "And what excuse am I going to give to Dick?"

"There's a general rule you ought to revisit here." Fiona re-filled our motley assortment of glasses. Alcohol would disinfect them, I thought, observing a cat hair on the rim of Heather's glass. Housekeeping, never high on Fiona's list of priorities, had gone by the wayside ever since little Laura Belle had been taken from her custody and arthritis had crippled her knees. "'To know, to dare, to will, to keep silent,' the good old cardinal rule of spell-craft. And I take that to mean, don't stir up the home cauldron unnecessarily."

"What *is* she saying?" Deidre whined in my ear.

"You mean, don't tell Dick anything?" Heather rephrased.

"When Rob Ritchie was alive, I found it saved a lot of tedious argument if I just went ahead and did whatever I wanted to do without running it up the mast to see if he would salute it. I don't know what it is with women needing approval for every little thing. Of course, my late husband, being a merchant marine like dear Cass's fiancé, was away a good bit of the time, so I'd become used to my independence. You'll like that part, Cass. Here's my little darling." Omar slid into the room, leaped onto the back of Fiona's chair, and hissed at us.

Phillipa was shaking her head as if she had water in her ear, as she often did after one of Fiona's meandering chats. "Okay, *don't ask, don't tell.* Whatever. There's a rumor going around that there's more than restaurant swill on the Pryde farm. Possibly something hazardous has been dumped there. If we could confirm that, the EPA might force him to clean up the place. Also, the citizens of Plymouth would be unlikely to vote for Iggy if he's polluting the town. I'd go myself, but Stone—"

"You'd better suit up for this expedition, sisters," Deidre interrupted. "Washable overalls. Disposable gloves. Masks. Cell phones, so I can call you if Iggy leaves the state park. I'm going to stick to his side like a Scotch thistle. But how do you know he won't leave someone else on watch?"

"So, be prepared to talk your way out, if you have to," Phillipa added. "Just drive in there as if you got lost or something, took the wrong road out of that little cluster of ranch houses."

"Captain Morgan's granddaughter get lost in Plymouth?" I mused. "Well, maybe—if she'd been hitting this Scotch of Fiona's. I think my legs are turning to jelly."

"I find it's quite an effective painkiller," Fiona said. "Now what about that poor creature you're worried about—Euphemia? What's she in there for?"

"Recuperating from hip replacement. Apparently, it's not going too well."

"Okay, let's do a visualization for her. Outside might be best." Fiona hobbled to the back door, and we all followed. Under the half-moon at perigee, we held hands and did the white-light thing for Euphemia and for our Pryde Farm expedition.

"*White lighters*—it's becoming something of a cliché," Phillipa complained as we trooped back into the cluttered living room.

"Clichés get that way from being true," Deidre said. "I like clichés myself. And white lights."

Phillipa merely raised her winged eyebrow at me. We were both thinking of Deidre's needlework pillows, "Friends are forever," "Love me, love my poodles," and the ever-popular "Home is where the heart is."

Chapter Fourteen

On Thursday I was back at the Manor with another cart full of books and a stack of macabre thrillers for Euphemia. Relieved to find her sitting up in bed looking perky and pretty in a pink satin bed jacket that matched the ribbon in her white curls, I smiled brightly and asked, "How are things around here?"

"Quiet as the grave. But Debbie Abrams says I'll be getting a new roommate today. I just hope she's got all her marbles. I could use someone to talk to—these nurses and aides don't have time for a decent word. Sorry I missed the fun with that doggie your friend brought in last week. I made it down to the sunroom yesterday, and everyone was gossiping about the critter attacking Miss Kane. We kinda figure that's the end of our canine therapy."

"Too bad, indeed, that you didn't get to meet Honeycomb. She's the friendliest dog you'd ever know. Although you look more like a cat person to me."

"You're a good guesser, Cassie. That's why I'm so anxious to get well enough to get out of here. I have two sweet little cats that are being boarded right now, and I worry about them all the time. Sugar and Spice. Sugar has a very delicate digestion, prone to hairballs, and Spice is liable to get himself into the worst predicaments when he flies around on a fantasy hunt."

"I know how it is to worry about a pet. When do you expect to be discharged?"

"That's what I'd like to know. I still can't get around without this darned walker."

I made a mental note to keep adding Euphemia's name to our healing work. The sooner she got out of the Manor, the less I'd have to worry about her. On the other hand, she was a bright spot in my rounds, and I'd miss her.

After my chat with Euphemia, I wheeled the cart back past the nurses' station, which was centered near the visitors' waiting area and the elevators, then continued trolling for customers at the opposite end of the floor. Most clients were more interested in talking than in reading new books, and some were disappointed with our offering.

One young woman, Gloria Gagan, who'd had knee surgery, wanted books about reincarnation, but she decided to borrow a new Danielle Steele anyway. I said I'd ask for books on reincarnation to be included on the cart for my next visit on Tuesday.

"Call me Gee-Gee," she said. "Atlantis, too. I feel a deep affinity for Atlantis. I don't know how long I'll be here, though. I hope to be discharged soon, if I can get my wimpy doctor to agree. The food here is awful—I can't eat a thing."

"The orange macaroni thing isn't too bad," her roommate, Rhoda Schott, piped up. The frowsy red-haired woman, who had declined my offer of books, was lying flat on her pillow with her gaze glued to the wall TV—Jenny Jones about to announce the results of some paternity tests. "Uh, oh—someone's in for a big surprise."

"Powdered cheese, ugh! How can you eat that stuff?" Gee-Gee looked at me and shrugged. "Dinner is at four-thirty, can you believe it? That's my ideas of a late lunch. I get terribly hungry at night. The night staff doesn't want to hear about it. One of the aides sometimes brings me a Jell-O, but, I ask you, what's a Jell-O going to do for a starving woman?"

Gee-Gee's zaftig body didn't appear to be starving, except for the hunger in her round blue eyes. They were compelling eyes, and her hair was a highlighted blond, artfully shaped, her hands expressive and the nails well-manicured, painted a deep coral. *She works in a salon*, I thought, but then glanced away quickly to avoid any uncomfortable clairvoyant episode. "You could look at this experience as if it were a trip to an exclusive spa," I suggested. "As they say, you can never be too rich or too thin."

"Oh, what crap," said Gee-Gee. "You can shove that spa cuisine. Besides I like being a size eighteen. Big girls have more fun, especially as eating is one of life's purest pleasures. They make great clothes for women my size now—lingerie as well. I've even done some modeling at Massasoit Mall. Besides, I have to keep snacking so I won't crave a smoke. Touch of emphysema queered that for me."

"You're not the only one complaining about the meals, Gee-Gee. Maybe I should be bringing in sandwiches instead of books."

"Yes, and how about a few boxes of Oreos? You could make a fortune selling real food to starving patients. God, I'll be glad to get out of here. The worst of it is, they tell me this operation is only good for about ten years, and repeats are limited—but I'm not even forty. I don't want to end up in a wheelchair."

"There'll be no wheelchair for you," I said, the confident words coming out of my mouth as a surprise to me. I did not feel well. I was far too impressionable for this work. "See you Tuesday. Reincarnation. Atlantis. I'll remember. You two take care now."

Feeling slightly nauseous, I waved vaguely at the two women and got out of their room in a hurry. I guessed the disinfectants were getting to me. It was now fifteen to eleven, so I left my cart in the reception area and strolled down the hall where the staff offices were located.

"Cass!" a pleased whisper cried out. I whirled around to find Rose holding a tray of jars that looked like urine samples. Her eyes were sparkling and her cheeks cherry red; she looked like a doll in her little white coat. "They told me you were the new bookmobile lady. Oh, you must come and see my laboratory. It's darling. And I'm so glad to be working again."

"I only have a few minutes before Miss Coots will be out in the driveway tapping her foot," I explained. "But let's have a quick look. How's Hari?"

She wrinkled her nose. "He misses his daddy, and he's not happy with the women who take care of him in the day. They're the mothers who don't have full-time jobs, so it's only natural if they favor their own children. And Hari's not used to being part of a group—sharing, doing little chores. But, we'll work it out. This is no time for me to heap my problems on you—you've done so much for me already. Come and see my little kingdom."

Rose's lab looked as if it had begun life as a storage closet, although there was one very small, high window, more like a transom. She had propped it open to invite in the pleasant September morning. The Formica counters, lab equipment, and small refrigerator looked new and were spotlessly clean. There was a tiny desk, a small computer, a high stool at the counter, and a visitor's chair with an armrest for taking blood samples from the ambulatory. I perched on the edge of the chair, conscious of the fleeting minutes. "This is wonderful, Rose. Your own office and laboratory. I'll bet you enjoy the autonomy."

Simply placing her tray on the counter, Rose had a lightness and grace to her movements that reminded me endearingly of Cathy—faerie gifts. "I have to admit I do enjoy working alone. It's so good to have a useful occupation, and to pursue it with no one looking over my shoulder," she said with a shy smile. "The room next to this is the little pharmacy, which I also keep in order. Locked, of course."

I noticed that she wore a key attached to her belt, and from there, my eye was drawn to the bruise on her bare shin. "What happened to your leg, Rose?"

The smile faded and a tiny frown appeared between her brows. "Hari is so frustrated sometimes, he flails out at me. Things will be better, I know, as soon as he feels less stress."

A chip off the old Saudi block, I thought. "You're probably right. I imagine a number of the children are troubled. Is there a psychologist or counselor on the staff?" I glanced at my watch. Five of eleven. "You might want to check with him about how best to help Hari."

"Yes, a friend of Serena's, Sister Mary Joseph, is our psychologist. You're right—I should talk to her. But just have a quick look next door before you go."

The pharmacy was a storage closet, too, and looked like one. Under Rose's management, it was spick-and-span, each shelf section labled with what looked like code to me. There was a narrow table for preparing medicines, and another computer. I assumed it kept track of inventory. "I can see you're doing a marvelous job here. I'm so proud of you, Rose, and I know Serena must feel the same. Promise to have a talk with Sister Mary Joseph, won't you?" I gave her narrow shoulders a big hug, sensing again the tenor of steel beneath her fragile exterior. Then I flew down the corridor, grabbed my cart in the reception area, and dashed out the front doors. Grace Coots was just turning the bookmobile van into the Manor's circular driveway.

The sunlight glinting off the van's windshield struck my eyes in that peculiar way that brings on a headache or a vision—sometimes both. In an instant, it was not the FLOTSAM vehicle I was seeing but Rasheed Abdul's black pickup truck, and in its passenger window, nose pressed against the glass, joyfully smiling, was Hari's little face. A moment later, Hari disappeared and Grace Coots was beside me, looking cross and worried. "Are you all right, Cassandra? You look as if you've seen a ghost." *I must warn Rose*, I thought.

On the day of the Pryde-for-Selectman Pig Roast, with some trepidation, I "suited up," as Deidre had recommended, in a pair of "paint" jeans, an old *Rainbow Warrior* sweatshirt, a Greenpeace cap, and my L. L. Bean work boots. I took a box of disposable latex gloves I use for handling some powerful essential oils, then drove over to the Morgan place to pick up Heather for Operation Chitlins.

"Oh, I see you brought the gloves. Well done." Heather was wearing her Lord & Taylor safari suit, a camouflage hat, and faux alligator boots (no reptile died so that Heather could be shod). Binoculars were slung on a cord around her neck, a small Nikon peeked out of her breast pocket, and a camouflage phone was hooked to her matching alligator belt. I felt like a grunge by comparison.

"Nice outfit," I said. "Understated. Who would guess we're on an undercover mission?"

"Thanks. At least I'm not covered with Greenpeace labels. This isn't my first foray into enemy country, you know. I've raided a few labs in my time, but Dick forbids me to talk about that. Don't you want to take the dog car?"

"Maybe the Jeep will be better if the roads are rutted," I said. Actually I thought her Mercedes might be too recognizable. The Morgans had figured prominently in Plymouth's maritime history, and longtime residents, like the Prydes, knew Heather by sight.

"Okay. I don't know quite what we're looking for, do you? But Phillipa seems to have her heart set on this expedition, and I'm always up for a meaningful sortie. If our morning's reconnoitering results in a cleanup, it will have been worth it. We never used to get that awful smell, but lately—"

"Did you tell Dick where we're going?"

"Upon reflection, Fiona's advice made such good sense. The part about avoiding a tedious argument, that is."

"Fiona is a font of wisdom, isn't she?"

"In her own pixilated way, yes."

Driving past the Kellihers' rambling ranch house, I could see several cats on the roof, just as Phillipa had described. Some were sprawled out in attitudes of feline abandon, and some were sitting up in the elegant poses of ancient Egyptian cat gods. "How marvelously decorative! They look like figureheads," I exclaimed. What an ideal life for a tribe of cats, I thought. A beauti-ful, bountiful home, freedom to roam the countryside in pursuit of adventure, and a group of one's peers to share exploits with. I hummed a few bars from *Born Free*.

"They'll be lucky if they survive, being allowed to go wild like that." Heather pressed her lips together in disapproval. "Eating parasite-ridden rodents and poisonous reptiles, being at the mercy of traffic and horrid sadistic boys and coyotes, possibly lying in-jured somewhere in the woods with no one to rescue them. Poor neglected critters!"

This was an argument not to pursue. Maybe dog people over-sentimentalized the joys of outdoor life. Just as I was wondering if I had chosen the right road, a whiff of noxious fumes traveling through the car's ventilation system suggested that we were nearing the farm. "It's off 3A, right? There's a sign?"

"Sort of," Heather said. "You'll see it in a minute."

And so I did. In large black letters on a rough-cut board, it read,

PRYDE COUNTRY.
PRIVATE PROPERTY. PROTECTED & MONITORED.
NO TRESPASSING. NO HUNTING. NO SOLICITING.
NOT AN ACCESS ROAD. DEAD END.
BEWARE OF THE DOGS.
I. PRYDE, OWNER

"I guess this is it," I said, driving onto a wide dirt road. "Why don't you give Deidre a call to make sure the coast is clear." When I came to a fork, I took the road more traveled. Passing an-other sign, NO ENTRY * POSTED AREA * POLICE TAKE NOTICE, nailed to a tree, I concluded that I'd chosen correctly.

"Okay. I'm getting nervous now," Heather said. "What do we say if there's somebody at the farm? I mean, I think they'll all be at the picnic, but . . ." She punched in Deidre's number. "Oh, shit. I *meant* to recharge this damn thing."

"I don't know. We could ask if they have any smoked hams for sale. Try my phone. Fish around in my bag." By now the acrid odor had become disgustingly strong. My eyes were watering. "And hand me one of those masks. Ugh."

Heather found my phone and punched in Deidre's number again. "Damn. She doesn't answer. I'll try again in a minute." She gave me a stiff white mask and put one on herself. It rather spoiled her camouflage look.

We arrived at a gated, fenced area with a forbidding pronged top. Stopping the Jeep, I slipped on my mask. It was only gauze, and it didn't help very much. I tried breathing through my mouth, but I worried that minute particles from that fetid air were zooming into my respiratory system.

Ahead of us, we saw a low-slung dwelling of indeterminate shape, mostly dark brown shakes with a few bottle green ones nailed among them, and several dark outbuildings sprawled between two rounded knolls that resembled ancient earthworks. The resulting compound had all the charm of an outcropping of giant toadstools. The moment we stepped out of the car, dogs began to bark. Pigs screamed. Cows bellowed. Hens started a ruckus of cackling. It sounded like the last verse of "Old MacDonald Had a Farm."

"So much for our sneak attack," Heather said. "Let's get out of here."

We jumped back into the Jeep, and I backed all the way to the fork in the road, where I pulled to a stop to reassess our options. "I admit that the front gate wasn't our wisest point of entry," I said, "but I don't like to get this far and give up. Why don't we walk around on foot and see what's in the back. Very, very quietly." I tucked my handbag under the seat and hooked my cell phone to the belt on my jeans.

"Okay. I just hope those guard dogs are chained up." We got out of the Jeep for a second time, and I found myself leading the way around through the woods. We couldn't see anything through the thick growth of trees and bushes, but I felt a kind of sixth sense kick in, and I knew we were moving parallel to the fence. Although we tried to maneuver carefully, there was an inevitable swish of branches and snapping of twigs as we crept forward, hunched over to blend into the brush.

When we'd been creeping along slowly for about ten minutes, the woods thinned out, and the fence became visible. There was another large gate on this side through which a truck might pass, heading into a half-hidden rutted road that accessed the rest of Pryde's woods. Through the wire mesh of the fence we could see the rear of the compound where, in a dozen or more pens, squealing piglets were rooting through despicable garbage. Each pen had a little sheltered area patched together from board or tin. One could hardly distinguish between the odor of pig manure and the ripeness of restaurant waste, especially seafood. Beyond the pens, an assortment of broken-down trucks and vans apparently were serving as chicken coops.

"Good. At least he lets the pigs wallow outdoors while he's fattening them for market," Heather said. "I've seen much worse."

"But not smelled worse, I bet. Let's see where this old road goes." I glanced at my watch. Noon. The pig roast should be in full swing by now. I wondered why we hadn't been able to reach Deidre. Well, it was too late to bother with that now.

This dirt road was much narrower than the entry road to Pryde's property. A thick growth of pines and oak trees, competing for space, were shutting out the overhead sun We slogged up a slight incline toward a lighter place that suggested a clearing.

"Oh, Great Goddess!" I exclaimed as we reached the highest point and looked down. Ahead of us there was another hollow, like the one where the compound was located, but this one was full of hundreds of huge old metal drums, leaning together like drunken trolls. Dented, rusted, and corroded, some of them appeared to be leaking a viscous green stuff. Bordering trenches ran with evil-smelling, multicolored liquids. Horrified, I simply stood and stared. What nerve to unload this noxious stuff here! I thought of children playing in the nearby development. Dogs licking water out of puddles. This was positively criminal.

Beside me, Heather sucked in her breath sharply and pulled up her binoculars for a closer look. "Eureka," she whispered. "I can see the letters on the side of one drum. I'm making out the word *Hygiechem*. Would that be American Hygiechem, Inc.?" She let go of the binoculars, letting them dangle on their cord, and whipped out her camera, moving purposefully from tree to tree, snapping the illicit dump from every angle.

"Come on," she said, moving forward with determination. "See those gulls screeching over there? Let's find out what's got their attention."

Moving around the drums, we kept to the derelict road and out of reach of the free-flowing stuff in the trenches. In the next large clearing, we found a disgusting dump of unidentifiable waste products. Gulls were dive-bombing some whitish stuff that might have been discarded diapers.

Heather picked her way gingerly around the perimeters of the dump, which was a surprisingly extensive one, much of it artificially green, taking more pictures. Finally satisfied, she said, "Okay, Cass. I have no idea where we are, but I think you do. Get us out of here and back to the Jeep. We have certainly got enough to hang Pryde."

Her faith in me was touching, but I have to admit I'd have never found my way if I hadn't had the old road and our own crashing trail to follow. Since we were moving faster now, it only took a few minutes to retrace our steps.

As we ducked under branches and trudged along, I muttered, "I don't know why Joe has to go all the way to Spain looking for environmental hazards. Pryde could keep him busy right here in Plymouth."

"Hecate protect us," Heather said, "Look there."

At the fork of the road, a rusty blue pickup truck was parked behind my Jeep, blocking retreat. It sported the Pryde logo, a pink pig wearing a smirk and a pilgrim hat. A big woman with a wild mop of orange hair, wearing black leather pants and a T-shirt with the legend "Kiss Mah Grits" written over her rather large bosom, was leaning on the door of the truck, holding a rifle. The rifle was aimed at us. We snatched off our masks.

"Well, if it isn't the Beverly Hills Girl Scouts! What the Christ are you two doing here?" she asked in the husky voice of a cabaret singer.

"And who do you think you are, Annie Oakley?" Heather demanded in an exaggerated Vassar accent.

"Please lower that rifle before someone gets hurt," I said firmly. "I can explain, of course."

"Let's hear it. I could use a laugh," Ms. Frizzy Hair said.

I took a deep breath, my thoughts scrambling madly. "Um . . . we're here to lend our support to Ignatius Pryde's campaign for selectman . . . and, um . . . we heard there's a rally being held today . . . so we thought it must be here. Apparently we were wrong. We couldn't find the pig picnic anywhere."

"Not bad," Heather whispered from behind my shoulder. She was attempting to stuff the Nikon back into her breast pocket.

"No shit, Sherlock," said the woman, lowering the rifle no more than two inches. "Hey, you in the Great White Huntress outfit. Step away from your Greenpeace friend."

"Do it," I muttered. With one last attempt to close the flap of her breast pocket, Heather moved around in front of me.

"I have my cell phone right here, and I'm calling nine-one-one," she said.

"Terrific. You can report your trespass to the police, for all the good it will do you. Whatcha got in that pocket?"

"What pocket?"

"Looks like a camera to me. Throw it over here, sister."

"It's a very delicate Nikon. I can't just throw it down," Heather demurred.

Ms. Frizzy Hair raised the rifle to her eye, sighted, and shot the limb off a tree about three feet away from Heather's head.

"Throw the damn camera," I said. Heather did.

The woman strode forward, grabbed the camera, and threw it backward without looking. It landed in the truck's bed. "Okay, now you two climb into that wagon of yours and get the hell out of here. Oh, and if you're interested in making a donation to the cause, you'll find the pig roast is being held at Myles Standish. I just came back for a few more kegs of beer. I'm going to drive to the house and get them. If you're still here when I come back this way, I'm going to shoot me a couple of trespassers looking to steal my pigs."

She turned and jumped into her pickup, spurting away to the main gate to the compound. It didn't have an electric opener, I noticed. She had to get out of the truck to open it. Had we known that, we probably could have gone into the compound the same way.

"Well, I guess that's that," I said. "Let's go make our report to Phil." When we got into the Jeep, my bag was sitting on the driver's seat.

"That Incredible Hulk-ess who stole my camera has been rooting through your bag. There goes *your* anonymity," Heather said. "Is she really going to heft beer kegs? They're awfully heavy." She was holding her hand over her empty breast pocket.

"Yes, I think she's fully capable of hurling beer kegs into the truck. Did you see her biceps? Looked to me as if she might be a lady wrestler. Iggy's girlfriend, I guess. She knows my name, but I don't know hers."

"Made for each other, those two. I think it's Wanda. Wanda Finch of the Finches who've operated a produce farm on the Carver line since the Year One. Nice source of fresh garbage for Iggy. They also run the Finch Farm Stand for sucker tourists over near Fiona's. They're an inbred, eccentric brood if ever there was one. Carrottops with burnt skin, freckles, and bad teeth, all of them. Clearly too many first-cousin couplings." As a native herself, Heather knew the lineage of every other old family in Plymouth. "We can't prove anything without those photos, you know."

"We can alert the DEM and EPA to get in there for a look, can't we?"

"Legal means of entry have been tried before, unsuccessfully," Heather said.

"Yeah? Well, my dear, when legal means fail, there's always magic. I'm opting for some intensive spellwork at Mabon. Something to bring about an open sesame at Pryde Farms. That'll still be in plenty of time to foil Iggy Pryde's political ambitions."

"Right on," Heather said. "Air, water, earth, or fire? That place could use an airing, don't you think?"

"Yes, but fire is so purifying."

"Not with all those animals. I wouldn't want any animals roasted."

We argued on the relative merits of elemental spells all the way back to her house, where we washed up thoroughly and changed clothes. Our commando-raid outfits smelled like pig manure and worse. I love borrowing Heather's clothes with their impressive labels and expensive tailoring—and they're only one size too small.

Lucrezia served us an excellent lunch of delectable eggplant, a Chianti Classico to die for, and for dessert, tiramisu. The housekeeper called the light-as-a-cloud concoction a "pick-me-up." After two helpings, I agreed. It's surprising how famished one feels after being threatened with grievous bodily harm. With the coffee, Lucrezia brought out a yellow liqueur and two tiny Waterford glasses.

"*Strega*," she said, looking at each of us meaningfully and smoothing the chef's apron over her black dress.

"No doubt the perfect ending to a beautiful lunch," I said. "Thank you, Lucrezia."

"*Prego, signora.*"

I noticed that the fingers of Lucrezia's right hand were making that good-luck sign that Heather had mentioned to me, the index and little finger like two horns against the whiteness of her apron.

The liqueur was nearly as strong-flavored as Chartreuse, perhaps herbal. Just as I was sipping a reviving shot of espresso, the cell phone on my belt began to beep. "It's about time," I said, punching in SEND. "Where in Hades have you been, Deidre? Thanks to you, we were run out of Pryde's by a wild woman with a rifle."

But it wasn't Deidre. It was Fiona. "Deidre never made it to the picnic," Fiona said. "Willy got one of those instant spiky fevers that kids run, and he's upchucking, too. So Deidre stayed home with Willy and Baby Anne, and sent Will off to the picnic with Jenny and Bobby. Deidre had her hands full, but she gave Will strict instructions to get in touch with me if Iggy or his girlfriend left the premises, and to tell me to call you. Which he did. As soon as the wild woman got back to the party with another keg of beer, he called me to say Wanda had run home for a minute but was back now and everything was cool. So I thought I'd better call and explain. I'm glad to hear you're okay. You ought to practice fading out, you know. It's the flip side of glamour. You should have been able to slip in and out of there undetected."

"In my dreams, Fiona."

"Let's not say anything to Deidre," she said. "Will meant well."

Chapter Fifteen

Although Joe returned from Spain before Mabon, on the night of the autumn equinox, he was summoned to a Greenpeace fundraiser being held at the Ritz in Boston. "I wish you were going with me," he murmured, watching me assemble supplies for the Sabbat, for which I would be hostess and priestess. I was wearing a filmy black and silver dress that he particularly admired, and I'd arranged my mop of sandy hair in the Grecian way, ornamented with a silver crescent moon.

"I know how you feel. You're looking incredibly handsome in that blue silk shirt, and I hate the thought of your wandering around unattached with those predatory females at a Ritz soiree."

"You mean you haven't put a hex on me to prevent that sort of encounter?"

"Well . . . just a little one."

His laugh was untroubled as he pulled me into his arms.

"Joe, honey," I whispered into his shoulder, inhaling the scent of summer hills that distinguished him from all other men. "Don't mess my hair. I'm trying for a goddess look."

"You don't have to try, sweetheart. You're there already. Now what is it you girls are going to do tonight? Draw down the moon, is it? And what's all this corn stuff mean?"

Deidre had supplied me with a basket of cornhusk dollies, who were now leering at us from the table's centerpiece and various other decorative perches. There were blueberry corn muffins heaped in a basket on the table. In the dining room, the centerpiece was a long wooden chopping bowl filled with green, yellow, and orange gourds. Representing the Earth Mother, a bundle of dried golden and Indian corn hung on the kitchen wall where it would remain until Imbolc in February. Bunches of dry cornstalks stood on each side of the doors. And on the windowsill over the kitchen sink were pots of rosemary, basil, and dill to snip fresh all winter. The sense of smell being the most direct route to the unconscious, its archetypes and hidden memories, I'd given some thought to evoking the divine aromas of the season.

"Balance is the theme of this Sabbat. The last harvest of earth's bounty, the turn of the wheel, rest and fulfillment." I might have said more, but then Joe was kissing me and all rational thought fled away. Good thing, since I didn't want to rattle on about saving lives at the Manor, exposing the illegal dump at Pryde's, and making ready for the death of the corn god. Who knows how he would have taken that last image? Though it was an inherent part of earth's cycle, from life to death, from death to life.

Later, after Joe had driven off, my friends arrived one by one—Heather bringing Fiona, who was finding it ever more difficult to drive—and we celebrated the Sabbat of Mabon. The night was fine and bright with stars, the breeze so slight it muted the waves' music to the soft swish of a whisk hitting a snare drum. But a chill in the September air warned of less felicitous weather to come. The beach fire and the dancing (alas, without Fiona, who clapped from the sidelines) served to keep us warm.

As priestess of this Sabbat, I drew down the moon into my body and my psyche. We spelled for healing and protection to surround everyone on our lists. Deciding to leave the Pryde spell open to whatever the cosmos would decide, we simply worked "for the good of all, and it harm none" that the cancerous dump in Pryde's woods would be cleansed and exorcised. But, of course, we were all looking at the fire, and our concentration on it might have sparked its own magic.

After that we returned to the house and feasted on honey mead, sweet corn muffins, and Phillipa's spicy cranberry bread. That honey mead, having no bite, went down rather too freely. Soon we were singing Victorian bawdy songs around the kitchen table, being totally merry and silly.

"We're making more noise than a revivalist meeting," Phillipa said, filling my kettle with fresh water. "It's time for a strong cup of tea, I think."

"Born-again pagans," Deidre said. "One thing I like about being a Wiccan is the fun of it."

"And the sense of power," Heather added. "The idea of twisting and bending reality into more beautiful shapes." She leaned over to admire the Mabon candle she'd made and brought for this Sabbat, pale yellow and filled with mysterious berries, tiny leaves, and fungi. "I blessed it with corn pollen, too—that's a Native American thing."

"Oh, yeah. Not to mention bending the law occasionally to catch a few serial killers," Phillipa said. "Where do you find the time to collect all that stuff? There aren't enough hours in my day as it is." Phillipa, who might lavish hours on preparing a special dish, scorned all other crafts.

"Oh, you should never say that, Phil." Dee made a quick banishing gesture. "That's so negative."

"Speaking of time, how about your teaching us your time tricks now, Dee," Fiona said while Phillipa made herself at home in my kitchen, spooning the Assam tea she'd brought with her into the pot. "Something we all should learn."

I took down five china cups and saucers from their high shelf (Phillipa would expect no less) and put them on the table with a dish of lemon slices, a pitcher of milk, honey, and sugar. "You have to see it to believe how much this girl can accomplish in one afternoon. She says that time expands to fit whatever got done that day. And I don't think she meant it in retrospect, did you, Dee?"

Deidre looked thoughtful for a moment, not an expression that sat naturally on her cute features—a snub nose and twinkling eyes. "I call it 'time out of mind.' Something I learned from my mom. 'We can do anything,' she used to say about whatever challenges we faced, 'if we don't waste time thinking.' I knew what she meant, but like her, I could hardly put it into words."

"Come now, dearie," Fiona said. "If I can explain the elusive state of a glamour, you can teach us your mom's wise ways."

"Well, here's one part of it," Deidre said. "You can sense in yourself a 'Stop and Think About This' button you push before every activity, even, say, brushing your teeth. You press that button, and an inner voice asks, *Do I really want to do this now? Is it necessary? Won't it be tiresome? How long will it take?* One thing I do is to bypass that internal monologue and move right on. Sounds easy but takes practice. That puts me in a state of mind that's pure action, even if what I'm doing involves planning and skill."

"I think that's called 'flow,' " Phillipa said. "As in, 'Go with the flow.' "

"Yes, but there's a magic component, too. Although Mom would never have called it that. *The wisdom of Saint Brigit,* she called it, but we know that Brigit came to sainthood by way of being a goddess all those previous centuries. This other thing is to envision yourself above the stream of time, look down and see as already done what you're about to do." Deidre sighed. "Gee, that's enough for now. I'm feeling my energy being drained away."

"Then don't speak from your own energy alone," Fiona advised. "Let the divine energy flow through you when you teach, and you'll never tire."

"Whew," Heather said. "I think my head is getting too full already. Does anyone know that old song Elsa Lancaster used to sing, 'Never Go Walking Out Without Your Hatpin?' "

* * *

I was getting so used to my biweekly bookmobile trips to the Manor, I was beginning to think of myself as an ordinary volunteer rather than an amateur crime-watcher. But then there was another incident, one that was personally very upsetting to me—because I should have seen it coming.

It was the start of October, such a delightful October when world environmental emergencies were at an all-time low, leaving Joe and me with a treasure of bright fall days to enjoy together. We'd walk on the beach in the early morning and again at sunset when the lowering light played "golden windows" with the curve of the shoreline. And when I rummaged for bayberries and roots of wild medicinal plants in Jenkins Park, Joe would come with me to carry the baskets. And then there were the moonlit nights, some of them not too chilly for a little outdoor romancing.

But I still had to keep up the business end of things, of course, or go broke. My Orgy of Love Massage Oil was doing really well, and the Calm Child Cambric Tea was perking along, too. While I was filling orders, Joe looked for jobs that needed doing around the house; and there were plenty. He mulched the herb gardens with salt hay, repainted the Adirondack chairs and the totem pole that gazed east from the top of the new beach stairs, and he cleaned the garage so that, amazingly, I could actually park the car inside it.

Scruffy enjoyed every moment of these activities, trotting after each of Joe's back-and-forth trips through the yard. The dog frolicked in the mulch, barked at the sea while Joe painted, and got himself spotted with paint in the process. He followed Joe in and out of the garage, with only an occasional complaint. *Hey, Guy, don't throw out that old bed, that's mine. Maybe it's still good.*

I knew how the dog felt as Joe dumped a number of items that I thought might have some usefulness left in them, but I bit my tongue. It was good magic in principle to clear out the old and make room for the new. I tried to explain this to Scruffy.

"That's okay, Scruffy. Maybe when we dump this old mildewy thing, a handsome new snuggle bed will appear in its place."

We dogs don't give a damn for new stuff. He gave me a disgusted look and proceeded to tug at some treasure among the discards, which trembled the whole pile like a game of Pick Up Sticks. It was a two-foot length of broken broomstick, round and slick. I'd saved it for working on the garbage disposal when it seized up. Scruffy pranced around the yard with his prize. *Look, here's a throwing stick I like. Let's have a game.*

The dog and I larked around the yard while Joe lugged, tugged, and swore, separating old tires and dried-up paint cans from nonhazardous rubbish. *How nice to have a man around doing manly things,* I thought. *I'd better not get in his way.* So I went in the house to start a savory beef stew, a nice hearty dish for an October eve. Just as I tossed my old green lumber jacket onto the hook by the door, I glanced out the window. Phillipa was coming up the porch stairs, carrying a basket.

"Guess what," she said as I opened the kitchen door. "Another death at the Manor, early morning hours, respiratory failure. And we are definitely ordering an autopsy for this one."

By "we" I figured she meant Stone. "Oh, Great Goddess . . . tell me it wasn't Euphemia Wilson."

"Your old doll? No, this was a younger woman, only about thirty-five. Knee replacement. Now I ask you, how could she possibly die of respiratory failure? Here"—she handed me her basket— "I've been testing pastry squares. Blackberry, fig and marscapone, chocolate tangerine."

"Joe will love them—me, too. What was the client's name?"

"Hmmm. Let me think. Grogan or Gagan."

"Sweet Isis! That's Gee-Gee. Now why didn't I pick up on that?"

"You're *not* going to blame yourself now, are you, Cass? You've always said that clairvoyance is not in your conscious control."

"Talk about ironic, Phil. Gee-Gee'd asked me for books on reincarnation and Atlantis. Grace Coots wasn't too happy, but she did provide a few that I could lend to her, and Gee-Gee was so pleased. So I got to know her a little. She was afraid she'd end up in a wheelchair, and I kept assuring her that would never happen. I absolutely knew that girl would never ride in a wheelchair. Now why didn't I realize the dark side of what that could mean?"

"All that reincarnation stuff—do you think maybe she had a sense of her own demise?"

"You mean like lining up the next life?"

"Well, whatever. You simply didn't have enough of a vision to go on. Do *not* get yourself all guilty and depressed. Let's use that energy to put a stop to whoever is the Angel of Death at the Manor."

"I know who. Or at least, I know one of them. Faye Kane. Only, as usual, I can't prove a thing."

"At least there will be an autopsy no matter what Dr. DeBoer writes on that death certificate. This wasn't some old person who might be expected to fail in the night. A young woman in apparent good health except for the knee surgery—very suspicious indeed."

"Poor Gee-Gee." I took the meat package out of the refrigerator and unwrapped it. Suddenly the bloody red stuff didn't look very appealing. I wished I had the strength of character to be a vegetarian. "You know, she did mention that she'd quit smoking because of 'a touch of emphysema.' I suppose that could be a tenuous connection to respiratory failure. But, frankly, I think she simply made herself too much of a nuisance over snacks. She told me that she often got hungry at night. Remember Mary Cork screaming for her meds in the middle of the night? Being a problem patient at the Manor can definitely be hazardous to a client's health. Promise you'll call me the minute you get the information on the autopsy?"

Phillipa was peering over my shoulder as I floured the beef. "What are you making there?"

"Stew. Want to stay?"

"No, thanks. Stone will be home eventually, and I have Boeuf à la Mode in the oven."

"Same thing, only drunker. Well, stay for a cup of coffee at least, so that you can gaze disapprovingly at my slapdash culinary style. I'm going for oregano, rosemary, garlic, and chickpeas."

"Chickpeas? I'm doing thyme, parsley, mushrooms, and Beaujolais. Coffee would be great. As soon as I hear anything, you'll be the first to know."

But two days later when Phillipa called me, the report was disappointing. "The medical examiner found nothing in Gagan's tissues to suggest poison and no signs of trauma from forcible asphyxiation with a pillow or folded fabric. It appears that she simply stopped breathing and her heart failed."

"I don't believe it," I said. "Not for a minute. Now what about the Pryde place? Is Stone at least going to get in there?"

"You have no idea the amount of red tape involved in sending in environmental inspectors. All I can tell you is that he's working on it."

"Meanwhile, Pryde's polluting his neighbors' wells and running for selectman."

"Town business as usual," Phillipa said.

I had to sit on myself not to rush right over to Manomet Manor, but I waited until my appointed day to make an appearance. Instead of my usual bookmobile route, however, I went straight to Gee-Gee's old room to talk to Rhoda. I found her in her customary position, lying on her pillows, her red hair sticking up strangely and showing an inch of gray at the roots. She was watching *Jerry Springer*. The other bed was already occupied, but a limp, flower-sprigged curtain had been drawn around that client.

"Hi, Rhoda. How're you doing?"

"I don't want any books. See that woman? The older one that Jerry's interviewing now? She just told her mean son that she's been sleeping with his wife. Son's more or less in shock."

"I know. I mean, I know you don't care to borrow a book. I just wondered how you are getting on since Gee-Gee—"

"It was pretty upsetting, I'll tell you. Big strapping girl like that, rosy cheeks and all. Who would have thought?"

"Who indeed? How did she seem to you the night before?"

"Fine, except for being royally pissed over her dinner. PMS, probably, although no one ever died of that. I don't think."

"Her dinner?"

"Yeah. Some fish in a gray sort of sauce. Gee-Gee said it smelled 'off.' Couldn't eat it, she said, so she hollered for something else to be brought, but it was one of those Spanish aides who just kept smiling and nodding. I ate my fish—it was okay. A little too fishy, but what do you expect? Anyway, I don't think the aide got Gee-Gee's drift, but she did bring a bunch of Hoodsies. I gave Gee-Gee mine." Rhoda sat up and for once looked away from the TV screen. "Gives me a good feeling when I think about it now. When I watched John Edward in *Crossing Over* last night, he stressed that those who have passed remember all the good things we did for them. They're all in a better place now, he said. Maybe so."

"Yeah, but maybe some of them would just have soon hung around on this earthly plane for a while. What happened after the Hoodsies?"

"Gee-Gee went without dinner, that's what happened. Then about eleven she started another big fuss, brought the nurse running. 'If I don't get something decent to eat this minute, I'm going to report this place to Blue Cross, the Board of Health, the AMA, and Channel Six."

"Wow. How'd they quiet her down?"

"Nurse Kane microwaved something for her. They keep frozen dinners and stuff in their own refrigerator. Smelled good, like eggs and sausage. Gee-Gee ate every scrap and drank down the Coke that came with it. I could have used a Coke myself. 'You gotta be the squeaky wheel,' she said to me later, about eleven, when we shut off the light."

How I wished now that I could have done more for Gee-Gee. Brought her a pizza. Warned her about kicking up a fuss with Nurse Kane. Something! I swore to myself that I would clip the wings of this Angel of Death before she disposed of any more of her restless clients. "Anyone come in later?"

"Oh, sure, the night nurse was in per usual. Gee-Gee barely woke up for her inhaler."

"Inhaler? Did Gee-Gee have respiratory therapy every night?"

"I didn't keep track. Maybe once in a while when the doc ordered it. Medicated mist, smelled nasty."

"Was it Nurse Kane again?"

"I really didn't notice. I just rolled over and went back to sleep. Say, why are you so interested anyway?"

"Just curious. She seemed so young. What time did she die?"

"Code Blue at five a.m. I remember that all right, what a racket."

"Who gave the alarm?"

"I did. I got myself into the bathroom. Had a stroke but I can get around pretty good now with these crutches. As I'm coming back to bed, I look over at Gee-Gee. Her eyes are open and her arms flung out stiff as boards. Any fool could tell there was something awfully wrong there. So I rang for the nurse. And I kept on ringing."

"Good for you, Rhoda."

"Hey, look, I'm missing this. Did the wife just say she slept with her husband's sister, too? His mother *and* his sister?"

"Okay, thanks. I won't take any more of your time. But I'll stop in and see you on Thursday. Maybe your new roommate would like to borrow a book."

"Yeah, maybe. Right now she's still out of it. Uh, oh . . . I think there's going to be a punching match pretty soon. Springer better duck out of the way." Rhoda fell back on the bed, the better to watch the high wall screen, and I trundled away to take up my usual route.

Euphemia didn't know anything, beyond the simple fact of

there having been a death in the other hall. "Poor thing. I heard she was really young, too. Maybe she was an athlete. Some athletes' hearts give out early."

"Not yet forty. I guess that's young. Well, let me know if you hear any gossip."

"You've got some kind of bee in your bonnet." Euphemia's bright eyes looked at me shrewdly. "You going to tell me what's going on?"

"Oh, nothing, dear. I'm just too darned curious, I guess. Now, look what I've brought for you today: *The Green Mile.*"

Before I left, I also stopped in at Rose's little office. She was sitting on a high stool, peering into a microscope, her cloud of dark hair piled up high on her head. She looked as sweet and pixieish as a water sprite sitting on a rock in an ad I remembered.

"Cass, how wonderful! Do you have time to have coffee?" she rasped out with a slight dry cough. She took a sip from the cup of water beside the microscope. "As you see, I'm having a great time getting back into lab work. I'm still grateful to you for helping me to escape from my old life. I could do nothing then but keep house, and I wasn't very good at that. After a while, I felt like a zombie. Some of Rasheed's friends thought I was not very bright."

I had ten minutes for a quick cup, which Rose had already brewed in the four-cup coffeemaker in her tiny lab. Before I left, I said, "I can't really explain this request, Rose, but there's something I want you to do for me."

"Of course, Cass . . . after all you've done for me!"

"Just keep an eye on your supplies and let me know if anything the least bit unusual occurs."

Her natural smile sobered in an instant, and she looked at me with complete seriousness. "I will. But to tell you the truth, Cass, everything here seems just fine to me."

I was folding twice as much laundry as usual—the flip side of having a live-in lover—when Deidre called me, all excited. "Will just got called back on duty, along with everyone else, including volunteers. There's a fire spreading in the woods back of Pryde's house. Worst thing you ever smelled. Can you believe this—Pryde didn't want to let the fire trucks in. Claimed it was just an excuse to intrude on his privacy, that the so-called fire was just the natural heat of composting. But some neighbor reported seeing flames, and the firemen said, 'You're endangering all those houses in Pilgrim Pines—out of the way or else.' The fire chief thinks it might have been a case of spontaneous combustion. *Ha ha*, I say."

I glanced at the kitchen wall clock. Nine-thirty. Joe was outdoors dealing with the garage trash in hopes that the collectors would take most of it—what a dreamer!

"Wait until the chief gets a look at those chemical drums. He'll be lucky if he doesn't have to evacuate those nearby homes to escape the noxious fumes," I said. "I hope that Will is wearing a mask."

"I'd already told him what you found in there, and Stone had given the chief a heads-up. And I did warn him again when he ran out of here."

"So this fire is, like, a blessing in disguise."

"Give me a break, Cass. Would you call that a blessing we were chanting at Mabon."

"I like to think it was. *Harm none.*"

"An important point. I certainly don't want Will to get injured. Or anyone else. Are you going to the fire?"

"You bet. See you there."

"As soon as I call the others."

Leaving Scruffy firmly closed in the house, fogging up the living room windows with complaints, Joe and I soon were racing down 3A in the Jeep. Fires were considered great sport on the South Shore, and it wasn't only teenagers who rushed to view the action.

With the wind coming briskly from the east, we could smell the disgusting odor—burning tires and manure, perhaps—from more than a mile away. We couldn't get as close as I would have liked, though. Iggy Pryde and Wanda Finch were standing by the sign at the entrance to his acreage, manning an impromptu gate made out of a long metal pipe, barring the way to all but official vehicles. Iggy looked positively apoplectic. That gave me a start. I certainly didn't want the pig farmer to keel over because of anything the circle may have set in motion.

"There must be another road going in there," my frustrated companion muttered.

I'd thought Joe was just humoring me, jumping into the car to chase fire trucks, but he seemed to be taking a personal interest in this conflagration. I'd filled him in, of course, on the mess we'd found in Pryde's woods, without being too specific on how I happened to see the two dumps. Perhaps he was programmed by Greenpeace to search out and confront toxic waste wherever he found it, like a superhero. For truth, justice, and clean air—*the Green Gladiator.*

"What are you smirking at," he said.

"Oh, nothing. I think if we drive around to the other side of Pryde's place, to that little cluster of ranch houses, we could park there and walk through the woods to the site of the fire. If you don't think that might be too dangerous. Or illegal."

"Since when do those minor concerns worry you?"

"A guy who's spent as much time in foreign jails as you have shouldn't talk."

He grinned but didn't snap at the bait. "I take it you know the way?"

"I have an idea that the fire is directly in back of the farm where the fenced area ends. There's an old road the trucks might have used to dump that illegal fill and toxic waste. If they drove into his front gate, probably late at night, they could have circled around the pens and gone through the back gate into the woods."

"You seem to have it all figured out." Joe was already backing up to follow my directions.

"Chalk it up to my clairvoyant skills," I suggested.

We found a road that led to the development known as Pilgrim Pines. The smell was intolerable, and the houses appeared to be deserted except for one guy who was hosing his roof and trees.

"Good move," Joe yelled out of the Jeep window. "Where's the fire from here?"

The homeowner pointed with a spray from the hose.

"Mind if we park here?" Joe had already stopped, and we were getting out of the Jeep. "I think you'll be okay. The wind's from the east; must be taking the fire in the opposite direction."

"Winds can change. It's a public way. You'll find most of the other idiots have filtered through those woods hoping to gawk at the fire. Iggy won't let anyone except firemen in the front gate."

"So we discovered." Joe took my hand, and we ventured forth in the general direction of the stink and steam. "We're going to be very careful."

Joe meant that. Whereas I would have bumbled on through, he stopped frequently to test the wind. Finally we got to where we could see great arcs of water falling on the burning mounds— not the corroded tin drums, but the other larger refuse dump. I felt a small glow of satisfaction. Now that the hazardous waste Pryde had hidden there would be a matter of public knowledge, he'd be forced to clean up his act. The Kellihers and Heather and Dick would be able to sit outside again without being gassed whenever they were downwind from Pryde's place.

"How did he ever get away with this?" Joe said with disgust.

"Pig manure makes a great cover."

Having seen for himself what was going on at Pryde's, Joe seemed satisfied. We trudged to the Jeep and drove back the way we'd come. Heather's Mercedes and Deidre's Plymouth Voyager were parked near each other on 3A. A bit farther down the road, Heather, Deidre, and Phillipa were all leaning on her BMW. It appeared that they hadn't gotten any farther than we had.

We stopped and got out. "Any news?" I asked.

"That Fiona!" Deidre shook her blond curls in disbelief. "Even I, married to a fireman, couldn't get past Iggy and that

Wanda Finch. I mean, what was I going to do, really? Blow on the flames to make them flare up?"

"It's been known," I said. "So what about Fiona?"

"Fiona didn't want to miss the fire, so Heather gave her a lift. Then she simply walked right down the road toward the fire while we were out here arguing with the Odd Couple," Phillipa said. "I don't think they even noticed her."

"It's the other side of glamour," I said. "If we'd learned to manifest that way, Fiona told me, Heather and I should have been able to slip into Pryde's place without getting threatened by that biker babe with the rifle."

"Are you saying that Fiona walked past Pryde without being seen? And what's this about a rifle?" Joe demanded. The look on his face spelled trouble. I sidestepped.

"Nothing. Just a joke. Fading into the background is one of Fiona's talents."

"Maybe we should recruit her for Greenpeace. Think of the gates she could unlock for our activists," Joe said.

"Sorry. We can't spare her," Phillipa said. "We have our own environmental challenges right here in Plymouth. Speaking of which, I suspect this is the end of Iggy's bid for that selectman's seat."

"Strange how it worked out for the good," Heather said. "Fire, and all. I trust the animals were spared."

"Yes, let's all pray that the little piggies are going to live long enough to become pork chops," was Phillipa's unkind comment. We were spared further argument by the appearance of a fire truck coming out of Pryde's road. The chief was driving, and sitting beside him was Fiona. As the fire truck edged by our parked cars, she nodded to us grandly and waved.

"Will you get a load of her royal majesty!" Heather said.

"Shades of the Queen Mum," Phillipa agreed.

"I guess it's just a mop-up operation now," Deidre said. "They'll leave Will and a few guys with the other truck, keep water on the fire until they're sure it's out. I might as well get along home and free my mother-in-law from her imprisonment with the kids. After Will gets home, I'll find out whatever he knows and call you."

"I'd better stop at the firehouse to see if Fiona needs a ride home," Heather said.

"I wouldn't," Deidre said. "Mick Finney is a widower, you know."

"You mean, just leave her there? Let her fend for herself?"

"Trust me," Deidre said. "The chief will be delighted to offer Fiona a ride home in that sexy bright red car of his. Might be a pleasant interlude for them both."

"Yeah? Wait till he sees that firetrap she lives in," Phillipa said.

Heather shook her head. "Matchmaking is fraught with unforeseen consequences, Dee."

Deidre grinned. "Yes, but that's what friends are for."

Chapter Sixteen

Our idyll in October lasted until a week before Samhain, when Joe was assigned to a ship off the coast of Adelaide, Australia, where activists planned a protest against ExxonMobil.

"Australia!" I wailed. "That's as far as you can go before you start coming back. If Greenpeace wants to protest Mobil, there's a station right here in Plymouth Center they can picket. Now that the tourist season is over, we could use a little excitement downtown."

"It's the way I make my living," Joe explained for the zillionth time. To his credit, his tone was loving not impatient. Having just hung up the kitchen phone, he was holding me in a comforting embrace while he delivered this bad news. "We did have a longer than usual layover this month. And you'll probably be busy with Halloween anyway—isn't that your big-time Sabbat?—then before you know it, I'll be home again."

"End of earth's cycle. A very solemn event. The veil between life and death is at its thinnest, and we honor those who have passed into Summerland. What in Hades are you going to do this time?"

"You're asking me for top-secret information here. What do you have to exchange?" He pulled me closer to him and brushed his mouth over my neck. His wiry beard tickled in a hot, teasing way.

Scruffy, who'd been waiting on the braided rug for whatever would happen next, his orange ball held at the ready between his paws, sighed deeply and flopped over for a nap. He knew where this scene was heading, and it wasn't outdoors for a fun game of ball.

"I must have something you want," I said, letting my hands roam over his back and thighs. Soon he was pushing me gently toward the bedroom.

"Okay, you win, Mata Hari. 'Eyes only,' and all that. One of the activists will lock himself to the anchor chain off the side of an oil tanker at the Port Stanvac refinery. He'll be holding a 'Don't Buy ExxonMobile' banner so huge as to be visible from shore."

"What if the oil tanker's captain gets irritated and orders the crew to drop the anchor chain a little farther under the surface of the ocean. Will the guy hanging off the chain be able to get free before he drowns?" I kept up this line of inquiry while being guided backward toward the bed.

"That will never happen. After all, Exxon is a civilized American company."

"The French are supposed to be civilized, with all those wines and cheeses, and still they blew up the *Rainbow Warrior* with someone aboard."

"We'll call the press beforehand. If they try to drown our man, there will be photographs not even a clever public relations person can explain."

"Goddess bless the press. That won't be you on the anchor, will it?"

"Not me. That's a young man's stunt."

By now we were lying on the bed, and he was pressing himself against me. That warm, yielding sensation swept over me. The sheik and his captive. Tarzan and Jane. "You feel young and strong to me," I said.

He chuckled wickedly. "And I intend to stay that way. All I'm going to do is keep things running on the ship." I didn't believe him, but this was no time for a full-scale discussion. We were just beginning our sweet good-byes, the next best thing to our sweeter helloes.

Later that afternoon, when I began to think again, it occurred to me that Joe's absence would be an ideal time to delve deeper into the Manomet Manor business without getting nagged about it. Just as Fiona had suggested, life with a seagoing adventurer did have its "up" side.

Joe and I took Scruffy for a long walk on the beach. With the east wind rolling up whitecaps, we had to keep moving briskly to ward off the chill, which suited the dog just fine. He'd brought his new treasure, the broken broomstick; Joe had smoothed the jagged end with sandpaper. I threw it for him until my arm got tired. "What's the weather like in Australia now?" I asked Joe.

"While you're celebrating the last harvest of the year in New England, keep in mind that it's always spring somewhere. Flowering trees and soft breezes where I'm going. New crops just starting to grow. But chances are, all I'll see is Port Stanvac and the oil refinery.

"It's our new year, too. At Samhain, we celebrate all that's gone before, and all that's yet to come."

" 'The best is yet to come,' as the poet says," Joe replied.

That called for more kisses, another pleasant way to warm up on a cold October afternoon. The days were getting noticeably shorter, the afternoon sun glinting on the gulls' wings for a few golden moments, then everything plunging rapidly into purple twilight. Wouldn't it be lovely just to follow springtime around the globe and escape winter's icy grip forever? For a constant traveler like Joe, the cycle of seasons must not feel inevitable at all. Snow in August, tulips in November—they're always out there somewhere.

The day after Joe headed off toward warmer climes, the temperature on the South Shore descended even more to an unseasonable low. Deciding to stock up on birdseed and dog chow, I drove out of town to an old-fashioned Feed & Grain establishment where these items could be bought cheaply in bulk. Scruffy went with me, obviously pleased to resume his rightful place in the passenger seat. He stuck his nose out the window, snuffling in the cold breeze, and barked sharply at pedestrian dogs who looked up at him in mild surprise as we passed.

I made my purchases, and got help loading the heavy bags in the back of the Jeep. Unfortunately, my strapping sailor wouldn't be there to unload them at home. Thinking to shore up my strength with a treat, I turned into Dunkin' Donuts at Plymouth Center, ordering through the drive-up window: coffee light and two crullers, one jelly and one plain. Scruffy was already drooling when I pulled into a parking place and handed him his treat cruller. The parking place faced the drive-through window, so I watched the customers idly as I sipped my coffee, which was delicious and restorative, just the thing to perk up the afternoon.

Then I saw him, what a shock! It was the same man I'd seen in my vision, Faye Kane's shadowy companion: nicely groomed gray hair, boyish features, and a small, neat mustache. How harmless he looked with that cute profile of his, the perfectly tilted nose. He turned his head toward the window, reaching for his bagged order and change. It was a navy blue van, very clean and shiny, the seat almost at the server's level. He must have treated the girl to a winning smile, because I could see her face light up in a flirtatious way. Perhaps he'd complimented her. She seemed to come to life, laughing and talking. The woman waiting in line in the car behind the van honked lightly. He turned, waved and smiled, then pulled away from the window.

As he drove past my car, I could read the small green-and-white lettering on the van's door: MANOMET MANOR. Not a doctor, I thought. A doctor wouldn't be driving that van. But what did he do? Pick up packages, provide security? Security! That's a laugh.

What could be more stupid than to follow this man whose name I didn't know and who was probably driving into town to run a perfectly ordinary errand for the Manor? Nothing to be learned by such foolishness. Immediately after thinking these sensible thoughts, I stuffed my coffee cup into the Dunkin' bag, quickly started the Jeep, and raced out of the parking lot to catch up with the van.

"I shouldn't be doing this. It's only a waste of time," I told the dog. "I can just as well find out what his job is the next time I'm at the Manor with the bookmobile cart."

Hey, Toots . . . can't we go any faster? This is fun. Scruffy's sensitive nose stuck out the window, taking in whatever news was borne on the breeze.

The van drove south on 3A, then turned off on Sandwich Street and Jordan Hospital, parking near the EMERGENCY entrance. I pulled in a few cars away. I watched the man walk through a side door. He was wearing a blue-and-green plaid flannel shirt over a turtleneck, tan chinos, and brown moccasins. After a few minutes, he came out carrying two cardboard boxes, not very large, one stacked on the other. They looked like some kind of medical supplies or small equipment. He laid the boxes on the passenger seat of the van, then got in.

Scruffy wiggled his head a little farther out the window and began barking furiously. The man in the van looked up, startled. I ducked down a bit while trying to pull Scruffy back from the window.

"Hey, you dope. We're on a stakeout here. Low profile."

You can't trust those bundle-carriers. He might throw them at us, like that guy who comes in the noisy truck. Scruffy's hostility toward the UPS delivery man was the real reason why the man tossed packages onto our porch and ran for his truck at full gallop.

This would be a great time to use Fiona's invisibility glamour. I wondered if it could be worked to include the Jeep as well as me. That's what I needed, a stealth vehicle. As soon as the blue van was a few cars away, I pulled out to follow. Clearly he was headed back to Manomet Manor. There was nothing to be learned, and anonymity to be lost if I persisted. Nevertheless, I kept on until he drove past the cemetery and funeral home, located so fortuitously next door to the Manor, and into the driveway. The van proceeded around to the service door. I parked in front in my usual spot, one of the spaces allotted to visitors.

Maybe I'd just drop in on Rose. She must know who this man was and what his role was at the Manor. "You stay in the car, Scruffy. I won't be long," I said, adjusting the front-seat windows to a two-inch opening.

That's what you always say. Deserting your loyal companion for hours and hours, freezing with cold and fainting with dehydration.

"Oh, be quiet, you mutt."

"Want to join me for a quick lunch?" I asked Rose. "How's the cafeteria here?"

I'd found her in the pharmacy, checking a new shipment of drugs against the shipping manifest. Her radiant smile lit up the small, cramped room. Amazing that nothing got lost on those deep, dark shelves, but everything seemed to be neatly labeled in Rose's precise handwriting, as clear as a first-grade teacher's, many of the medicines' names unknown to me. I supposed a visitor would be just as confused looking around my own storage area, once my grandma's cellar cold room, rows of bottles labeled with the names of obscure herbs, a few with no names at all or pseudonyms because I didn't want to advertise their presence. Hemlock, for instance, was labeled Soc. for Socrates.

"Oh, Cass. What can I say about our cafeteria?" Rose raised an eyebrow, shrugged, and made a little moue of dismay.

"One of the clients told me that the food here is terrible. The gal who died last week. No connection, one assumes, but maybe we'd better not risk it. How about if we go out for some artery-clogging fast food instead? Scruffy's in the car—he'll be thrilled if we do takeout."

We brought back robust burgers and anemic salads in plastic tubs. Rose said she'd make tea on the Bunsen burner, much better for us than shakes. This time when I left Scruffy in the car, he was too busy munching his burger to complain about being abandoned again.

Once we got settled with our lunch in Rose's tiny lab, I described the gray-haired, baby-faced man to her. "He drives the Manor's van on errands. He's been seen in the halls at night wearing a white coat, but when I saw him today he wasn't in uniform. I don't think he's a doctor."

"Does he have hazel eyes and rather a small mouth?" Rose deftly removed the tea bags from our mugs and pressed the moisture out of them on spoons without spilling a drop. "Sugar?" she asked. "Sorry, I have no milk."

"No thanks. Plain will be just fine. Small mouth, yes. I didn't see his eyes. He may be a special friend of Faye Kane."

"Yes, I know just who you mean. Randy. Randolph Wallace. He's a sweetheart. Gentle eyes with the longest lashes, and the nicest, warmest smile." She smiled to herself at the pleasant recollection.

In that instant it was clear to me that Rose had no protective sixth sense where men were concerned, which may have been the reason that she fell for Rasheed Abdul. We would have to wrap her in some kind of spell against future involvement with creeps like her husband and this Randy character.

"What's Randolph Wallace do?"

"Respiratory therapist. We have a few people here with chronic emphysema or cystic fibrosis who are just too ill to be cared for at home, or they may have some other complication. And, of course, if anyone is on oxygen, Randy monitors that. He's a doll. Everyone loves him. I sure wish he hadn't gotten involved with that Faye Kane. She's not his type at all."

"What makes you say that?" I wrapped up my greasy papers into a neat package and stuffed it into the wastebasket. I really should have been rescuing Scruffy, but the conversation was just getting interesting.

"Well, she's always so strict and proper, not at all like Randy. He's soft-spoken and easygoing."

"Appearances can be deceptive. Maybe she's not all that proper, and he's not quite the sweetheart you imagine."

"Oh, I don't believe that. Randy's a wonderful listener, too—really draws out a person's thoughts and responds so sincerely," Rose said in her whispery voice, the characteristic blush on her cheeks growing rosier. "Randy says he might be able to help me with my voice. He's studied speech therapy as well as respiration."

It appeared that Rose was already mooning over the charming coconspirator. Talk about out of the frying pan . . . !

I leaned forward and took her slim little hand in both of my own, meaning only to warn her off Randolph Wallace. For a moment I had forgotten how the touch of someone's hand is liable to trigger a clairvoyant episode in me. In the blink of an eye, the little laboratory faded from my vision. Instead, I was watching Rose run through the reception area in the Manor. It was late at night. The receptionist was no longer on duty, and the security guard was sleeping in a corner, curled up in one of the waiting-room chairs. Rose's mouth opened to scream, but only her rasping whisper was coming out. "Stop her, oh, someone please stop her." She dove into the pharmacy and grabbed something off the shelf so hastily that several bottles fell to the floor.

"Cass, Cass . . ." Rose was patting my hands and my face. "Are you all right, Cass?"

I came back to reality feeling sick with the usual nausea and headache that follow one of these episodes. "I'll be all right in a minute. I really should leave now. Scruffy's been stuck in the car for over a half hour." Actually, I wanted to get away and sort out these impressions, try to make sense of them. I always hesitated to disclose the substance of a vision, which might not come true at all. If I kept track, I think the ratio would be about sixty-forty between genuine clairvoyance and craziness. So I wouldn't tell Rose about this latest vision, unless there turned out to be some relevance to it. I hadn't even revealed all the details of the last vision I'd had about her, the one with Hari being driven away in

Abdul's pickup. I'd merely warned her to take extra care not to let her son leave St. Rita's unless she herself was with him. I decided to reinforce that now.

"Rose, you are being very cautious about Hari, aren't you? I'm afraid that Rasheed may be planning something."

"I think Rasheed is trying in his own way to be a better man." Even talking about Rasheed, her voice got harsher, as if every word made her throat sorer. Maybe Randolph Wallace was on to something about Rose's speech, I thought, giving the devil his due. How much of Rose's ruined voice was caused by physical trauma and how much was psychological? "Since the court case, he's visited Hari twice at St. Rita's with me and Serena Dove present. I have to say he's been very good about not getting the boy overexcited and restless." Rose looked at me earnestly, as if I were the one needing reassurance. "He brings presents. Not terribly expensive ones. Just ordinary, nonviolent toys that Hari can enjoy without making the other youngsters jealous. Rasheed hasn't asked to take Hari away from St. Rita's, like to a movie or anything. And Hari is never allowed out of the gate without me."

"What about school? Doesn't Hari go to kindergarten?"

"He did, before . . . before I ran away. But Serena has a nun who comes in to teach the small children, Sister Mary Vincent. She's quite jolly, loves to introduce the children to new songs and number games. So there's no need for them to go out even for nursery school and kindergarten. The older children, first grade and up, are transported to school and back by Ken Wakahiro, the gardener. I guess you remember about Ken—he's also a martial arts expert. Anyway, Hari won't be in first grade until next year. Maybe by then Rasheed will have fulfilled his plan of returning to Saudi Arabia."

I certainly didn't want to be the one to dash Rose's hopes, but I couldn't imagine that Abdul would leave the States, possibly forever, without making one all-out effort to take his son with him. I turned away from Rose's eager, trusting expression.

Finishing the last swallow of tea, I stood up. Rose stood up, too, and we hugged good-bye. I had turned to leave when, as an afterthought, she said, "There is one thing I've wondered about. When I asked Randy, he said not to worry about it."

I whirled back. "And what's that?"

"I can't understand why we have Pavulon in stock. That's pancuronium bromide, used to immobilize anesthetized patients in surgery, so they won't make any involuntary motion that might be harmful. But we don't perform any surgeries here. And yet I find we stock a supply of Pavulon, and, look, according to this manifest, we just received another shipment. I was going to finish unpacking after lunch. I only mention this because you asked me to tell you if anything in pharmaceuticals seemed odd."

I was silent for a moment, trying to remember if I knew anything about Pavulon. I didn't. "I'm glad you brought that up, Rose. It's just the sort of information that might help us figure out what's going on here."

"I feel there *is* something going on," Rose said, her face puzzled, "but I can't seem to grasp what it is. That's why I'm mentioning this to you. I don't think I should be questioning the drug supply here to anyone else, do you?"

"Absolutely not. Eyes open, mouth shut. No matter how friendly anyone seems to be—and that includes Randy Wallace—don't discuss your doubts or my inquiries. Sometime, when we both have more time, I'll tell you everything I know, I promise."

"And there's one more thing, Cass. The Pavulon we had, that we don't need—some of the vials have gone missing."

"Rose, you are a treasure. Now remember: not a word. I don't want to get you into trouble." *Or danger,* I thought.

Instead of driving home, I went straight to Phillipa's.

"You look like a witch with a mission. Come in and tell me everything. But do you have to bring Scruffy in?" Phillipa asked.

"Now I'm going to have to find Zelda and close her into the bedroom. He won't whiz on any of the furniture legs, will he?"

"I've already walked him. And I guarantee he won't bother Zelda. It's Omar he can't stand."

"Oh yeah? The last time that dog visited us, when he left, Zelda was too nervous to eat her dinner. And I'd made her favorite, salmon with egg sauce."

No wonder that black hairball smells like a fish factory. Scruffy looked around for Phillipa's cat, sniffing the air lightly for a clue.

"Don't you dare chase after Zelda or you'll go right back into the car," I warned.

Scruffy looked away, yawned, and nonchalantly pattered off toward the living room. *I need to stretch my legs after all those hours locked in the car.*

As always at Phillipa's, we were soon conferring at the long marble table in her kitchen over cups of frothy cappuccino. A delicious aroma was wafting from her oven, and there was a tray of tiny tarts cooling on the marble counter. Following my glance, she arranged a few on a plate and set them right in front of me. "Chocolate bourbon pecan," she said.

"Mmmm," I said, my mouth already full of crumbly crust and delectable filling.

"So, what's the big news. I know you've discovered something—you've got that cat-swallowed-canary smile on your face. No to mention a little smear of chocolate."

I swallowed and dabbed at my cheek. "What do you know about Pavulon?" I asked.

Phillipa looked puzzled. "Is that some new restaurant?"

"It's a drug. Rose says that the Manor pharmacy has a stock of Pavulon that they don't need, because Pavulon is only used to immobilize patients in surgery. And that the Pavulon stock is being depleted."

"Bingo! That girl is worth her weight in search warrants. Why don't you and I look up Pavulon on the computer, and then I'll call Stone."

"What a good idea. Then at least we'll know what we've discovered before we go running off at the mouth."

"Which will make a change, won't it?"

A few minutes later we were hunched over Phillipa's office computer, scrolling through a prescription-drug database. "Great Goddess, look at this, Cass. It's like curare. Paralyzes the nerves. Incorrectly administered, Pavulon can cause respiratory failure in a few minutes, especially in the weak or elderly."

"And this," I said, pointing to the bottom of the page. " 'Partially hydroxylated by the liver, 40 percent excreted unchanged in the urine.' Maybe that's why it wasn't noted in Gloria Gagan's autopsy."

"Sounds as if you have to know what you're looking for." Phillipa picked up her cell phone and punched the first button. "Hi, darling! How's your day? . . . I'm just having a coffee break with Cass . . . Yes, she does have a bee in her bonnet. . . . Pavulon." Phillipa related all that we'd learned about the drug from Rose and the Internet database. "Good, you do that. What time do you think . . . ? Oh, that's nice. Mmmmm. I'll be waiting."

It was always a pleasure to watch Phillipa's sharp features soften and glow whenever she was talking to Stone. I might call it a match made in Heaven, if I didn't know it was magicked by Deidre two years ago this Yule. Deidre's urge to marry off her friends never slackened. Come to think of it, there was only Fiona left to splice to some likely lover.

"Stone says he'll have a talk with the M.E. Maybe call in a forensic pathologist. He'll mention Pavulon, ask if it could have been involved in the Gagan case. Also, he reminded me that Rose may be a little rusty on her pharmaceuticals. Her career as a laboratory technician lasted only a few months before Abdul took her off the market. He hadn't wanted his wife working in a place where she might be in the company of males, whether coworkers or clients."

"I wonder if Dr. DeBoer knows that his staff is ordering Pavulon," I said.

"I'm not on a chatting basis with Dr. D. Are you?"

"Stone could be," I suggested.

"I can only make so many suggestions, Cass. Stone is wonderfully understanding, but . . . Hey, how about if I read the tarot for you? See what that turns up."

"Splendid idea!"

From her desk drawer, Phillipa took out a package wrapped in red silk and unveiled her tarot, the Waite deck. We sat in two small easy chairs in a corner of her office, a little square table between us. It was a warm, familiar place where we'd sat many times for readings, although usually we were seeking answers about love and family concerns, not murder. She shuffled, I cut, and she laid the cards out for the Celtic Cross reading, with the sandy-haired Queen of Wands, as usual, representing me.

"Uh oh." She frowned at the cards. There seemed to be an inordinate number of swords. "Well, see this card that covers you? The Moon? The truth of the matter is hidden from you."

"You don't say, Sherlock."

"Great Isis, the Ten of Swords, crossing The Moon—a very great danger of illness or death." I didn't like the look of that card, a shrouded figure prone on the ground with all those swords sticking into her.

As she laid down each card, Phillipa murmured its meaning, almost as if talking to herself. "Beneath you is The Fool, no surprises here—a time of decision and danger. Behind you, the Two of Swords, tension and stalemate. Crowning you, The Star. Well, that's a good one. Insight. Spiritual gifts. Your clairvoyance is your crown. And over here, immediate future, The Tower . . . well! Complete overthrow of something or someone. What you fear, *strange*. The Four of Wands is a festive, romantic occasion. A few reservations about your coming marriage, my dear? But here, what others believe about you, it's The Hanged Man, the quintessential sacrifice Oh, at least, for what you hope: seems to be the dashing Knight of Swords to the rescue."

"That ought to be my hero, Joe. Are you sure he isn't dashing away to clean up some toxic hazard on the other side of the globe?"

She ignored me. "Well, there *is* a ray of hope in this last card, the Six of Swords. Passage away from trouble." She looked up suddenly and put both palms flat against the cards on the desk. It was time for "the real reading," the one where she didn't even glance at the cards on the table. "If you persist in this crusade, you're going to be in mortal danger, Cass. I mean, really. Something very bad is going to happen at the Manor. But that's not all: just when you think you're safe, *you won't be.* You know what I'd like to do right now?"

I felt the blood draining away from my face. Phillipa's voice had gone Oracle-of-Delphi spooky. "What?"

"Send you right around to the other side of the globe with Joe. You're in too deep this time, Cass."

"I can't quit. You know that."

"Crazy woman. We all love you, you know that."

We might have got a bit maudlin right then if a black streak hadn't flown across the little hall that separated Phillipa's office from her kitchen. With her ears flattened, Zelda jumped into one of Phillipa's copper planters, crushing several fresh herbs that had been growing in perfect array. From this fragrant perch, she leaped up on top of the glass-fronted cherry cabinets, rocking a Meissen platter on its wooden stand and rattling a soup tureen. Scruffy sauntered in after her. We rushed into the kitchen.

"I told you that big oaf was after my little Zelda," Phillipa scolded.

"Okay, that's it, Scruffy. Out to the car with you."

Everyone blames the dog! If you ask me, that little hairball is as nutty as a squirrel.

"No one is asking you," I said.

"Do you really think he's talking to you?" Phillipa watched the two of us with a perplexed expression. "It's not easy to explain," I said, clipping the leash to Scruffy's collar. "But, yes, I do."

That's how much she knows. Scruffy nosed my elbow affectionately. *What'd you say, Toots . . . let's go home and get us some dinner.*

My friend's face looked suddenly tired; that tarot session must
have drained her the way a vision does me. "Thanks, Phil dear,
for the scary reading."

"Something's coming down soon," she said. "You be damned
careful."

Chapter Seventeen

It had been a disturbing day, and I was glad to relax in my kitchen rocker with a glass of wine and the radio tuned to WCRB, even if they would insist on playing those double-trumpet concerti. Meanwhile, Scruffy made up for loafing around in the Jeep half the day by running pell-mell outdoors, barking at anything that stirred. I contemplated dinner without excitement. No robust Greek guy to cook for, with my hand heavy on the garlic and oregano. Putting my feet up on the little footstool, I sighed and sipped, letting my imagination drift out over the oceans to where Joe might just now be waking up to a hard day's environmental protest. Experience should have taught me that this is exactly the moment of reverie when the phone will ring. As it did.

It was Heather. "Come for dinner! We're rescuing the Kellihers from the lingering fumes. It's not bad at my house, but it's still a problem at their place. Do you know that disgusting fire is still smoldering? Lucrezia is making some amazing rolled beef stuff—and a shrimp thing with pasta. She's in a snit, though, because I won't let her buy veal. I showed her the pictures of calves in crates, and now she won't let me in the kitchen. She's in there banging beef fillets with a wooden mallet so viciously even the dogs won't go near her. Oh, and of course, bring Scruffy!"

"Oh, why not," I said ungraciously. "It's very dull here without Joe, and Scruffy's had a terrible day stuck in the car. It would be nice to visit with the Kellihers. And you, of course. I do have some news, too, about the Manor. Not good. We ought to see if we can talk Maeve out of getting herself admitted. And Fiona."

"I don't know. She's a stubborn little thing. You'll have an easier time, I think, convincing Brian. I invited Fiona, too, but she said she's going out to dinner with a gentleman friend. Can you imagine? So . . . see you about six?"

Although Scruffy groaned when I announced my plans, he brightened visibly when I reminded him that Honeycomb would be there, too. I wrapped up a container of my Canine Calm Down, vitamin B–laced liver-fudge dog treats for Heather's crew. Maybe she'd allow her dogs to enjoy a snack that actually tasted good to them. I used Scruffy as a guinea pig to taste-test my canine products and only marketed his favorites.

A short time later, the two of us were slicked up and ready to join the party in Heather's conservatory, where the usual rubber bones and mangled tennis balls had been cleared away for company. A long oval table covered with a green linen cloth had been set for dinner. Pots of flowering mums stood between ficus and palm trees that had been pushed back to give Maeve's chair more room to move about. Although it was not yet dark, an inevitable array of Heather's homemade candles, all different heights and widths, were casting their wavering lights on the white Victorian stoneware dinner plates.

Dick had just opened some wonderful white wine, and Heather was, as usual, pouring it with a generous hand. A tray of delectable antipasti drew Scruffy's immediate attention. I ushered him directly toward the glass doors that opened onto the so-called dog yard, really a lovely stretch of lawn and trees, protectively fenced.

"Play nice," I admonished.

With these mangy flea-hounds? A purebred French briard like moi? Where's Honeycomb, anyway?

"Purebred on your mother's side only. Your father was a Don Juan of dubious pedigree. So go mingle. She's out there somewhere." I pushed his rump through the door and firmly slid it shut, gratefully accepting a glass of wine.

"We're celebrating the completion of Maeve and Brian's manuscript," Heather said. *"Living the Druid Life* is on its way to the publisher at last, artwork and all."

"Congratulations! I bet it's going to be a winner," I said. "I'm looking forward to learning more about Druid lore."

"Druid lore is not much different from Wicca lore," Maeve said. The blue smudges under her eyes more pronounced than usual. Although curly brown hair softened her features, they were angled with pain. But still, the sweetness, patience, and good humor that glowed within gave her a serene beauty.

Brian, who was hanging over his wife's chair, explained. "Druids celebrate the same high holidays. Many important goddesses, too, Brigit et al. I expect you already know their names."

"Ah, Brigit, now," Maeve continued, "she's a goddess after your own hearts, guardian of poets, healers, mothers, and craftspersons like myself. But you also must become acquainted with Fintan, the divine salmon, survivor of the flood and a symbol of immortality." Maeve's impish smile dispelled for a moment the aura of illness.

"I think we have Fintan on our totem at home. A gift to Joe. I seem to remember that the Native Americans had a flood myth, also."

"It's all written in our archetypes," Brian said. "The Druids taught a glamour not unlike Fiona's. Shapeshifting, it could be called. And I think you gals will be interested in Druid weather magic, and the mist of invisibility."

Looking over Maeve's shoulder, Heather raised an eyebrow at me. "We could have used a bit of mist last week when we got caught snooping at Pryde's."

Did those ancient Druid warriors and priests look like Brian—blond, bearded, and so robustly healthy that you had to wonder that he and Maeve became a couple. But she had nerve and spiritual force to make up for her fragile body. I thought of Elizabeth Barrett having the strength to run away from her Victorian father and elope with her exciting poet to Italy, even rescuing her dog as well.

"Maeve," I said abruptly, "I wish you'd stay away from the Manor, at least until Stone clears up a few things related to recent deaths."

"I know you mean well, Cass, but my heart is set on working with a physical therapist who's recently joined their staff. He thinks he can get me out of this damned chair and into a walker." Maeve's smile held not a hint of flexibility. "And Fiona's going to be there with me. She's hoping for her own little miracle, some remission of her arthritis. We're both being admitted the Monday after Samhain so that we can keep each other company. Our original admitting date was postponed so that I'd be assured of some quality time with the new therapist, and then Fiona didn't want to miss the holiday. So there you are—November 2nd it is!"

I groaned inwardly. How much should I tell Maeve? "Listen, we have a little friend working in the laboratory. You'll probably meet her if you have any blood work done—her name is Rose. Rose is disturbed by the presence of drugs in the pharmacy for which a rehabilitation center should have no use."

Brian's grip on Maeve's chair tightened. "I wish you would listen to reason," he said to his wife. She reached back and stroked his tightly clasped fingers with her thin hand. "I'll be fine, darling. I promise you. I think when the investigation has been completed, you'll find that there's simply been a series of unfortunate coincidences and misunderstandings."

"How are you at the mist of invisibility?" I asked Maeve. "It might come in handy."

Before she could answer, Lucrezia came in bearing an enormous platter of shrimp over linguine flecked with chopped fresh tomatoes, olives, and fragrant herbs. A sigh went up from all of us as we hurried to take our places at the table.

"*Primo piatto*," Lucrezia said, setting it down in the center of the table as carefully as if it were a new baby. She drew herself up to her full five-foot height, smoothed her black dress, and bowed slightly with a stiff little smile of satisfaction. A true artist, sure of her mastery.

"Thank you, Lucrezia. It's a masterpiece," Heather said, then to us she warned, "*Primo piatto* means the main course is still to come." It would not be easy, however, to resist overindulging in this first course.

We found our places, Maeve at one end of the table that had been left clear of chairs for her. As we twirled linguine around forks, it didn't seem mannerly to return to the subject of how Pavulon might have been used to dispatch troublesome patients at Manomet Manor. We dined and drank and laughed. From time to time, an envious dog would press its nose against the French doors, looking longingly at the table. As it got darker, automatically timed floodlights, meant to ward off skunks and coyotes, lit up the hungry faces of the horde outside. It was like dining at an open-air café in India.

"Now don't you feel sorry for them, Cass," Heather said firmly. "Lucrezia has put out bowls of nourishing, scientifically balanced chow with a little canned dog food mixed in for flavor. It's the nature of dogs to beg no matter how well they're fed."

I thought I would hear a different version of this from Scruffy, and so I did, all the way home. *Ugh, eck! That stuff tasted like the bottom of a birdcage. I'd rather starve. I hope you've got a decent meal for me at home.*

"Didn't you warn Maeve at all?" Phillipa demanded when we talked on the phone the next day, ostensibly to discuss Samhain. It was Deidre's turn to hostess, but since her mother-in-law was kicking up a fuss about having the children overnight, we'd decided to celebrate the holiday at Phillipa's. It was to be hoped that the usual chicanery of Halloween would keep Stone busy for most of the evening. We did like to keep the Sabbats for us five

alone—not that Stone would interfere. He had the admirable quality of not being unduly curious about our doings. Perhaps his job
as a detective siphoned off most of his investigative zeal.

"It didn't seem fair to Lucrezia's fabulous meal to harp on poisons," I said, knowing full well that Phillipa of all people would
understand giving our full attention to the chef's accomplish-
ments.

"Hummph. Well, you can count on me to give Fiona an earful
before she gets herself admitted. But speaking of Lucrezia, guess
what I found out? Only you have to keep it absolutely secret.
Lives at stake, you know."

"Hey. Witches' *omerta* and all that. What about Lucrezia, and,
for that matter, her brother Caesare?"

"Material witnesses," Phillipa whispered. "They've fingered
some mob bigwig. Poor Heather doesn't even know that her
ideal couple may have to be spirited away at any moment to a
safe house."

"Oh, now I understand. I had this crazy vision. . . . You remember, when Lucrezia and Caesare took their little holiday in town?"

"You didn't say anything."

"To tell you the truth, I was afraid to contemplate what the
Malatestas might be up to, seeing as I visioned them crouched
down in Heather's Mercedes, waiting for someone to emerge
from Luciano's Villa in the North End. I mean, they told Heather
it was a *commissione*, and then they left toting some big suitcase.
What would you think?"

"You see too many Mafia movies."

"*Au contraire*, Phil. I'm really not into the Italian cowboy scene
at all, and I never thought Marlon Brando looked very good with
jowls. But your story brings up an important point about clairvoyance: it's not enough to see psychically; interpretation is everything."

"Very profound, Cass. But personally, I've found your visions
to be quite reliable—although likely to get us into trouble. But . . .
don't you want to know the rest of the Malatesta story?"

"There's *more?*"

"Oh, yes. There's a trial in the U.S. District Court in Boston, starts December 1st. U.S. versus Walter Santamaria. Conspiracy and murder. A federal judge was shot down while enjoying an espresso at an outdoor café in the North End last summer. The waiter was Caesare Malatesta. Behind the counter, the pastry chef, Lucrezia, was just arranging a tray of wine biscuits. Both of them caught a glimpse of the shooter but couldn't find his mug in the mug books they were shown. When the prosecutor in Boston was looking for a quiet place to stash these two material witnesses to the shooting, a colleague in Plymouth suggested that Lucrezia get herself some kind of invisible job hereabouts, and Plymouth law enforcement would keep an eye on her well-being. Heather's hiring Caesare as well as Lucrezia was a bonus. On the weekend you mentioned, the Malatestas, in the company of FBI agents, at last succeeded in identifying the shooter. They fingered him coming out of Luciano's Villa in the company of Albert Familia, whose son Jimmy was recently sentenced for drug trafficking by that same judge."

"Did Stone know about the Malatestas being stashed in Plymouth? That Heather had hired herself a 'hot' couple?"

"He swears not until it was fait accompli. I grilled him pretty thoroughly."

"Well, it's simply not fair," I cried. "Heather's already had one housekeeper blown up with a package bomb. Now what? Her new couple mowed down in a Valentine's Day–style massacre?"

"I have said as much to Stone. I think he got the message." Phillipa's severe tone of voice put me in mind of one of those no-nonsense matrons from the Greek tragedies having a word with an erring husband. "Do you think we should tip off Heather? And Dick? At least we can hint that if the Malatestas are spirited away suddenly some night, their employers should have no cause for alarm, they haven't departed with the family silver."

"I'm not sure that's a good idea. Dick will be wild if he gets the notion that their household has been put into the least bit of danger. He might just blow the Malatestas' cover, or force them to decamp. Heather's really going to miss Lucrezia. She's a fabulous cook and, in her tight-lipped fashion, tolerant of the Devlin menagerie. Honestly, Heather has about as much luck with housekeepers as she used to have with husbands. I have to give this some thought."

"At Samhain, we could send out a call for the perfect housekeeper-and-cook for Heather. It might be rather interesting to see who shows up." Phillipa laughed wickedly. "But here's the moral dilemma: does friendship require absolute truth in all cases?"

"The truth," I said, "is not only relative, it's highly overrated."

"If you were Heather, wouldn't you expect your friends to tell you that you were inadvertently hiding in your home material witnesses possibly targeted by some mob kingpin?" was the way Joe put the matter when he returned from Australia and got an earful of the latest news. He was right, of course. And it was all my fault—I'd talked Phillipa out of giving the Devlins a heads-up. So right after breakfast, I drove over to Heather's to reveal all we knew. I'd leave it to her whether Dick should be told, too.

"Come out to lunch," I insisted. "We need to talk."

"Why can't we talk here over bowls of Lucrezia's amazing *zuppa di pesce.*"

"No way. And don't ask me why. Just let me treat you to lunch at Winston's."

"Are you crazy? After I picketed the place over serving Provimi veal?"

"Okay—then how about The Walrus?"

"All right. They do have a decent wine list," she said dubiously. "I suppose you have your reasons, 'which reason knows not of.' "

So I told her. We'd ordered our scallops and were sipping chilled Conundrum. She screamed aloud when she heard the news, but fortunately the place wasn't all that crowded. "Lucrezia! And Caesare! Do you mean to say that Stone let me hire people who were fleeing from the Mafia?"

"Shhhh. Stone didn't know."

"Oh shit." Heather drained her glass and reached for the bottle. "What will I tell Dick?"

"If I were you, I'd take a leaf out of Fiona's grimoire and keep my mouth shut. Say nothing to Dick or to the Malatestas. This revolting development does mean, however, that you'll soon be losing those delectable pastas and pastries. So we thought, at Samhain, we'd put in the call for a new housekeeper, and maybe even a gardener, too—some couple who would be absolutely perfectly suited to your needs."

Heather smiled uncertainly. "Yes, all right. We'll let the Universe of Infinite Solutions work it all out. I mean, look how well things turned out in the case of Iggy Pryde. Now that everyone knows what he's got festering in his woods, seeping into the groundwater, I doubt he could get three votes for dogcatcher."

"Right. Keep the good thought. And see if you can get Lucrezia to put a few casseroles down in the freezer."

"Well, I did it. I told Heather," I bragged to Joe later. We were sprawled on the bed watching the local news at six o'clock. There was some passing reference to bail being denied to Walter "the Saint" Santamaria but, thank Goddess, no reports from Manomet Manor. I supposed I'd have to make dinner soon, although I was still stuffed from lunch at The Walrus and the Carpenter. This is what happened when you had a family. Spontaneous grazing, one of the joys of singlehood, went out the window when love walked in. I rolled over and put my head on Joe's chest. It was a muscular, protective chest, and he smelled good. I guessed it was an okay trade-off. Maybe I could make something easy and light, like sandwiches from that leftover roast leg of lamb.

Hey, Toots, I could go for some roast lamb. Scruffy was lying on the floor at the foot of the bed, seeming to nap but with ears pricked for any stirring into action of the chief cook.

"Okay, okay . . . cold lamb it is," I said.

"Are you reading my mind again?" asked Joe.

"You have to be really careful of your thoughts when I'm around." I might as well take advantage of my reputation as a magic-worker. "Speaking of which, tomorrow night is Samhain, so. I'll be at Phillipa's for the evening. You'll be okay by yourself?"

"Of course. Scruffy and I will keep an eye out for trick-or-treaters. Do they call here? Will I need to stock up on candy?"

"I think the neighborhood children rather steer clear of my place. They don't know how I may react to, say, a green, warty witch's mask. What if I were to take offense?"

"Right. Turn the little buggers into toads on the spot. Well, don't you worry about us—you just go ahead and have fun."

Ah, the ultimate guilt trip!

Deep into the Samhain ceremony, we lit candles for those dear to us who had died. The older we got, the more candles there were to light. Especially when Heather insisted on lighting a candle for each of the beloved dogs she had lost. "When at last I go to Summerland," she said, "may they all come to greet me with barks of joy."

"A regular stampede," Phillipa whispered to me. "Like the running of the bulls."

"Hush. Be a priestess for once. Banish that sharp tongue."

We were seated on floor pillows (except for Fiona, who insisted on a chair as befitting her dignity, wisdom, and arthritis) in the circle Phillipa had cast in her luxurious living room. With its apricot and cream silks, golden Afghan rugs on a slate floor, and huge copper-hooded fireplace, now blazing with fragrant apple logs, it always reminded me of a fifties movie set.

After honoring the dead, we began our healing spellwork, for

Fiona, for Maeve, and for Euphemia, whom I had added to the
list. We did visualizations, each in her own way, then wrote our
healing wishes on slips of paper we would later consign to flames.
The candles were leaf green; the incense was sandlewood and
cinnamon. Deidre had made amulets of amber and rose quartz. I
tucked one away to give to Euphemia on my next bookmobile
visit. Fiona worried that she was already hung 'round with so
many of Deidre's amulets, if she signed up for water therapy at
the Manor she might sink right to the bottom of the pool.

"Now we are going to do a little calling for Heather, too,"
Phillipa said.

"What do you call for the woman who has everything?" Deidre
asked.

"Possibly I will need a housekeeper," Heather said. "The
Malatestas may be taking a trip one day soon. To Italy. To see
their relatives. Just in case that happens, I don't want to be left to
my own devices. I wouldn't want Dick to suffer through my adventures in cooking."

"Poor baby," Phillipa said.

"You're not telling us everything." Fiona complained.

"Oh, all right, Fiona. You are too much." And with a little coax-
ing from Fiona and Deidre, Heather told the real story of Lucrezia
and Caesare identifying Walter the Saint as the shooter in a mob
hit, how the couple, now in hiding in Plymouth, might have to be
moved to a safer place without any niceties such as a two-week
notice.

Phillipa groaned. "Stone is going to be *really* angry with me.
When he told me about the Malatestas, he swore me to secrecy. I
should have known better than to tell you anything, Cass. I'll bet
you've told Joe, too, haven't you?"

"I wouldn't want to give him anything else to worry about.
He's already carrying the weight of worldwide environmental
hazards on his shoulders," I lied.

"None of us is going to breathe a word," Deidre defended me.

Her mischievous blue eyes could take on quite a blaze when she was riled up. "This is a circle of sisterhood, of friendship, of magic, and, above all, of silence."

"Besides, what did you swear on?" Fiona asked.

"Nothing, I just gave my word. And we see what that's worth," Phillipa wailed, something she rarely did.

"Doesn't count," Fiona said. "If you want a Wiccan to give her word, you have to get her to swear on her Book of Shadows."

"I don't have a Book of Shadows," Phillipa protested. "I have a plain ordinary Torah. You're the only one in the circle who's brave enough to actually write down any of this stuff."

"There you go, then," Fiona reassured her. "No promise given, no promise broken."

"Fiona has her own ethical system," Heather said. "And it's beginning to make a lot of sense to me."

"Okay, let's get at it then," Phillipa said. "We will each visualize the perfect resolution to Heather's household problems without specifying what form that solution might take." We took a minute of silence to imagine without picturing, not the easiest thing to do. Then Phillipa went on: "Time to raise a little energy and send our spells out into the Infinite. There is one source, one power, one spirit, one creator, to whom we are all connected. What good things we desire, as they harm none, fly out on the wings of our desire and are fulfilled in ways so unexpected and marvelous, we cannot even conceive of them. Let that energy build among us as we hold hands here."

Pressing hand upon hand around the circle, we began to pass that feeling of warmth and electricity faster and faster until it felt nearly uncontainable. At a signal from Phillipa, *"Now!"* we threw up our hands and let go of every hope and dream we had conjured all evening. What a release! It made me feel positively light-headed.

And so it did to everyone else. Soon we were into our "cakes and ale" festivities, which Phillipa had interpreted as freshly baked "white" foccaccias with Verdiccio and a marvelous dry Marsala wine.

"What an amazing stove this Viking is." Deidre admired the two ovens that had produced the savory flatbreads.

"This is not just a stove—it's a trophy," Phillipa said. "One can hardly be a cookbook author without a restaurant-size range that costs as much as a small car."

"And is almost as big," I added.

Chapter Eighteen

"I brought you a good-luck charm," I said to Euphemia on my next visit. "Look, this rose quartz matches the ribbon in your hair today!"

"Oh, that's lovely! You're such a thoughtful person. I had a cousin named Cassie, did I ever tell you that? We used to have such good times together." Euphemia was sitting up in bed wearing a rose ribbon in her hair and a rose-sprigged hospital gown. She carefully marked her place in *Portrait of a Killer: Jack the Ripper* with a prayer card.

"You can wear the charm as a bracelet or, if you prefer, keep it in your night table. The rose quartz is said to confer a blessing, and the amber bead has healing properties."

"Well, I could use some of each, Cassie. Think I'll just wear this around my wrist. It sure is prettier than the hospital's name band. Did you bring me a new batch of mysteries, too?"

"Tami Hoag and Lisa Gardner," I said. "Chills and thrills, I guarantee."

Euphemia stretched out her hands for the books with an expression of greedy anticipation. "I am getting around a little better," she said. "I've been practicing with a cane, you know. Maybe I'll get to go home soon."

"That ought to please Sugar and Spice. I bet they miss you."

"You never know with cats. Independent cusses. If they really missed me, they'll find some way to punish me for deserting them, so's I'll know they're serious."

"Speaking of getting around more easily, I have two friends being admitted this week for physical therapy," I said. "I think they'll be roomed together on this hall. One of these gals, Maeve Kelliher, is in a wheelchair now, but she hopes to graduate to a walker, and the other, Fiona Ritchie, is half-crippled with arthritis."

"I've got a new roommate myself." Euphemia swung her legs over the side of the bed. She stood up in her walker and thumped a few steps toward the window, looking out at the cheerless November landscape. "She's down in the sunroom right now, not that she's going to catch a whole lot of rays out of this sky. But you don't have to worry about bringing her any books. All she reads is her Bible and the *Daily Word*. Reads it straight through out loud and at top volume, too, because she's a little deaf herself. I swear, they must be able to hear her down at the nurse's station. She's at the Song of Solomon right now—it's pretty racy stuff, if you ask me, but Mad says it's just full of symbols of God's love for man and vice versa. Madeline Coffin. A fine New England name. Lots of Coffins in Plymouth."

Too many these days! I thought. "I hope Madeline Coffin doesn't read aloud at night and disturb the patients. Or the nurses," I said.

"That's one thing I got to thank God for. Mad falls asleep about eight every night and I don't hear a peep out of her until breakfast. Gives me a chance to watch some grown-up television without her calling down the Lord to cleanse my heart."

I glanced at the chart on the other bed, but not fast enough to elude the bright eyes of my little friend. "You're wondering what Mad's here for. Advanced emphysema. She's getting breathing therapy from that nice Dr. Wallace."

"Oh yes, Randolph Wallace. I didn't know he's an M.D."

"Says so on his name tag, Cassie. Cute little guy, isn't he?"

"I don't exactly know Dr. Wallace, but everyone seems to speak well of him. I guess he's quite a lady-killer." An unconscious pun. I'd have to watch out for that.

Euphemia looked as if she'd just bitten into a lemon. "No chance of that." She lowered her voice to a whisper. "There's someone on the staff who has him roped and tied, poor guy. Talk about the Odd Couple!"

"Faye Kane?"

"So you've heard, then. She's a stickler for timely care, proper procedure, and all that, but there's just something about that woman that sets my teeth on edge. I wouldn't dream of buzzing for a nurse when I know she's on duty."

"I'm a great believer myself in following one's instincts. I hope you'll keep on avoiding Nurse Kane. Especially at night." This cryptic statement earned me a sharp look from Euphemia. All those horror books she read had probably quickened her sense of danger. To change a subject I was not prepared to pursue, I picked up her returns and marked my little record book. "Can I get you anything before I go? Hoodsie? Jell-O?"

"No thanks, Cassie. Bless you for looking out for me. If I can ever return the favor, you can count on me. And now that I'm walking better, I'll pop in and visit your friends, show them around a bit. Take this gown right here." She patted the pretty rose pattern. "I had to help myself to this one, instead of that faded blue thing the aide brought me this morning. The Manor keeps a stack of fresh gowns on shelves in the connector between the two halls. Mad, now—she likes to wears her own nighties, but she's got a daughter to wash and iron 'em. When did you say your friends are coming?"

"Thursday." I could hardly say the word without a sinking feeling in the region of my heart.

Having to rendezvous with Grace Coots by eleven, I missed visiting with Fiona and Maeve on Thursday morning. Apparently they were still occupied with admitting forms and various X rays and tests. But I did have a chance to visit with Rose and ask her to be especially alert for any irregularities while my friends were in residence.

"If there's any blood work ordered for Ms. Kelliher and Ms. Ritchie, I'll have a chance to introduce myself," Rose said. "Of course, I've met Ms. Ritchie before, at the custody hearing, but I was so upset, I barely spoke to her. I was really grateful, though, for your presence, all five of you. 'The Five Angels' is how I remember you that day. And I will always believe that somehow your prayers for me caused Rasheed to ruin his own chances." With her dark hair pulled back into a neat knot, her crisp white coat (R. Fiorello embroidered on the pocket), and her eyes shining with confidence, Rose looked radiant, a new woman, not to be compared to the waif in a flowered head scarf to whom I'd given shelter a few months ago. Not only had she reverted to her maiden name, I noticed she was no longer wearing her wedding band.

"Great. They'd love to talk to you. I'll be around visiting myself. How's Hari doing?"

"He's really settling in at last. I have to credit Sister Mary Joseph for teaching me how to manage his moods and tantrums. I'm afraid I've been far too permissive with Hari. His father . . . well, you know . . . whatever Hari did, even bullying me, Rasheed always said something in Arabic that means the same as 'boys will be boys.' Anyway, all that's changed now."

"Good for you. And I don't doubt that Hari will be happier, too."

"Yes, but we're still living in a group home. If only Rasheed would go back to his family and that native land he loves so much, I'd feel free to rent an apartment for Hari and me." Rose sighed. "Until then, it's just too much of a risk. But I'm not discouraged. It's wonderful to have something to hope and plan for. Before, with Rasheed, I felt so defeated and depressed I could hardly go out of the house to shop for the everyday things we needed. We'd run out; then everyone would be so angry with me. Now Dr. DeBoer has promised me a raise as soon as I've been here for six months. I have to be very careful to do everything exactly right during this trial period, and then . . . So you won't say anything, will you, Cass, about my questions concerning Pavulon?"

"No, of course not. I would never want to get you into trouble, Rose. But I do appreciate your keeping an eye out for my concerns."

"Dr. Wallace came back to talk to me about the Pavulon. You remember that I had asked him about it and he said that I needn't worry?" She blushed, her normally pink cheeks going scarlet. In that instant I knew that what Wallace had really said was, "Don't worry *your pretty head*."

"Did he give you a reason why the drug had been ordered?"

"He said Pavulon *is* used principally during surgery, but there are certain types of respiratory emergencies during which it might be necessary to immobilize the patient completely, which is what Pavulon does. He said he was glad to have someone in the lab and pharmacy who was really on the ball and knew what she was doing, and he would say so to Dr. DeBoer."

"You really like Wallace, don't you?"

The blush, which had nearly faded, flooded back into her face. "He's so different from Rasheed," she whispered, her raspy voice getting even lower than usual. "He really listens and cares. And he took the time to teach me some breathing and other exercises to bring back my voice."

The term *lady-killer* popped right back into my mind. All the truly successful Don Juans had in common this trait of being a good listener. Once you can fake sincerity and gaze into a woman's eyes as if she's the most fascinating person in the world, you're already a mile ahead of the guy who thinks the way to a woman's heart is to amaze her with stories of his skill with a carburetor, a rifle, or a stock portfolio. "Are the voice exercises working?" I hadn't really noticed any change.

Rose looked down shyly. "Perhaps I haven't practiced them enough. I'm so busy now, not only here but at St. Rita's with Hari, and I have to do my share in the family. But I'm sure Dr. Wallace will be able to help me. He said he would come by to see how I was getting along."

I ought to nip this one in the bud. "One of the clients told me that Wallace and Faye Kane are still an item. But you probably know about that. You mentioned it to me once before."

Rose's quick look told all. She busied herself rearranging empty vials. "I'm not interested in him that way," she declared. "I know Randy and Faye have something hot and heavy going. One of the nurses on the same floor, Debbie Abrams, said . . . Well, she said that once she found the two of them in a storage room together. She thought it was odd because it was late at night, right after a Code Blue had been called. Randy wasn't even supposed to be there. But I went away before Debbie could tell me any more. I didn't think it was very nice of her to gossip about her friend."

"Not very nice, but very interesting, Rose. Faye Kane is the same nurse who had that unfortunate encounter with Heather's Therapy Dog Honeycomb. She's certainly not a tolerant person, so you want to be careful not to make her jealous. She's very close with Dr. DeBoer, and her recommendation, or lack of it, would count with him."

Rose looked crestfallen. What a sensitive flower she was! I was sorry to seem to be scolding her, so before I could puncture any more of her dreams, I gave her a big hug and made my way back to my cart and Grace Coots. I would come back to the Manor after lunch to visit with Fiona and Maeve. That Code Blue love scene was interesting and worth reporting.

At home I found Scruffy draped on the window seat, looking forlorn. *The furry-faced guy forgot to take me running with him.* There was a note from Joe on the kitchen table.

Greenpeace ship docked in Boston. Catching up with some old friends. Be back by five. Don't get into any trouble, okay? I love you. Joe.

"So, you're beginning to like those morning jogs with Joe. Well, don't think I'm going to carry on when he goes away on another assignment. I'm too old for all that flapping." Nevertheless, I took Scruffy out for a good long walk, after which I ate my lunch in front of the computer, reading a few additional references to Pavulon.

When I turned off the computer, I called Phil, barely saying hello before launching into my concerns. "You did tell Stone that Pavulon doesn't necessarily show up in an autopsy?"

"Yes, Cass. He's not relying on you entirely to keep him current. They know this particular drug may be partly excreted with urine and missed in a routine autopsy."

"Who's 'they'?"

"Stone and his partner Billy aren't the only detectives who are concerned about incidents at the Manor. One of the other guys has an aunt who's in residence. She's been incapacitated by a stroke, needs physical and speech therapy. Anyway, they've got a line on this forensic pathologist who's developed a method of detecting the smallest traces of Pavulon in the remains even after some time has elapsed."

"Are they going to exhume some of those suspicious respiratory failures?" I was staring at reflections of sunlight in the screen of my darkened monitor. The reflections shimmied and floated, reminding me of a crystal ball.

"Well, not yet. At the moment this guy—Dr. Edward Lockett— is in Great Britain giving lectures to other pathologists at New Scotland Yard, Oxford, and other important places. He won't be back in the States for a few weeks. And even then, it's going to take some fast talking to get him interested in our little problems."

I didn't answer right away because my attention was riveted by the scene developing on my monitor, something like a photograph taking shape in a chemical bath. An Asian man, wearing a white coat, was leaning over a table where a body lay under a sheet. He was smiling. I felt as if I were reading his thoughts.

"Is Dr. Lockett an Asian?" I asked.

"Yes. Half-Chinese. Edward Liang Lockett. Do you know him?"

Finally, I said, "No, I never heard of him. But don't worry. By the time he gets back to this country, he'll be quite willing to step into the spotlight. He's got his grant application to consider."

"Cass! Are you having a vision right this minute?" Phillipa demanded. "What's going on there?"

The scene faded away like the Cheshire Cat. Dr. Lockett's smile was the last thing to go.

"It's not explainable. Trust me on this."

"I'll tell Stone. He'll be thrilled, I'm sure."

Before I left for the Manor, Scruffy and I went out again, down to the beach on stairs that still smelled new. Joe's newly painted totem presided over the scene. Eagle, bear, and salmon looked out protectively over the Atlantic. Although it wasn't windy and the sun shone brightly, it was still a November day.

Run . . . run . . . let's run! Scruffy dashed ahead joyously, waiting for me to throw his new favorite, the broken broomstick. *C'mon, Toots. I'm trying to warm you up here.*

I hadn't bothered to leave a note on Joe's note, because I'd be leaving the Manor before its unbelievably early four-thirty dinner hour. It wouldn't hurt, I thought, to bring a Care package of sandwiches, so I did. Brie and smoked turkey on seven-grain bread. I added a small container of my Stomach-Soothing Ginger and Raspberry Leaf Tea and a few *Joe Froggers* (molasses cookies). *Just call me Earth Mother,* I thought, packing the food neatly into a plain brown paper bag.

Fiona and Maeve were installed three doors down the hall from Euphemia in a crowded double room painted the Manor's signature pink. Its large windows overlooked the arborvitae that masked the neighboring Asher Brothers Funeral Home. The two women were giggling and chattering away like teenagers at a slumber party. The television was on, the sound muted. Maeve's chair, folded at her bedside, added to the clutter. Propped against Fiona's night table were two silver-headed canes, a bobcat and an owl; her bulky old green reticule was lying beside her.

Maneuvering through the tables, chairs, and other equipment, I held out my little bag of goodies. "Here, dears. I've been told that you'll be fearfully hungry by bedtime at this lean-cuisine spa. But you two seem to be in high good humor. How's it going?"

"Just lovely," Maeve said. "Brian got off to his editorial conference in New York, so I don't have to listen to any more dour pronouncements, and my wonderful physical therapist was here to greet me and map out our program. He thinks he can guarantee some improvement in ten days, if I will work very hard. And Fiona and I are having the grandest gossip. She's been telling me all about some of the circle's escapades."

"Gee, Fiona—what happened to 'keep silent,' the fourth rule of spellcraft?"

"Oh, Cass, these look terrific." Fiona rummaged through the bag. "I'll just tuck them away for later." She whisked the package into her reticule. I couldn't help wondering if it was wedged beside her pistol, or if that item had been left at home. In these insecure times, who knew when one would be subject to a search? "I don't think I'm giving away any state secrets," Fiona continued. "Just a few highlights of our previous campaigns for Truth, Justice, and the Wiccan Way."

Maeve giggled again. In the midst of all this good humor and optimism, the pink walls damping down anxiety, the bustle of aides and carts in the hall, the murmur of dozens of TVs tuned to afternoon talk shows, it was almost impossible to believe that anything sinister lurked in the shadows of Manomet Manor.

Still I said, "You have two people to watch out for: Faye Kane and her male friend, Randolph Wallace. He's the respiratory therapist, so unless one of you suddenly needs oxygen, you may not even meet him. I don't know when Kane's shift is this month—

that's one thing you could find out for me. If she's on nights, please *do not* buzz for any extra care or painkillers. Also, if you hear a Code Blue called, see if you can find out what happened, but *don't get caught spying.* You both have cell phones?"

"Not allowed," Maeve said. "But these bedside phones are sufficient."

"Of course, I'd forgotten that." I jotted their phone numbers in the little spiral-bound notebook crammed with indecipherable notes to myself that I always carry in my bag. "May your therapies be marvelously successful. I'll be looking in on you again tomorrow. *Be careful!*"

"Don't you worry about us, my dear." I noted with alarm that Fiona was patting her reticule in a reassuring manner.

"Fiona? You didn't!"

"Never leave home without it." Fiona was pulling herself up into a full glamour, the queen who will not be disputed, so I left without further argument.

Everything will work out for the best, I told myself as I walked out through the chilly parking lot. It's a Libran pep talk I use from time to time, being a firm believer in positive thinking. At that precise moment, I could feel hidden influences coming to light soon. In my mind's eye, I glimpsed that tarot card, the one called Hope that had turned up for me in Phillipa's reading.

Joe had brought home clams and lobsters. He was busying himself in the kitchen, getting ready to cook them. I went into my office, the former borning room, where I wouldn't have to hear the crustaceans scream as they were boiled alive. I could deal with them okay when they were cooked and cracked open. Melt butter. Nuke potatoes. Toss a salad. Musing on the menu, I booted up my computer to check for e-mail orders.

There were several orders, but an e-mail from Freddie, my former protégée, took precedence.

From: witch freddie   freddie13@hotmail.net
To: witch cass   shiptonherbs@earthlink.net
Subject: new job!

it's me again.

guess where i am! atlanta! guess what I'm doing! junior junior programmer. your hunk-son adam got me an awesome job at iconomics, just three floors below his office. god(dess), is he hot! okay, okay—i know he's ancient. ☺

where am i living, you ask. got fixed up with a studio apt. don't know how long that will last, since i already busted a few lightbulbs. and a minor incident with the washing machines. you know how things happen when i'm high. (ON LIFE, that is. don't get nervous.) & kitty shadow might be a prob—the creep (landlord) is really on my case.

ANYHOW, everything is super. do me a good spell, okay? see you at yule when you & joe tie the knot or jump the fire or whatever it is we wiccans do. adam promised me a ride. ☺☺☺

love & XXX to you & all the witches. f

Reading the note was like flinging open a window and having a fresh spring breeze waft through the gray November scene. How I missed Freddie and her irreverent view of the world! Still, I wondered how she'd managed to maneuver a job out of Adam, and what else she'd be after next. That girl had some powerful physical magic—more than even she herself knew. But she was much too young for him, in every way.

With all else I had on my mind, I decided to postpone worrying about Adam and Freddie for the time being. When I saw them together at the wedding, I'd know. Printing out Freddie's letter to show Joe, I continued scrolling down through my messages, looking for new orders. I reminded myself that I had the two of them to thank for the ease with which I could manage my on-line herbal shop and for the resulting increase in my income. *Bless them both!*

By Friday the crowded room was even more so. A chrome walker stood beside Maeve's folded wheelchair, and there were several floral displays on the wide window ledges. I wedged my way through to admire them and, incidentally, to read the cards. One from Brian, of course, with a gorgeous fall arrangement. A basket of exotic fruit from Phil and Stone. "And what's this? 'To Fiery Fiona from her ardent admirer.' " I read aloud the card clipped onto the plastic holder that displayed it amid a stand of red roses.

"He's a one with the poetic phrases, isn't he?" Fiona said. "Don't read too much into all that, Cass. At my age, I'm immune to messing up my life with a new man."

"Oh, sure," I said. "Everyone know there's an age limit on that sort of thing."

Maeve giggled. "I think the chief is doing Fiona more good than the therapy."

"I wouldn't be surprised," I agreed. In fact, I was thinking that a little lovemaking can do wonders for joint flexibility. Unfortunately, I could just imagine Deidre's self-satisfied smirk when she heard that the chief was sending Fiona passionate floral tributes. Much as I would enjoy grilling Fiona for details, I changed the subject to one of more immediate concern. "Now what about Faye Kane and Randy Wallace?"

"Kane is on duty from noon to eight this week. I inquired," Maeve said. "Wallace's shift is eight to two daily, with a return tour in the evening for special breathing cases that need more therapy. He gets the two-shift deal because he's the one and only respiratory specialist at the Manor."

"Sure he does. Especially if it's Kane who needs his personal attention. Well, I'll sleep better knowing you won't have Kane on nights while you're here. Still, if there's any problem at all, call me. Or nine-one-one, if it's a real emergency, of course."

"You're sure about Kane?" Maeve asked. "This is really a cheerful place, and I've been here before without any unpleasant incidents, other than Brian hauling me home when he got worried about that flurry of sudden deaths. But I'm finding it hard to believe that anything so depraved as dispatching helpless patients is really going on here."

"Cass has the second sight, Mae," Fiona defended me. "Especially where evildoers are concerned. Her clairvoyant visions have unmasked murderers twice—seemingly nice guys living right here among us in the Plymouth area. It's not a pleasant thing for her to do, and it can be dangerous. I, for one, tend to listen to her warnings."

"Ah yes, a seeress." Maeve nodded. "The Druids called them *ueledas*. How aptly you are named, Cass."

"I share the fate of all Cassandras, not to be heeded," I said. "As a case in point, why are the two of you here, right smack in the path of danger, after I begged and pleaded with you not to get yourselves admitted until we clear up this Kane business?"

"Well, to snoop around, naturally," Fiona said. "Isn't that what we always do when we get suspicious of someone? You don't have the corner on crime fighting, you know."

It's impossible to argue with Fiona, who always manages to veer deftly away from the point. So I asked about their courses of therapy, and we chatted about that for a while. Maeve was thrilled to be up in a walker. With the encouragement of the new physical therapist, she'd gone a few steps in the hall on her very first try. And Fiona was enjoying the buoyancy of limbering up with water therapy in the Manor's basement pool.

"What's it like down there?" I asked, handing over a new offering of sandwiches and fruit. "Sounds as if it might be dank and mildewy."

"Your sandwiches have been saving our lives." Fiona looked inside the bag with interest. "Neither of us could go that so-called pot roast they served us last night. Maybe it was beef, but I doubt it. We flushed ours down the toilet. We wouldn't want to have the dietician haranguing us for not consuming proper nourishment—if they have a dietician. They certainly don't have a chef. That reminds me, Phillipa said to tell you *she's* bringing a hamper of goodies tomorrow, so don't you. So nice to be pampered and cosseted by everyone this way!"

"The pool room?" I steered Fiona back to the subject.

"Oh, the pool room's not too bad, actually. There are little windows all around three sides, and it's painted aquamarine of a shade never seen in New England waterways. The water therapist is a peppy blond gal who wears a whistle on a hemp braid around her neck and cheers us on like a camp counselor. Seems to know her stuff."

"Are you feeling any improvement?"

"I think I'm moving around more easily," Fiona said.

"Especially since those roses arrived," Maeve added.

The change in the Manor's pink cheeriness began on Monday. As usual, I skipped the magazines and flowers and instead brought a paper-bag lunch for two. Maeve pointed to a small insulated hamper on her night table. "Thanks to you and Phil, Fiona and I have had the luxury of turning down every one of the Manor's more unsavory entrees—knowing we had our own little food bank right here. Which is good, because I do think that Salisbury Steak with Gravy was manufactured by Alpo and tested by wolfhounds."

"Hmmmm. What did Phillipa bring you?" I peeked in the cooler, looking for something truffled. All that remained, however, was a peppered cheese ball, somewhat ravaged. I put in two containers of my Orient Express chicken salad, rolls, and some frozen fruit to keep everything fresh.

"I have news!" Maeve sounded quite pleased with herself.

I pulled my head out of the cooler, and whirled around. "Yes? What?"

"Kane's shift has changed. Eight p.m. to four in the morning starting tonight. One of the aides who speaks a little English told me. Seems the aide's relieved to have Abrams managing the floor during her day shift. Kane, she said, 'is *muy particular, muy escrupuloso.*' "

"I am not happy about this," I said. "I want you to promise me that you won't ring for the nurse at night, no matter what."

"Have you had another vision?" Fiona asked.

"No. I'm operating on another Wiccan sense now: common sense."

On my way out, I went across the reception area to see if Rose was on duty. She was. I found her with Randolph Wallace. Sitting on the lab's high stool, she was wearing her name-labeled white coat, her hair coming loose from its neat bun, her cheeks scarlet. Wallace was leaning forward, one arm on each side of her, his hands pushed against the counter at her back—yet not quite touching her. She looked both pleased and flustered to be so enclosed.

I cleared my throat. "Hi, Rose. Am I stopping by at a bad moment?" What an ideal time for me to meet Wallace and incidentally to break up his predatory tête-à-tête.

Wallace removed one arm, swung around, and leaned against the counter beside Rose's perch.

"Cass! Of course not!" Rose twisted the unruly strands of her hair back into their proper place. "Cass, this is our respiratory therapist, Randolph Wallace. He's been giving me exercises to help my speech," she rasped worse than ever. "Randy, this is Cass, my good friend, and—"

Before Rose could say more, perhaps too much, I interrupted. "I'm the bookmobile lady. Tuesday and Thursdays, usually, only today I'm here visiting a friend. So you're giving Rose speech therapy?"

"Hello. So nice to meet a friend of Rose's," Wallace said in the exact tolerant, disinterested tone he might have used if he were her big brother being introduced to a school friend. He smiled in a debonair, charming fashion, showing perfect white teeth under his movie-star mustache. His gentle deer eyes, fringed with long eyelashes any woman would die to possess, gazed into mine a shade too long. Obviously, this was a guy who had to feel his power with every woman he met. The full effect of his attention was, if not overwhelming, at least whelming.

He held out his hand. I took it. What a mistake! As sometimes happens to me, immediately the full weight of his emotional life landed on me like an avalanche, cold and stifling—I could hardly breathe. In some dim corner of my brain, I decided to go all the way and looked him full in those soft hazel eyes. An instant later, my own consciousness fell away, and I found myself in the Manor. I felt it was late at night, perhaps just past midnight. I could look out the window and see that the sliver of moon had risen high in the sky. Then I looked in the other direction. Wallace had Nurse Kane pressed against the shelves of clients' gowns in the dark connector between the two halls. He was rubbing against her, his face in her breasts. "Do it," he said. "Do it now, and let me watch. Then we'll go into one of the empty rooms. I'll take care of you good." I knew they were going to kill someone.

"Cass! Cass!" Rose was screaming in my ear and patting my wrists. I was on the floor. I had fainted.

"I'll get her a whiff of oxygen," Wallace said, moving purposefully toward the door.

"*No.* I'm all right. I'm fine," I cried out. And I was fine. At the thought of Wallace giving me a whiff of anything, a shot of pure adrenaline coursed through my veins. In a moment, I was fully awake. Headachy and nauseous, I struggled to my feet, little Rose giving me her surprisingly strong support. Falling rather than sitting in the chair reserved for clients needing blood work, I took several deep breaths and told myself silently what the vision had shown. It's always important to describe a fleeting vision in words. Not that there was much of a chance that I'd forget this one.

So there it was. Clearly, Wallace needed something very grisly to get it off, and Kane was willing to provide it so that she could enjoy him sexually. I was glad my vision hadn't included the two of them going at it on one of the hospital beds. This truly was sick.

"I'm just overtired," I lied to a worried Rose. "I'll be fine as soon as I get outdoors."

"Oh, you mustn't drive. Not after fainting like that. Please come into one of the treatment rooms and lie down for a few minutes. Then we will ask Randy to drive you home."

"No way!" I hoped my tone was not too abrupt. "I promise I'll just sit in my car and rest until I feel perfectly all right. I don't want anyone to drive me home. In fact, I'm going to leave before Wallace comes back. You take care now, Rose. The way Wallace was looking at you when I arrived was not exactly therapeutic. Remember if you take the word *therapist* apart, you get *the rapist*. I wouldn't want Nurse Kane to walk in on her lover leaning over you."

Rose actually laughed merrily. "Oh, Cass, you are so funny sometimes. *The rapist*, indeed! All right, but I'm going to walk with you to your car, and see that you rest for a few minutes." She took my arm as if I were her elderly aunt. As soon as we went out of the lab, she locked that door, and the adjacent door, too, that led to the pharmaceutical supply closet. We moved together slowly across the reception area and out the front entrance. The air did revive me a bit. I was thankful, too, to sink into the front seat of my Jeep, and even to detach myself from Rose with many promises to be careful. Being a clairvoyant is not all the fun and games the other people suppose, not when you fall into the depths of a murderer's psyche. I would need time and solitude to collect my wits.

But then, of course, I would need to share what I'd experienced with the circle. I fished in my bag for the cell phone and punched in the familiar numbers.

Chapter Nineteen

Four of us held an impromptu council in Deidre's yellow kitchen. We missed Fiona's wacky wisdom; she was certainly in the thick of the Manor's problems.

But it was a magic moment of semi-peacefulness at the Ryan home. Jenny and Willy were at school. Bobby was playing Demolition Derby in the living room and watching out the window for the school bus that would disgorge his older siblings. Baby Anne was sweetly asleep upstairs in the nursery. Pushing aside her baskets of dolly fixings—this time she was making cute witches that looked remarkably like herself—Deidre poured hot water over tea bags in mugs and put out a plate of arrowroot cookies.

"It's unusual to see a witch with this mop of yellow curls," Phillipa commented, taking a sample out of the overflowing basket of finished dolls. "How long does it take you to make all these?"

"Oh, a few hours in the morning," Deidre said vaguely. "I try never to watch the clock. That's how you get into trouble with managing time."

Heather leaned over, counting the morning's product. "Tell that to the time-motion engineers. Eighteen . . . nineteen. No way! I think Deidre has some arrangement with the Little

People that she's not telling us about. At night, she leaves out tiny glasses of milk and mini-Oreos. The next morning, *voila!* Another basket of soft dollies ready for market."

"We of all people should not be demanding an explanation for psychic skills," Phillipa lectured. "Obviously, Deidre has a handle on time the rest of us would kill to possess. Let's just observe, listen, and learn."

"Oh, it's nothing too special." Deidre's mischievous grin belied her innocence. She knew she was on to something we were all dying to learn. "But if I were to give you the first commandment, it would be, get rid of your wristwatches and clocks. Start operating by internal time. For one thing, it puts you more in tune with nature. For another, you won't waste any energy, which is time in another form, on worrying about your schedule."

"I thought that little Earth Mother types like you had to keep a very finely tuned schedule for the kiddies." Phillipa glanced at her own wristwatch as if it might disappear and leave her timeless.

Deidre laughed merrily. "Don't you think Annie knows when it's time for her next bottle or a nap? I just follow nature. It's much less stressful than trying to get her to sleep when she's not in the mood for it."

"Dogs, too." Heather's expression was thoughtful as she fished the tea bag out of her mug and dumped it onto the saucer Deidre handed her. "They keep their own schedule for food, sleep, and romps. But what if you have, say, a dentist appointment for three p.m. Are you telling me that nature will get you into the mood to have your teeth drilled?"

"Sure. It's called 'a toothache.'" Deidre had picked up her workbasket and, with barely a glance at her busy fingers, was stuffing doll bodies. "And don't worry about the three p.m. problem. You'll soon learn to read your internal clock. But even if you don't, there are other clues. For instance, look outside right now. See how the sun is hitting the top of that maple tree? That's three-fifteen in November. In December at three-fifteen the sun will be glinting on the top metal knob of that jungle gym. Simple observation, my dear Watson."

Phillipa peered out the window and studied the sun in the maple tree, then turned abruptly back to the room. "I won't ask you what you do, Dee, on cloudy days. But I'm sure you have your own mysterious system. Come on now, sisters. Let's hear what Cass has to tell us and get on with our crime watch."

"Clairvoyant episodes are so amorphous," I said in apology for the sketchy details they'd be hearing regarding my encounter with Wallace and the ensuing vision. "The way I see it, the killings are a sexual turn-on for Wallace. I think he likes to watch. Perhaps he lets Kane choose and dispatch the victim—probably whoever has been getting on her nerves."

"Sounds like a flaccid libido to me," Phillipa said. "And not much in the way of equipment, either. Needs to whip it up, so to speak." Our expressions must have registered some surprise, because she gave us her most wicked grin and added, "I guess you girls haven't read up much on fetishes and other deviant sex in Krafft-Ebing's *Psychopathis Sexualis.*"

"It's not my favorite bedtime reading," Heather said. "I've seen Kane, and she's a big, good-looking woman. It takes a mature golden retriever at full gallop to bowl her over. Why would she let herself become besotted with a weak guy like that?"

"You haven't met Randolph Wallace," I said. "Wallace has an undeniable force of masculine charm that he turns on like a searchlight to dazzle every woman he meets. Poor Rose is completely blinded. She's relying on him to give her speech therapy. I just hope Kane never finds out that he's turning on the big amps for Rose!"

"I fear that murder may be nothing new to Kane," Phillipa said. "I have a late-breaking bulletin."

We sat up straighter in our chairs and looked at her with attention.

"Stone sent for Kane's personnel records from all the hospitals where she's worked before, and he finally spilled the results.

Hospital administrators tend to be cagey, but there's a definite pattern that emerges. Take the Macree Women & Infants Hospital in Philadelphia, for instance. First there was an unexplained rash of deaths in the nursery; then the nursery staff was 'reorganized' so that Kane's senior position was eliminated. Berkshire let her go with regret—and a glowing recommendation, of course."

"That's criminal!" Heather exclaimed.

"Exactly," Phillipa said. "But difficult to prove. Stone's trying to get in touch with nurses who may have worked with Kane at Macree. Perhaps they will be more willing to talk than their supervisors."

"So, what can we do meanwhile, Phil? We simply have to stop her," Heather said.

"I have the feeling that something may be coming down tonight," I said slowly. Flashes of my earlier vision kept popping up in my mind's eye. The position of the moon. The moon calendar on my office wall at home. "I'm not happy with the thought of Fiona and Maeve asleep and unprotected on Kane's shift. Maybe I could get there tonight and have a look around."

"Are you crazy?" Phillipa exclaimed. "If you're thinking of a break-in, I don't want to know about it. If I knew about it, I'd feel honor-bound to tell Stone."

"Oh dear," Deidre said. "You're simply going to have to get yourself out of that West Point mind-set, Phil. Fiona says it's the ruin of so many marriages."

"Maybe so, but I'd like to know how Cass is going to explain herself to Joe when she tries to slip out of the house tonight with her face blackened and a coil of rope over her arm."

"And how are you going to get past the security guard, that's what I want to know." Deidre put down her work and went to one of the kitchen cabinets. She took out a bottle of whiskey. In moments of stress, Deidre was wont to sweeten her tea with a drop of the Irish.

"Maybe I'll get Rose to go with me. She won't have any problem with Security." My plan was evolving even as I spoke, as if it were being channeled to me from the spirit world. I didn't know how I'd get away with sneaking out on Joe, but somehow I felt sure that this was the night to act. Something would turn up. "Guess I'd better get going, then."

I had been entirely occupied with my plan. When I looked up, I saw varying degrees of worry and concern in the faces around Deidre's Formica table. Heather was reaching for the bottle in Deidre's hand. Phil was casting her eyes heavenward.

"I didn't much like what I saw in the cards the last time I read for you," she said.

Sipping her fortified tea, Deidre smiled and nodded. "You go, girl! We'll all surround you with the brilliant light of protection."

"Oh, cliché!" Phillipa moaned.

"But it works, Phil," Deidre said. "What time will you be going over the top?"

"Midnight, I guess. The witching hour, you know."

Phillipa moaned again.

Driving home, I thought about how Joe's whole career with Greenpeace had involved exposing environmental dangers. As a crusader himself, surely he would understand my need to investigate the Manor. He'd see that the wheels of justice were turning far too slowly and that more people would die if Kane weren't stopped. How many babies, wrapped up in all their parents' hopes and dreams, had perished at Macree because of her? An infant's life is so fragile, it doesn't take very much to end it.

When the law dragged its heels and greedy corporations availed themselves of loopholes, Greenpeace waded right in regardless of any threat. The thing to do, then, was to share my plans for tonight with Joe, and ask for his help! Before they were married, Dick Devlin had helped Heather on a few of her escapades to rescue laboratory animals. Now, of course, he had warned her never to discuss those incidents, not even with us. What a laugh that was! Heather's predilection for grand gestures and her general openness rather jeopardized any clandestine operation. Hecate, no doubt, had her hands full protecting Heather.

Perhaps I, too, should leave the matter of what to do about Joe to the guidance of whatever angel or goddess was looking out for me. I hoped it would be Maeve's Brigit, whose sphere of influence fit our circle so well. Brigit appealed to me strongly. "Dear Brigit," I tested the words aloud, "please guide me tonight. If it's the right thing to tell Joe and invite him to go with me, let there be a sign. And if it's not a good idea, if he'll try to stop me, find a way to warn me. I'm depending on you, dear Brigit." It may have been my imagination, but for a moment I felt an aura of warmth swirl around my shoulders like a soft woolen cloak.

When I arrived home, I found Joe in the kitchen, his head in the refrigerator. He stood up, looking sheepish, and pulled me into his arms. "You've been gone for *hours*, honey. I was just thinking maybe I should start dinner. How were the girls? Still grateful for your Care packages?"

Scruffy came trotting downstairs from his pre-dinner nap and jumped around us until Joe and I finished smooching and I could turn my attention to him. *Where were you? It's time for my dinner, Toots!*

"Down, Scruffy. What a nag! The girls were perky but hungry. Apparently, the Manor's cuisine is the lean and mean sort. Someone should really have a word with Dr. DeBoer. It shouldn't cost any more to cook foods properly."

"Not necessarily. DeBoer might have to hire a better chef."

"Speaking of which, just stand clear and let me see what's for dinner." Actually, I'd forgotten to thaw the chops I'd planned to broil. What could be cooked while in a semi-frozen state? *Ah, salmon, how appropriate!* Inspiring Druid fare for us commando types. "Anyway, Maeve's taken a few steps in her walker, Fiona's been enjoying water therapy, and, incidentally, acting cool about an enormous bouquet of red roses from Mick Finney, the fire chief." I wrestled the wrapper off the fish and laid it in a baking pan with olive oil and scallions. "When I left the Manor, I stopped over at Deidre's for tea. Phillipa and Heather were there, too. That's why I was gone so long. Any phone calls?" I would have to call Rose, and soon. Should I tell Joe?

Scruffy sniffed rapturously. *Fish! It's fish!*

"Scruff and I went for a jog. As soon as we got back, he went upstairs and flopped on one of the beds." Joe gave me a rundown of events I'd missed. "Becky called. Said she and Ron were going on an anniversary cruise, she'd call back after dinner, meanwhile don't worry. Adam called. Said Freddie was working out fine, no need to worry. Cathy called. Said she'd spoken to Rose and wanted to get in touch, nothing to worry about. A Greenpeace guy called, Russell Deck. Wanted to know if I could drive up tonight to be on hand for a fundraising tour of the harbor first thing tomorrow morning. I said I didn't think I could make it. Rusty said not to worry."

I put the salmon into the microwave and pressed DEFROST. "All these people not wanting us to worry—doesn't that give you the heebie-jeebies?"

"Must be something in the air. Negative ions. High tension wires. Radio waves from Mars." There was an undercurrent of disappointment in Joe's light remarks. He was sacrificing himself so I wouldn't accuse him of constantly running out on me for any old Greenpeace affair.

It occurred to me then that Greenpeace's fundraiser might be the Goddess-sent answer to my dilemma. I would see how this played out. "Don't you want to lend a hand to the tour boat? Won't they need an old salt like you to keep from running aground on one of those harbor islands?" The edges of the salmon were beginning to soften. I snatched the dish out of the microwave, slathered it with Dijon mustard and crumbs, and put it into the oven at 400 degrees F. Less than a half hour to get the rest of dinner cooking. Rice! And a big salad.

"I'm shocked that you're urging me on to that fundraiser." Joe came up behind me and put his chin on my shoulder, breathing into my neck, his arms around my waist. "I'd have to stay the night. Or get up at the crack of dawn."

"Mmmm. I will miss you, honey. But I think you'll feel better if you got settled in town tonight, so you'll be raring to go tomorrow."

"I'm raring to go right now." He pressed in closer.

"Don't crowd the cook, dear. Shall we have a glass of wine? That won't interfere with your driving later, will it?"

"Cass! Do you have something planned tonight that you're not telling me about?"

"Who . . . me?"

While Joe was packing his duffel bag after dinner, I sneaked upstairs and called Rose from one of the guest-room phones. "I need you to let me into the Manor tonight," I said. "Could you tell the guard that you left your wallet in the lab?"

"But I don't have a car, Cass. Ken Wakahiro drives us to work in St. Rita's van."

"I'm bringing the Jeep, dear. Pick you up at the front gate. Eleven—okay? Have to go now. I'll explain everything later."

"So there's no big Sabbat or Esbat or nude dancing in the woods going on tonight for which you require my absence?" Joe asked. We had finished dinner and were standing at the doorway with our arms around each other, delivering our usual last-minute admonitions to drive carefully (me) and not to forget to lock up properly (him).

"It's called sky-clad, sweetie, and even if it weren't November, it's not our style. No, nothing special. I just thought I'd catch up with Rose and see how she's doing." This was so nearly the truth, there was hardly a ripple on my conscience as we kissed good-bye.

As he drove away in the rented Chevy, I thought of how fortuitous it was that Joe always insisted on hanging on to his rental no matter how long it was between assignments, although normally I thought him stubborn and wasteful not to simply use my car.

Come to think of it, he was a rather strong-minded guy who generally did as he wanted without much discussion. No conferring and debating and decision by consensus for Joe, whereas I myself was the soul of openness. Well . . . except perhaps for the little charade I was pulling this evening. I could almost see the vague shape of future confrontations between Joe and me, so I shook my head and my hands to scatter that negativity. *Get married first. Worry about compromises later.*

I glanced at the kitchen clock. I'd given up wearing a wristwatch according to Deidre's metaphysical time-management system, but I was fond of my green kitchen clock, which had belonged to my mother and had an herbal theme. It was nine. Possibly a good time to call Becky.

"An anniversary cruise!" I enthused. "What a grand prospect! Especially this time of year, when everything is gray and bottle green in New England. The Bahamas will be a feast of pink and aqua! A perfect way to celebrate your second anniversary."

"Third, Mom," Becky said.

"Oh, right. I don't know what I was thinking of. Cathy called this afternoon, too, but unfortunately I was out visiting some friends at the rehabilitation center and missed her. I guess she just wanted an update on Rose—you remember the young runaway wife Cathy sent me a few months ago?"

"You're an easy touch, Mom. Maybe I should send you a few of the gals I've been counseling."

"Don't you dare! But . . . if you ever have a difficult custody case, my friends and I might be able to—" I caught myself in time. Becky was not liable to credit Fiona's humming spell as a family-law strategy. "So, how's the new job going? I'll bet Ron misses working with you."

"I love being at K and K. I'm not making as much money, but I'm not working sixty-hour weeks, either. My bosses are good guys, my schedule is doable, and my clients need me a lot more than some corporate sleaze who's looking for a legal way to cheat on his taxes. I'm learning about real-life law and getting some great courtroom experience as well. Ron is adjusting. Actually, I think we have more to talk about than when we used to be in the same boring meetings day after day."

She sounded so thrilled with her work and hopeful about her marriage, it gladdened my heart. Maybe when those revealing credit card receipts had come to light, Ron had learned his lesson. I thought of all the good magic I could do to enhance Becky's happiness, but maybe it would be better to keep my psychic hands off this time. *No micromanaged magic! If it ain't broke, don't do a spell to fix it.*

"I can't understand why you're doing this . . . and why tonight." As we drove to the Manor, Rose hunched over, arms across her chest as if holding herself together. "I know you're a person of deep concern and compassion, Cass, but maybe this time you're being a little overprotective. In all the time I've been working at the Manor, I really haven't seen anything suspicious going on."

"I really appreciate this, Rose. I know you're worried about getting into trouble with Dr. DeBoer by helping me," I said. "But remember how you wondered why the pharmacy was stocking Pavulon, a drug used to immobilize patients during surgery, and then you found your stock of it was being depleted for no good reason? Well, I just know I have to be at the Manor tonight to prevent that drug being used illegally."

To tell the truth, I wasn't quite sure myself why I was hurtling along in the middle of the night on this quixotic mission. Clairvoyants like me never get the whole picture in a coherent way. It's more like a clue here and a clue there, then an irresistible impulse to do something crazy. But if you don't follow that impulse and something terrible happens, you blame yourself for turning your back on a gift from the cosmos. But I hoped this escapade wouldn't result in poor Rose losing her promised raise—or worse, the job she was so proud of. "Once you get me inside, perhaps you should get out of there. Borrow my car and drive yourself back to St. Rita's."

"And then what would *you* do?"

"I have my cell. I'll call one of my friends for a lift." It would have to be Heather, I thought. Phillipa had Stone to contend with, Deidre was burdened with a houseful of kids, and Fiona was at present a client of the suspect institution herself.

"No, Cass," Rose said. Again I sensed the strength of her resolve, that slender steel backbone, surprising in one who seemed pliable. "I will not take your car and leave you to hitch any old ride home. I'll just slip into my office and catch up on my lab work. Chances are the security guard will go back to sleep and never know whether I've left or not. He's just an old duffer in need of a few dollars—everyone knows he sleeps behind an open newspaper in the lobby. Once in a while when there's a code called in the middle of the night, they say he nearly has a heart attack himself."

I smiled. This was sounding easier and easier. If I could just stay out of Faye Kane's path.

"Do you at least know the antidote to Pavulon?" As she said this, Rose sat up straighter and folded her hands in her lap, looking out on the dark road before us with her chin raised resolutely.

"I didn't even know there is one."

"It's reversed by neostigmine and atropine." Her raspy whisper was even lower and more grating than usual.

"You looked that up?"

"Yes. In case. Also, if Pavulon is administered as a medicated mist for someone with, say, emphysema, if you get there fast enough with a ventilator, the victim may be saved."

"But it's Randolph Wallace who administers such remedies. I thought you'd accepted him as a friend."

Even though I was driving, in my mind's eye I could see a blush rising across her face. *Rose Red.*

"That speech therapy," she said. "Just an excuse to hit on me.

He asked me to meet him in the woods behind the cemetery on my lunch break. 'So no one would talk,' he said."

"Specifically to Faye Kane," I said. "I take it you turned down the rendezvous?"

"I'm still a married woman," Rose said. "I wouldn't want to do anything that might jeopardize the custody agreement. And besides . . ."

"Besides?"

"*In the woods?* What does he think I am?"

I didn't tell her that making love in the woods, if you're in a safe place, can be quite a spiritual experience. Instead I said, "Quite wise. I sense an evil in that man. Randolph Wallace is one of the reasons I'm here tonight."

I pulled into my usual parking place in front, but then thought better of it and drove around the Manor to the back lot. It was lit with floodlights, but I chose a dark area near the Dumpster. I didn't lock the car, thinking I might have to jump into it for a fast getaway.

Rose and I walked around to the big double front doors, which she opened with her key, admitting us to the lobby. The reception area was lit only by table lamps; the overhead light had been switched off. As predicted, the security guard sprang up out of the chair where he'd been sleeping, the newspaper that had covered his eyes cascading to the floor in an untidy heap. His hand was on the gun at his hip.

"It's only me, George," Rose said. "And this is my friend, Cass. We were just on our way home from a movie. Cass had to pay for both of us because I couldn't find my wallet. Now I think I must have left it in the lab. So I just thought I'd stop by—see if I can find it and reimburse her."

George mumbled something incomprehensible and fell back into the comfortable waiting-room chair.

"We may be a while, so you just relax," Rose said. "As long as I'm here, I'm going to make us a cup of tea while I have a look around for my wallet. I sure hope I find it. I'd hate to have to replace my license and credit cards." She tugged me along in the direction of her lab. "Come on," she whispered. "He'll be back asleep in a few minutes. Dr. DeBoer doesn't know this, but George has a day job, too, down at the fish house, so he's always exhausted, poor guy."

"Yes, but I'm going to have to cross the reception area to get to the clients' rooms. He'll hear me."

"Not to worry," Rose said. "I'll show you the back way around through the kitchen."

Rose was turning out to be a very savvy coconspirator.

Chapter Twenty

Rose went ahead and checked out the kitchen. "No one's there," she reported. "I haven't a clue as to who may be on night duty elsewhere in the building. But I believe that the kitchen crew won't be in until five. The cleaners whisk through the offices and common areas between nine and midnight, so they're gone. Two Spanish girls do the clients' rooms first thing in the morning. So the coast should be clear. Let's go."

The kitchen smelled of overfried fat, overripe citrus, and pine disinfectant. Rose led me through to an area where the trays, silverware, dishes, and uniforms were stored, something like a butler's pantry. She indicated the swinging doors at the other end of this storage area. "Go through here, take the door on the left, and you'll be in A Hall. The nurses' station is in the B Hall where there's a little lobby, a waiting room for visitors, and a connector between the two halls. It's all female clients here, as you know; males on the second floor. Your friends are beyond the station in B Hall, but if you go straight to the end of A Hall to the sunroom, you can come around on the far side and maybe the nurse on duty won't see you."

"Euphemia Wilson is in A Hall. I may just check on her as well."

"I don't know what you'll find. If anything." Rose was back in her dubious frame of mind. "I'll be in the lab. I guess I might as well make tea while I wait. Or maybe coffee. I could use a pick-me-up."

Something about that idea disturbed me, but I didn't know what, and I didn't have time to allow the picture to rise to consciousness. Shrugging off my jacket, I handed it to Rose, grabbed one of the heavily starched white tops from the shelf, and slipped it on. "Manomet Manor" was embroidered in blue on the pocket, the same kind of coat I'd seen the aides wear. "Have a look at that notebook in my pocket. I've made a list of clients who may have been victims of Kane and Wallace." I pushed through the swinging doors.

I was in a small landing with a door on each side. "The lady or the tiger?" I muttered to myself. Taking a deep breath, I pushed through the left door to the familiar realm of A Hall. It was much too well lit for comfort. If there were any other aides on duty at night, I didn't see them, but I hoped the uniform would give me anonymity. As I passed a cart rolled against the wall, I spotted a small steel tray with some empty paper cups on it. I picked that up and took it with me, an extra bit of protective coloring. Still, if I were caught here, this would definitely be the end of my Book Lady career. Honeycomb and I—failed volunteers!

I glanced in Euphemia's room as I passed and saw that she was reading *The Silence of the Lambs* with a tiny pen light, the heavy book propped open on her thin chest in such a way that she didn't see me. *Just as well.* As Rose had suggested, I passed by the connector and went to the sunroom-end of A and turned the corner to B. Three doors more and I'd be in the relative safety of Fiona and Maeve's room.

I edged forward, moving in the shadows from doorway to doorway. Before I could reach my objective, however, a dark figure stepped out of the connector between the two halls. As he came under the hall lights, I saw that it was Wallace. He was rolling some kind of a cart with what looked like gas masks and a cylinder on it.

Immediately I ducked into the nearest room. The lights were dimmed. The client in the first bed was sleeping. The other, near the window, was watching TV with the sound turned so low as to be barely audible. She glanced over at me without any evidence of surprise. I smiled reassuringly. "Hi. Just checking that you have enough blankets."

"You're not Spanish," she said.

"Ah . . . no. I'm new," I said, peeking back out into the hall. What had become of Wallace? What was he up to? The cart he'd been rolling was parked in the hall near the connector. His white-coated back was strolling down to the nurses' station. Oh, Great Hecate! I glimpsed him leaning over a shining blond coiffure—Faye Kane! He was kissing her neck. If this romantic interlude continued as I had envisioned it, they'd soon be looking for some sadistic fillip to whet their appetites for each other.

Well it sure as Summerland wouldn't be my friends who supplied the thrills! Without another thought of being discovered, I hurried down the hall and turned into Fiona and Maeve's room. They were both sound asleep, the lights turned as low as they could go. But Fiona instantly opened her eyes and sat up, looking dazed and disoriented as she grasped for her reticule.

"Don't shoot," I whispered, throwing my hands up. "It's me, Cass."

"Oh, *Cass*. My goodness gracious, I was just dreaming of you. What time is it?"

"Shhhhh. Midnight, I believe. I feel that something's coming down here tonight, and I'm here to prevent it, if I can."

Now Maeve sat up, reaching for her walker. "Cass! What's up?"

"Her thumbs are pricking, so to speak," Fiona said. "*Something evil this way comes*. We'll have to help her, if we can."

Maeve smiled. "Of course." She shook her abundant hair, rubbed her eyes, and took a sip of water from the glass on her night table. Then she recited some rhyming words I couldn't understand.

"Gaelic," Fiona said.

"You'll be needing a mist," Maeve said. "Come over here for a minute."

When I'd moved over near Maeve, she ran her hands over my head and shoulders, still repeating the Gaelic rhyme. "Can't hurt, might help," she said in English.

"Where are all the nurses? All I saw was Faye Kane at the nurses' station, and Randolph Wallace lurking around her."

"Upstairs probably," Maeve said. "As far as I can figure, the guys rate two nurses on the night shift, and we get one. There's a couple of Spanish girls, too, but they don't have much to do after the last juice cart. I see you've acquired one of their white coats."

Fiona looked toward the door nervously, still clutching her reticule, not a good sign. "I've seen the night aides playing cards in that little room with the microwave and refrigerator where the nurses have their snacks. It's a wonder they didn't spot you. It's only a couple of doors down the hall."

"I came around by the sunroom," I explained. I peeked out the door cautiously. No one in sight. No Faye Kane, no Wallace, and *his cart was gone, too*. "Hey, see you girls later. I've got to follow that cart."

"What cart?" asked Maeve.

"My guess is it's the death cart," I said.

"You don't think you're letting your imagination run away with you?" Fiona asked, swinging her plump legs out of bed. She felt for her slippers and reached for her owl-headed cane.

"You stay here!" I insisted in a whisper. But I could sense that she was putting on a commanding glamour, so I eased out the door before she could overrule me.

"Oh, do be careful," Maeve pleaded. As I left, she, too, was struggling up in bed, although considerably more hampered than Fiona.

Still no one in sight! Where could they have gone? At this

hour, the clients were sleeping or close to it, nothing to be heard but a quiet cough, a muffled snore. I thought of poor Mary Cork and her senile night-screaming sessions. Gee-Gee and her cries for *more food*. No wonder it was so peaceful and quiet on this floor! Anyone who broke the silence was silenced.

At that point, I didn't so much have a vision in my mind's eye as a sick feeling clutching the pit of my stomach. Euphemia! Up every night reading! Without another moment's hesitation, I crept down toward the sunroom and around to A Hall. Great Goddess, I spotted Wallace's cart right outside the door of my little friend's room!

"I'm sorry. I just couldn't get to sleep," I heard Euphemia's voice explaining. "I'm not disturbing anyone. Look, I don't even have a roommate this week."

"Now, now," Wallace was saying. "Just let me slip this mask on, darlin'. A few breaths of this will give you a *really* good night's sleep."

"I don't need that thing," Euphemia pleaded. "Please, I'll turn out my light now, I promise."

Where was Faye Kane?

I soon found out. She was coming up right behind me!

"What are you doing here?" Kane demanded in her strident voice. Mistaking me for an aide, I hoped. Maeve's Druid mist of invisibility had obviously been a failure.

I didn't turn around. "*Gracias, gracias,*" I murmured the only word of Spanish I knew, other than *via con Dios*, which seemed a bit too appropriate somehow. I made as if to move down the corridor, feeling Kane's gaze boring into my back.

"Just who the hell are you," the nurse said, her fingers grasping the soft flesh between my neck and my shoulder in a steel-claw grip. She was surprisingly strong. She whirled me around to face her, somehow keeping her gorilla grip. I think I grinned stupidly.

"You! I've seen you before." Kane was scowling at me, trying to remember our last encounter. "Randy, come out here."

In a nanosecond Wallace was in the hall, standing beside Kane, glaring at me, none of his boyish charm in evidence. "I know you," he said. "This is Rose's crony, the book person. Cass, is it?"

"Cass!" Euphemia shrieked when she heard my name. "Cass, they want me to breathe that medicated stuff, and I don't want to. That's what they gave Gee-Gee."

I grabbed one of Kane's fingers and bent it back as far as I could. "Jesus Christ!" she yelled, instantly letting go of my shoulder. "I think she broke my damned finger. Randy . . ."

Before she could issue her attack orders, I stuck out my elbows and forged between the two angry people to reach Euphemia's bedside. "You'd better get this respirator thing out of here and leave Ms. Wilson alone, or I'm calling nine-one-one."

Then I remembered. Shit! My cell was in my coat pocket, and my coat was with Rose in her lab.

I reached for Euphemia's phone. Wallace lunged toward me, knocking the phone out of my hand, a menacing expression darkening his boyish features. "I think you're the intruder here, missy. Maybe you need a few whiffs yourself, to calm you down while *we* call the police."

"No!" Kane, who was standing right behind Wallace, blocked the door. "Let me call the guard, complain about an intruder. Then I'll give that interfering bitch a shot."

"What about this one?" Wallace gestured toward Euphemia, who had pulled the blanket over her head. The small huddled pile of her was trembling with fear.

"Later," said Kane. "You stay here, and don't let them out of this room." She strode down the hall to the house phone and barked a few urgent words into the receiver. I would have tried to bolt, but how could I leave Euphemia quaking in her cocoon?

"Did that little tramp Rose come in with you tonight?" Wallace put his hands out to grab hold of me, but I ducked behind an IV pole and kept dancing around, keeping the stand in motion between us. "I *thought* I smelled coffee over near the lab! Christ, what a mess you've made, you interfering bitch."

"It's all over for you now, Wallace. Why don't you help me expose Kane's murders, and I'll put in a good word for you." *Oh, sure . . . like I've been watching too many police dramas. I might as well offer him a plea bargain.*

A nasty laugh. "Who do you and your pal think you are? The Odd Squad?"

Kane was back. In her hand gleamed a wicked needle. I heard the guard's heavy footsteps hurrying down the hall. There was an excited squabble in Spanish as the aides' card game was interrupted. Soon there were several new faces in the door, jamming any possibility of escape.

"George! Grab that woman. She's gone berserk." Kane ordered. "You hold her still so that I can give her a shot to calm her down."

"Oh no you don't. George, they're murderers. Help! Help!" I screamed, ramming the IV cart forward against George's advance. It was clear from the guard's expression that he didn't believe me. But why wasn't anyone coming to help me? What did the clients think, that my screams were some kind of Code Blue? That they should all just roll over, go back to sleep, and leave the action to the professionals?

Maybe the two aides would have seen my plight and helped me, but Kane barked out some orders in Spanish, and the women backed away.

I like to think I put up a good fight, but between George and Wallace, I was soon thrown across the other empty bed. George held my feet and Wallace had one hand on my throat, the other holding down one arm. I flailed at him with my free hand, but I was losing my breath from his grip on my windpipe. Kane approached with the needle, a smile of anticipation on her face. At the last moment, I heaved myself away, but she stuck me anyway.

A searing, brutal pain. Seconds later, I turned to stone.

It was the single most terrifying thing that had ever happened to me. I couldn't seem to move a muscle. But I could feel my neck aching where Wallace had grabbed me, the bruises on my arms and legs where the two men had held me down, every body blow I'd suffered in my struggle. Although I couldn't cry out or move a finger, the pain of my injuries seared mind and body. And I could hardly breathe. It felt as if someone had put a pillow over my head, and I was smothering. With all my remaining energy, I sent out a call for help, for protection, for the marvelous light and love that created the universe to grant me one breath after another. I lay on the bed, barely breathing, unable even to look away from the ceiling. But I could hear. The men's heavy footsteps. Then an enormous thud as someone's body hit the floor.

"Faye, what did you do?" Wallace whispered urgently.

"We can't have George calling the police to report an intruder, now can we? I gave him the rest of the shot."

"What are we going to do with this one? Her eyes are still open. You didn't give her enough." Wallace was beginning to whine. Mommy's boy. "And what about Rose? I think they came in together, used Rose's key. This problem has spread too far. I don't think we'll be able to contain it. What will we do?"

"That interfering bitch wiggled away from the full load. But don't worry, love, her breathing will shut down soon. And we'll get us out of this, one way or another. I have an idea," Kane said. "Unplug that phone over there and bring it with you. We wouldn't want Wilson to make any outside calls, now would we?"

"What about Teresa and Maria?"

"I sent them to the cellar to clean out that little cement storeroom behind the furnace and make up a cot for this crazy woman. They think I'm going to keep her there until the police come to take her away. But listen, I want you to go down there and . . ."

The conversation faded away. Kane and Wallace were leaving. *To do what?* my consciousness screamed. At least George was out of the picture, in a heap on the floor somewhere. I wondered if Euphemia still had her head under the blanket. I wouldn't blame her.

Rose! She would have no warning. What would they do to Rose?

I don't know how long I lay there, forcing myself to release my fear and wrap myself in healing light. Just to breathe was good fortune, I told myself. The smothering feeling was getting worse, a black miasma was closing in on me. If Kane could have managed it, she'd have given me the full dose and I'd have been as dead as the others. *Where there's life . . .* I thought of Joe, my children, sending them love with all my being. *Thoughts are things.*

My eyes were beginning to close. I struggled to keep them open, but my mind was not in touch with my nerves any more. The ceiling had a stain in it, like a yellow rose. Perhaps it would be the last rose I ever saw.

My forced contemplation of the yellow rose was abruptly interrupted. Apparently, I'd retained my sense of smell. And I was smelling smoke! Sweet Isis, what had Kane done? A smoke alarm screeched urgently somewhere. *Sprinklers! Why weren't the sprinklers working?* Would I have to lie here, frying and sizzling, not even able to call out?

Another sound! *Clump, clump, clump . . .* What was that?

"Where in Hades is that hideous noise coming from?" Thank the goddess, it was Fiona limping in on her cane. Soon her concerned face was leaning over me. "Cass! Cass! What happened to you?" I couldn't answer, couldn't even blink my eyes. I must have looked comatose. If someone shut my eyelids, would I be able to open them again? Is this how people wound up being buried alive?

"It was that Nurse Kane," a quavery voice said. Euphemia had come out from under her blanket. "I think she gave Cass some kind of shot. Oh, I hope she isn't dead. Is she dead?"

"She's alive, but she's in a bad way, the poor dear girl. Seems to be in some kind of trance." Fiona's concern and anxiety were apparent in her voice. If she'd taken my pulse, I hadn't felt it. "Is that a smoke alarm I hear? And who's this guy on the floor?"

"I think his name is George. He's the security guard. Smoke alarms go off all the time here in the kitchen. The chef burns a lot of food," Euphemia said.

"It's almost one a.m. No one's cooking now. And that alarm is sounding right down the hall. Give me your phone, dear. My cell is down, and I need to call for help." Fiona's voice was calm and assured. "Cass, I'm holding your hand. I'm sending you healing and love. You are going to be all right. Trust me, dear. Believe in the light."

Clients were beginning to wake up and call out from their rooms. Euphemia began to sob quietly. "He . . . he took my phone . . . Randy Wallace."

A loud metallic whack. Might have been Fiona's cane hitting at something in frustration. Good. Her energy was revving up. I wished she'd lean back over me where I could see her face. Maybe she could say a few more words, one of her protective incantations. Did she know any words to douse a fire? Did she think I wasn't aware of what was going on? Small wonder, since I'd turned into a pillar, like Lot's wife.

"Don't let them near Cass again, you hear? I'm going out to the phone in the hall. Cass, you hang on there, dear."

Clump, clump, clump . . . moving away.

Light footsteps, running toward us. "Oh, Ms. Ritchie." Rose's voice. "Help me, please. They're coming after me. And there's a fire somewhere!"

"Don't you worry, dear. Just calm down and tell me, *who* is coming after you?"

"Kane and Wallace. I think Kane started a fire in the snack room. I was just going to investigate. Then Randy showed up. From the cellar, I think And I saw from his face that he wanted to hurt me. I asked him, '*Where's Cass?*' and he said Kane had taken care of her. So I grabbed my microscope and hit him on the side of the head. I need to find Cass. Did they give her anything? An injection? An inhaler?"

"In here! She's in here," Fiona said. "I don't know. What would they have given her?"

"Let me have a look. If they gave her Pavulon... I didn't know what I should do. Then Randy started to get up. Still dazed, but he grabbed the microscope. So I whacked him with the centrifuge this time. I needed to grab some reversal drugs out of the storeroom. In case. Then I went to find George, but he was gone."

Running footsteps in the hall. Heavier than Rose's. Oh, Rose, hurry up with that stuff. In my mind's eye, I could see the fire clearly now, leaping from a pile of papers in the corner up onto the curtain and across the ceiling. Great time for a vision!

"Rose, you little bitch. What do you think you're playing at? I'll fix that throat of yours for good." Wallace! He'd come back to get Rose.

"Randy, hurry up with them. We've got to get out of here." Kane's voice, breathless from running.

"Stop right where you are." That was Fiona. "If you come one step closer to this room, you and your lady friend are both going to be candidates for knee replacement. And I'm an excellent shot."

Ah. Goddess bless old Rob Ritchie for arming Fiona.

Then Rose was leaning over me again, her raspy voice crooning, "It's okay, Cass. I'm getting you on a respirator. You'll be breathing easier in a moment. Now I'm giving you an injection. I think I've got it right. They gave you Pavulon, right? Oh dear, I wish you could answer!"

Not as much as I wished it! I would have said, *"Yes, try anything."* Because anything was better than this living death. But I *was* breathing easier now, the blackness receding. Deep full breaths. What joy!

Fire alarm! Someone had set off the main fire alarm. Clients in the other rooms all over the Manor were beginning to cry for help. Some of them were yelling loudly, crashing about in walkers, others moaning. Voices of nurses, must be from the second floor, yelling instructions. "If you can walk, come out into the hall." "Don't get into the elevators." "Someone will help you down the stairs." "Don't panic. If you can't get out of bed, you'll be carried." The Manor's beds were on wheels, so clients on the first floor could be rolled out through the sunroom or the reception area. But that didn't help the male clients on the second floor when the elevators couldn't be used. How would they get everyone out of the building? How fast would the fire spread? Why didn't the sprinklers work? *And where were Kane and Wallace?*

I didn't feel the shot Rose gave me, but I did feel my eyes blink at last. As I struggled to move, I thought maybe my right hand had lifted off the bed. Rose was watching me intently. "Fiona, I think she's coming around."

Now Fiona's face was beside Rose's. She began chanting something in low melodic tones. "Her goodness and power have no end, Begone all evil from my friend." Then her whole manner changed, and she became Fiona the warrior goddess! Waving her pistol, she turned to Rose, and announced, "They were after you, too, Rose. Kill the witnesses and torch the evidence. Do you think we can roll Cass onto one of those stretchers with wheels? We have to get her and Maeve out of this place this minute!"

Oh, how I wanted to speak! *Go after Kane and Wallace. Don't let them get away.*

Rose's face disappeared from view. "I'm trying to revive George, but I don't know . . ." she said. "I've got him on a respirator, too, I've given him an injection, but he doesn't seem to be responding."

Euphemia began to whimper. "Don't forget about me."

Heavy footsteps were running down the hall. Shock after shock, this time it was Joe who was leaning over me. Was I dreaming? "What did they do to you, love," he cried.

"I think she's going to be okay," Rose said. "Her breathing is normal now, and I've given her an antidote to reverse the drug. God, I'm glad to see you, but how did you get here?"

My very question!

"Cass's call to you. I overheard it. The more I thought about it, the more it bugged me." Joe was gathering me into his arms. "I'll explain later, Rose. That fire's moving fast. One of the aides from the second floor is trying to slow it down with extinguishers, but I don't know . . . Right now you've got to get yourself out of here—and take this lady with you."

"Oh thank you, dear," Euphemia whispered.

"Never mind your walker," Rose was saying. "Just lean on me."

"Fiona, can you get your roommate into her chair?" Joe said. "I got the sunroom door open, and you can wheel her right through it. Back to help you!"

At last I was moving, because Joe was carrying me in his arms down the hall toward the sunroom, murmuring sweet words in my ear the whole while. I could feel my mouth flooding with moisture at last. My lips moved. "Joe," I said.

"You're going to be all right, darling."

Sirens were screaming. Fire trucks roared into the driveway, closely followed by police and rescue vehicles. After making sure that I was in the hands of paramedics, Joe raced to help with the evacuation of the Manor. Then Rose hurried up, stumbling a little as she supported Euphemia. She was eager to explain to the medics about the Pavulon and the antidote she'd administered. "George, the security guard. He got shot full of Pavulon, too. The firemen are carrying him out now." She pointed George out to the team, then Rose, too, was gone. She would leave Euphemia in a safe place so that she could help with the rest of the clients.

The paramedics were thorough but quick in checking out my vital signs and setting me aside. "She's coming out of it," one of them said. "We'd better attend to those chest pains over there next. Guy in the plaid bathrobe."

"Christ!" A gruff voice I took to be a fireman's. "Isn't this place supposed to have sprinklers? Finney better call for more men! Those people inside are helpless."

"Someone shut off the damned water," was the indignant reply. "Finney is over there hollering about it to the chief of police. Ryan went in to check the main valve. Found it jammed shut."

I wondered if that Ryan was Deidre's Will. Must be.

"Get it fixed?" asked the first guy. "Here, give me a hand with this hose, will you?"

The second fireman laughed sardonically. "Hell, no. Before Ryan could get to work on it, a couple of hysterical broads started screaming blue murder in Spanish. They were in a room behind the furnace—somehow they got locked in. Ryan breaks through the door to let them out of there. They grab hold of him like they're drowning and won't let go till he hauls them out of the building. He's back in the cellar now, though, still trying to free up that valve." Their voices faded away as they dragged another hose into action.

Lying on a stretcher beside the rescue wagon, with my own little oxygen inhaler, I could turn my head a fraction, so I tried to see where everyone was. Maeve? Fiona? Joe? I couldn't locate the two women, but I did see Joe among the volunteers carrying people out of the Manor. And then I noticed two shadows ducking down the side of the building and around to the back lot. Everyone else was running to help, but these two figures were running away. They must be Kane and Wallace. I tried to talk, to say, *Someone stop them!* But my mouth had dried up again, and, anyway, no one had time now.

Sirens continued to wail as more fire trucks and cruisers rumbled up the drive. Firemen were running inside with hoses. Other hoses were being played on the outside of the building and through the windows. I could see flames in one window, billows of black smoke in others. Dr. DeBoer and his wife arrived, their little Mercedes roadster managing to scoot between the larger vehicles. Whether it was the light or not, I don't know, but

DeBoer looked absolutely apoplectic, like he might have a stroke at any moment. He yelled at Mick Finney that the sprinklers should have everything under control in a few minutes, and Mick Finney yelled back that the fucking sprinkers weren't working.

Ignoring the heated exchange, DeBoer's wife hurried to assist with the clients who were being led, carried, or rolled out of the hospital. The front lawn filled up with refugees in hospital gowns. An aide was circulating with a stack of blankets to cover their shivering forms. Where could they bring all these invalids? Jordan Hospital would be swamped.

I leaned back and closed my eyes. *Closed my eyes!* What a wonderful feeling just to blink away the burning sensation.

"Cass . . . Cass! It's me, Dee." I looked up into my friend's concerned face. "When Will got the call for the Manor, I had to see if Fiona and Maeve were okay. Woke up my neighbor to stay with the kids. And now I find you! What happened!"

I tried to get enough saliva into my mouth to speak. "Joe's here," I said. "Tell you later. Go . . . find . . ." My voice failed.

"Yes, dear, don't you worry. I'm going to make sure those two gals are safe, then I'll be right back. We all ought to be together." As she hurried away, I saw she had her cell phone pressed up against her ear. Calling Heather and Phillipa, I didn't doubt. I sure would like to talk to Stone, if only I could get the words out.

When Fiona finally came into view, pushing Maeve's chair, I found my voice at last. "Thank Goddess. Fiona, I think you saved my life. Where's your cane?"

"Dropped it somewhere looking for Maeve," Fiona said. "I thought I'd lost her. Turns out she saw Kane and Wallace run by, got scared, and wrapped herself up in that Druid thing. The mist. It's a lot like a glamour."

"It *is* a glamour. Look at how well you're walking, Fiona," Maeve exclaimed. Huddled in her chair, she smiled bravely, but she was shivering in a thin hospital blanket. "Isn't she a wonder? Are you okay now, Cass?"

"I had Mae's chair to lean on, don't forget." Fiona was wearing a faded blue terrycloth robe with the Manor's logo stitched on the pocket. I noticed she hadn't run off without her green reticule, though; it was looped over her arm.

"Listen, you have to do something. Kane and Wallace are out back, probably driving away this very minute. They tried to kill Euphemia, the guard, me—and Rose was in danger, too. Kane started the fire, and Wallace turned off the water. Fiona, you've got to alert Mick and Chief Fogg."

"Don't worry, wherever they go to ground, I'll find them," Fiona the Finder said in a grim tone.

"What kind of car were they driving?" Maeve asked.

"Probably Kane's car. All I've ever seen Wallace drive is the Manor's van. Tell Chief Fogg to broadcast Kane's license plate number," I didn't doubt Fiona could zero in on them, too, given enough time and her good dowsing crystal. But right now Kane and Wallace might be apprehended by law enforcement, if they got cracking right away.

"Don't you worry—I'll give Mick an earful." Fiona was already turning Maeve's chair around for an assault on the authorities. "When Phil gets here, be sure she calls Stone. I don't know about this Fogg."

"Finney and Fogg—sounds like a vaudeville team. I ought to call Brian, I suppose." Maeve said as she was wheeled away. Her tone was not too enthusiastic as she anticipated a well-earned scolding.

"We'll have to borrow a cell phone. The battery's too low on mine. Must have turned itself on by accident, banging around in my bag." Fiona said. I wouldn't have been surprised if she had a fire extinguisher in there, too, nestled beside that ever useful pistol. Ever since Stone had made her get a permit for that thing, she'd turned into a regular Annie Oakley and wouldn't even go to a librarians' convention unarmed.

Having hitched a ride in a cruiser, Phillipa and Heather were by my side within a half hour. By then the fire was subsiding, more steam than smoke issuing from the A Hall windows, scene of the worst of the conflagration.

"I can't imagine what kind of a warped mind would do a thing like this," Heather said, gazing at the ruined building with disbelief.

"Faye Kane, the angel of death, started this, with a little help from her friend Randy," I said.

"I suppose a woman who doesn't like dogs is probably capable of any malfeasance," Heather said. "But I'm so glad no animals were involved in this. I can stand anything but pets in mortal danger—especially from fire."

"What about our heroine here? I suppose you *can* stand to see someone turn her into a toasted marshmallow?" Phillipa asked.

"You just don't understand." Heather took the Hermes scarf from around her neck and wiped my forehead with it.. "Dogs and cats are so dependent and trusting. But of course I care about Cass. And I don't think this sooty air is doing her any good, do you? I mean, if her lungs were at all affected . . ."

"But it's going to take hours to get everyone over to the hospital," Phillipa explained. "There aren't enough ambulances, so they're concentrating on transporting the most serious cases."

Fiona returned from her mission to brief the chiefs. "Why don't we drape Cass in the back seat of one of the cruisers," she suggested. "Phil can get one of the uniforms to drive."

"Are you kidding me?" Phillipa said. "Just because I'm married to Stone doesn't mean . . ."

Heather punched in a number on her cell phone and wandered away, speaking quietly and earnestly into the receiver. "It'll be okay," she said when she returned. "Dick is coming with the Wee Angels Rescue Wagon. All we have to do is to get Cass out onto the main road. Oh good, there's Rose. We'd better tell her to let Joe know where we're taking his bride-to-be."

So it was that I got a wild ride through the mass of vehicles jammed in the Manor's front driveway, with Heather and Phillipa pushing the gurney and Deidre draped across my body to keep me in place.

The Wee Angels Rescue Wagon turned out to be quite comfortable. A bit small for a full-size human being, but with plenty of doggie blankets to keep me warm.

Dick careened the van with the cute winged canines painted on it into Jordan's emergency entrance with the cluster of other arriving ambulances. Emergency teams rushing out looked at us dubiously. "Not a dog, not a dog!" Heather called out. "We have a poison victim here. Is your chief of medicine on duty?"

Chapter Twenty-one

After the mix-up about my insurance card—back with my wallet in the jacket Rose had stashed somewhere in the burning Manor—it seemed as if I spent hours in the bustling environs of Jordan Hospital, lying on a gurney in the corridor, judged by the emergency team and the chief of medicine to be out of danger but not well enough to release just yet. Satisfied that I was in good hands, Heather, Dick, and Phillipa had gone home. It had been past two in the morning when they left; we were all exhausted.

I was feeling terribly depressed and didn't know if it was more of a chemical reaction or a psychological one. The screams of the Manor's clients were still in my head, terrified people who were pinned in their rooms, unable to move out of the fire's path. The fire was under control now, but my feelings were still red hot.

Snippets of information came my way as medical personnel and family members hurried by. Two female clients from A Hall had suffered serious burns, a male patient had died of a heart attack, and the security guard, George, had succumbed to respiratory failure despite Rose's efforts to save him.

Joe was beside me—I could feel his hand squeezing mine; what a marvelous sensation that was! And I could wiggle my toes, lift my head, talk as much as I wanted. And I wanted to talk, to ask questions, to find out everything!

"I got some information from Finney and Fogg," Joe replied in response to my eager questions. "Most of the Manor's furnishings and wall coverings were flame-retardant. But those damned curtains in the snack alcove went up like a torch and caught onto the piece of fancy wood molding that runs along the ceiling throughout the first floor. An architectural feature from the Manor's past that DeBoer had decided to retain. Worse, it had been refinished with some kind of flammable varnish. I don't know why the inspectors never cracked down on that detail. Fire kept creeping from room to room on that damned molding, then sparks would fall on someone's bedclothes. What a horror show!"

"It could have been even worse," I said. "What Kane and Wallace really wanted to do was to gut the whole floor and us with it."

"Yeah. Fogg wants to talk to you, and Phil says Stone will be along, too. Right now he's at the scene, getting up to speed."

Not five minutes later the tall, scholarly detective himself arrived. As he leaned over me, his eyes behind oval, metal-rimmed glasses showed deep concern and considerable fatigue, rather the way I think doctors should look, although they rarely do. When he took my hand, I half expected him to feel for the pulse. Even in my weakened state, that touch brought visions to my mind's eye, some of the most pleasant a seer can hope to encounter. (Not counting, of course, the electrifying visions I've often experienced when Joe and I held hands, right from that first night.) These images were full of Stone's kindness, his love for Phillipa, and his determination to hunt down this mad couple who had threatened her friends.

"Oh, Stone, I'm so glad to see you," was my feeble response to the warmth and resolve I perceived in him.

"And I you," he said. "From all I learned at the Manor, you've had a very narrow escape. Are you up to telling me what you know about Kane and Wallace, and especially where they may go next?"

I told Stone everything I had observed in the terrifying hours just past. In his reassuring way, he gave me his complete attention, absorbing every detail. Finally I let my head fall back on the gurney. "You've got to apprehend those two before they get away—or do something worse," I concluded.

After Stone left I had uttered just about one deep sigh of relief when the most sickening idea hit me. How vengeful might that deadly pair feel? My third eye was giving me some weird pictures, flashing them too fast to register. And I was getting one hell of a headache.

"Joe! Help me up. I've got to get home right away."

You really don't need permission to leave a hospital. Just gumption and a willing confederate. By now Joe had enough faith in my prescience to put aside his misgivings and help me to my feet. My feet! They were there after all, mine to command once more! Still, I was glad to lean on Joe's strong shoulder while I dragged myself along the hall to the front door. No one threatened to stop us. Everyone was much too busy to bother with one escapee.

Joe insisted that I stay in the entryway where there were chairs provided while he picked up his rental in the crowded parking lot and drove it to the front door. It seemed to take forever. I kept glancing over my shoulder, expecting someone to wrestle me back onto a gurney. But there Joe was at last, jumping out of the Chevy to run around and help me into the passenger seat.

He arranged his jacket over my shoulders, fastened my seat belt, and kissed me. That was sweet, but I wanted to get going. "Honey, I'm worried about Scruffy," I said.

We drove home at invalid speed, not at all the way I would have driven myself. From the outside, my dear little house looked just as it should—except there was no dog in the window sitting bolt upright waiting for my return.

"Something's wrong," I said.

"What?"

"Where's Scruffy? He always knows when I'm coming home and waits for me on the window seat."

"You stay here. I'll go investigate."

"I want to go, too." I struggled into an alert posture and opened my door.

"*Jesu Christos!* You can hardly walk. You stay here." And Joe was out of the car without waiting for any further argument, moving swiftly through the shadows of trees toward the seaside porch, our usual entrance.

A bolt of sandy fur came charging out of the lilac bushes beside the garage, barking furiously. Scruffy jumped up to put both paws on my knee. *Help! Help! Something's wrong! A stranger opened the door. I ran out to frighten him away. But he got inside and I can't get at him. Hurry! Hurry!*

Hearing the commotion, Joe came running back to the car.

"Scruffy says there's someone in the house," I told him.

"Oh sure. And I suppose the dog can describe him? Assuming it's a him," Joe said. "Do you happen to have your cell?"

"Nope. It's back in the Manor. I gave Rose my jacket before I went to find Fiona and Maeve."

Scruffy decided the better part of valor was to jump into my lap. The big shaggy fellow ended up draped across me like a bear rug. He swiveled his head around to look at me. Dogs don't blush, or he would have been red-faced. *Don't think I'm scared. I'm worried about you, Toots.* I leaned toward him, and he licked my face all over. *You sick? You smell funny.*

"I was sick, but I'm better now."

"Are you talking to Scruffy again?" Joe demanded. "*Jesu Christos!* We have an emergency here, honey. We need to phone the cops."

"Nothing's open at this time of the morning," I said.

"There's always the phone in the house."

"Haven't you been paying attention? We have intruders in the house."

"I'm going to have a look around, check things out."

"Please, Joe. Don't."

"Hang on to Scruffy. I don't think I can make a stealthy approach with the dog barking like crazy."

I grabbed Joe's sleeve, anything to delay him. "How did whoever it is get here? There's no car."

"Could be parked anywhere up on the main road. It's not very well lit. We might have driven right past and not noticed a car on one of those dark shoulders. Okay. I'm going." He picked up the heavy flashlight he keeps in the car, holding it like a club. "And I'll be careful."

Scruffy woofed. "You have to be quiet now," I told him. "Like when you stalk a squirrel."

My naturally superior hunting skills are shot. Toots. Woof . . . woof. Scruffy's ears were pricked with worry, and he couldn't seem to stop barking from time to time, which was a rather dead giveaway that we were out here, casing the situation.

I closed the door so that Scruffy couldn't get out, pushing him off my lap onto the floor, and I slid over to the driver's seat. "Get your butt in back," I ordered him in my deepest alpha voice. Startled, he immediately jumped into the back seat and lay down, nose between paws. If the intruder looked out the window, he might think I had driven home alone and not realize that Joe was slinking around to the back porch. It was ominously quiet in the bleak predawn hour. Even the November winds seemed to be exhausted; not a dry leaf moved. I couldn't stand not knowing what was going on.

To distract myself from following after Joe, I visualized the intruder or intruders being bound up hand and foot by a rope of light. I saw it winding around and around them like a spider's silk until they were unable to move. For this to work, I should have been in a semi-trance, alpha brain waves serene and aware, which is fairly impossible to do in an emergency. Still I tried—the instant version, fingers crossed.

I heard a woman's scream in the house! Joe's shout. Something crashing. I was about to leap out of the car when the passenger-side door was wrenched open. It was Wallace! He jumped in and slammed the door shut.

He had a hypodermic needle in his hand. Pointing it right at my arm, he held it like a weapon, which I knew all too well it was. "Start the car, but keep it in Park," he ordered.

The next thing that happened was a confused scuffle of attacking dog and screaming man. Without even a warning snarl, Scruffy simply jumped halfway over the seat back and grabbed Wallace's arm in his teeth. The needle dropped on the seat between us. "Get him off! Get him off!" Wallace yelled.

I picked up the needle gingerly, opened my door, and jumped out. "Hold him!" I said to Scruffy. "Good boy. I'm going to find Joe and call the police."

"He's biting my arm off," Wallace moaned, flailing at the dog with his other hand. He managed to open the passenger door and fell to the ground, with Scruffy on top of him. Letting go of the man's arm, Scruffy landed both paws on Wallace's shoulders and began barking and growling.

"Hold the man, Scruffy. Don't let him go."

Don't worry, Toots. This wimp's not going anywhere. The dog's teeth clicked menacingly as he made little snappy passes at the enemy's throat.

"If I were you, I wouldn't move a muscle, Randy," I said. I think I may even have laughed. Although my balance was upset and my gait unsteady, I crept toward the back porch where I'd last seen Joe. The kitchen door was standing open. I'd left only two lights turned on, low, one in the kitchen and one in my office. They were sufficient to see that Joe was lying on the floor, knocked out cold. The figure standing over him was Faye Kane. She'd just dropped my cast-iron frying pan and was reaching into the nurse's bag that hung over her shoulder. Looking up, her face registered shocked recognition.

I didn't hesitate for a moment. The needle was in my hand, and I stuck it straight into her upper arm with all my strength, pushing the plunger halfway. I remember thinking, *Don't go all the way. Don't kill her.* That was definitely my higher self speaking, because I really wanted to obliterate her from the face of the earth.

With a half cry, "You . . ." she toppled to the floor like a felled tree. What on earth were those two doing here!

I fell to my knees to check on Joe. *Please, to the mother of all living things, may he not be badly hurt.* He was breathing, and I heard him groan—two good signs. I laid my hands around his dear head, then flat on his chest, sending him all the healing energy in my heart, feeling its warmth race through my fingers into his body. After a few moments, I thought his breathing had become more normal.

Then I dialed nine-one-one on the wall phone. I might have been a tad incoherent as I tried to explain about my unconscious friend, the break-in, the assassin in my car, Scruffy, and some unknown drug I'd just used on Kane, which I hoped was a barbiturate but might be Pavulon. Only I didn't exactly say that it was I who had administered the drug. "Don't hang up," the woman's voice said. "All available cruisers are otherwise deployed at the moment. I'll see if I can divert one of them to your location. Are you in any immediate danger?"

I had another look at Kane. She was lying with her leg twisted under her in what looked like a painful position; she appeared to be unconscious but breathing. Maybe the drug *had* been a barbiturate. "Yes, yes I am," I said, answering the emergency operator, "And I know about the Manomet fire, but that's nearly under control now. On the other hand, my situation is precarious, to say the least. There's a lunatic outside who wants to kill me and my friend. I don't know how long my dog will be able to keep him at bay. He might get free at any moment. So, please, do what you can to get cops here in a hurry!"

I let go of the phone, allowing it to dangle by its cord. I straightened Kane's leg, felt for the pulse in her neck. Slow but pumping. A good thing, probably. After all, killing someone might really screw up my karma. Her shoulder bag was half spilled out on the floor. A familiar item caught my gaze, and I picked it up—my notebook, the one in which I'd made a little list of Kane's victims. It probably hadn't been an outstanding idea to carry that with me. A quick rummage through the rest of Kane's stuff uncovered my wallet. I stuffed the wallet and notebook into the pocket of Joe's jacket, which he'd insisted I wear.

First chance I get, I thought, *I'd better figure out what mischief Kane had in mind when she came here tonight. Eliminate the busybody, I don't doubt.*

I checked Joe again—his color seemed better—then ran outside to see if Scruffy was still keeping Wallace on hold.

He was, barely. Wallace had got one hand on a rock and, uttering a stream of curses, was trying to bang at Scruffy's head. Scruffy still had both paws on Wallace's shoulders, but the dog appeared slightly dazed, as if he'd been hit at least once. How thankful I was that he hadn't gone for Wallace's throat but had kept to the hold command! Crouching down, I grabbed the man's arm, and gave him the rest of the needle he'd used to threaten me. In an instant he was as quiet as a corpse. Scruffy rolled off and lay beside him, panting and snuffling. Taking the dog's head into my lap, I murmured, "Good boy, good boy."

The siren wailing in the distance came nearer and louder until it seemed only a few moments before two uniformed officers, a man and a woman, were jumping out of the cruiser. They assumed a straight-armed defensive posture with guns drawn. The weapons were aimed at me. The female cop's head came up to her partner's shoulder. With her mousy ponytail and fresh-scrubbed face, she looked like a kid. The guy, too, looked far too young for the job—but these days, everyone did. Not wanting to make these two nervous, I sent out the calmest vibes I could muster.

"Stand up and put your hands in the air," the woman demanded.

"You've got it wrong." Gently I laid Scruffy's head back on the lawn and got to my feet, hands raised as directed. "This is my house, and the man lying on the ground is an intruder who broke in."

"Yeah? So what happened here?" Lowering his weapon, the male officer began checking Wallace for vital signs. "This one's alive, but he isn't moving," he told his companion, whose gun was still pointed my way.

"His name is Randolph Wallace. He's a doctor, sort of, and he's wanted for the Manomet Manor fire. He threatened me with a hypodermic needle, but he got stuck with it himself. Might be a barbiturate of some kind. Works fast, whatever it is. We'll need an ambulance for my friend, the man inside the house, who's suffered a blow on the head. I'd like to call the vet, too. My dog may need attention."

"Watch her, Barb." Leaving his partner to cope with us, the male officer drew his gun again and moved cautiously toward the house.

My arms were tired and wobbly. "Stay as you are," Barb warned.

We waited a moment until her partner reappeared. "Jesus, they're both zombies in there. What is this? You're the only one left standing, and you tell us you're the victim?"

"Please, can I put my hands down? I'm unarmed, and I'm just out of the hospital myself. I was inside the Manor when it caught fire."

"Okay, Ken?" Barb said, relenting. I eased my arms down slowly so as not to alarm these two edgy cops.

Barbie and Ken! I wondered if the cruiser's trunk was full of alternate outfits—ballet tights, evening clothes. Maybe I was getting a little hysterical. "The woman is Faye Kane, also wanted for the fire. She's been dosed with half the stuff in the needle. The man is my companion who lives with me. Apparently Kane knocked him out with a frying pan. And he needs *immediate* medical attention. He could have a concussion. So could you please make those calls *now*."

The two cops finally holstered their weapons. Ken kept a careful watch on me while Barb began talking into her cell phone.

"Oh, and the two intruders will need a doctor, too," I added. "When you get around to it."

Another car was approaching at top speed. A Mercedes! With a splat of gravel, Heather's "dog car" came to a crashing stop behind the cruiser. Barb stopped talking on her cell, and both officers put their hands back on their weapons. Heather jumped out. She was wearing blue silk pajamas and a Burberry trench coat. Her usually neat bronze braid looked disheveled. "I knew it!" she screamed. "My head had just hit the pillow when I had this most awful dream about you and Kane and Wallace. They're here, aren't they?"

"Barb . . . Ken . . . This is Heather Morgan." I introduced her by her maiden name because everyone in Plymouth knew the family—and the Morgans carried some clout. Turning back to Heather, I exclaimed, "Am I ever glad to see you! Joe's in the house, unconscious. He needs medical attention. There may be a concussion. Scruffy got banged on the head, too, but he seems to be recovering. I'll want Dick to have a look at him anyway. It wasn't that long ago that Scruffy got conked by Abdul, remember? Where is Dick? Did he let you run out of the house alone like this?"

"Stone called and asked Dick to transport Lucrezia and Caesare someplace. Big emergency. Dick wouldn't even tell me where he was going. Don't you just hate it when men get all officious and protective? Sweet Isis, what a night this has been!" Heather pushed escaping tendrils of hair out of her eyes and looked around, for the first time taking in the whole scene. "Poor little pup!" she said, spotting Scruffy. Then, "Is that Wallace over there? What happened to him?"

"It's a long story. Your dream was clairvoyant, dear—dead on target. I'm going in to Joe now. Would you keep an eye on Scruffy for me?"

"Where's Kane?"

"She's knocked out, too. In the house."

"What in Hades did you do, Cass? That must have been some fancy spellwork."

I looked nervously at the two policemen. I hadn't yet confessed to being the agent of the knockout needle. Barb was on the phone again. Ken was closing in to accompany me into the house.

"Hold it a minute," Barb ordered. She glanced up from her call. "It's no use. There isn't a free ambulance anywhere on the South Shore right now. Best thing would be if we transport this lot in the cruiser. Maybe have to make a couple of trips."

"I can take Joe and Scruffy in the Mercedes, no problem." Heather rushed to open the backseat of her commodious sedan. "I'm leaving the bad guys to you, officers. This should be quite a collar, by the way. Faye Kane and Randolph Wallace set the Manomet Manor fire, and they're wanted for questioning in several murders besides."

Barb's cheeks seemed to get a little pinker, and Ken straightened up manfully.

It took our combined strength of four, of which I had the least, to dump Kane and Wallace in the cruiser. They were as limp as Raggedy Ann and Andy. Barb cuffed them anyway.

Meanwhile, Ken and Heather eased Joe into the backseat of the Mercedes, and I held Scruffy half in my lap in the passenger seat. The cruiser's siren cleared our way to the hospital; it was no more than a ten-minute trip.

"Barbie and Ken?" Heather's tone was incredulous.

"They probably take a lot of kidding at HQ, poor babies. It made me really anxious to see them waving those guns around."

"Do you suppose they live in a little dollhouse somewhere?"

"That was my very thought."

Now we were both laughing, hysterical with relief and exhaustion.

"*Jesu Christos*, my head aches! Will you two cut out that racket?" Joe was coming to life! I turned around in my seat, as much as

I could with an exhausted dog in my lap, and grabbed my lover's hand, the nearest part I could reach. "Oh, darling. You're going to be all right."

"I remember now. I'd just got into the kitchen when some huge guy hit me over the head with a club." Joe was rubbing the top of his head, a crease of pain between his eyes.

"The guy was Faye Kane. She hit you with my frying pan. Cast iron makes quite a weapon. But she's out of it now. I gave her a shot of her own stuff. Wallace, too."

Joe fell back on the seat. Probably too much to absorb in his weakened state.

"Good for you," Heather said. "Didn't kill them, did you?"

"No, thank Goddess. But to tell you the truth, I didn't know *what* was in that needle, and I didn't care. Wallace used that needle to threaten me, so he deserved whatever—"

"Justice was served, as they say. Get the cell out of my bag and press one," Heather said. "Maybe Dick's back." He was, and he offered to meet us at the hospital with the Wee Angels Rescue Wagon so he could check out Scruffy.

Scruffy moaned. *I was very brave, wasn't I?*

"I don't know what I would have done without you." I hugged him, but not too much. Dogs like their space. But scratches between the ears or on the chest are always acceptable. Especially when they come with murmurs of loving praise.

When we arrived at the hospital, we found the place was still a zoo of refugees from the fire, some ambulatory with walkers or canes, others on gurneys. It took some time to get a doctor to glance at Joe and talk with him for a minute.

Dr. Blitz was a small, neat man with a dark mustache and a brisk manner. "Bad bump, but he's alert and sensible," he said. "You can take him home now, okay? No room here anyway. Bufferin for the pain, okay? If he sleeps, wake him up once in a while, just to be sure he's not unconscious. Any problems, bring him back for a scan, okay? Right now it would be impossible.

We've not only got all of Manomet Manor here, we've even got the police taking up two rooms."

Barbie and Ken must have brought in their prisoners while we were waiting to be seen. What a coup for them! "Oh, yes? What happened?" I asked. Miss Innocence.

"I hear they've arrested the arsonists, a couple of bad guys who somehow got themselves drugged. Don't know with what, just that they're being revived now. But you didn't hear it from me, okay? Four or five cops up there guarding them. I'll tell you, this has been a night to remember."

"One for the books, all right," I agreed.

"Or the tabloids," Heather said. "I guess no one's caught on yet to how those two got aced."

"'To keep silent.'" I warned, quoting from the familiar formula for spellcraft. "Hey, what about Fiona and Maeve?"

"Good question!" Heather turned to Dr. Blitz. "Two of our friends were in the Manomet fire. They got out okay, we saw them outside, but we need to locate them now. They weren't recuperating from anything—they were at the Manor for physical therapy. Who's keeping track of the admittances here?"

"Try the front desk, the girl you talked to when you brought in your friend. He's doing fine, but keep an eye on him, okay?"

As Dr. Blitz hurried off to his next emergency, we found a vacant chair for Joe while we checked with the weary young woman at the computer. In response to our questions, she pounded a few keys. I expected to see her head fall upon the keyboard at any moment, and I knew exactly how she felt. My knees were buckling with fatigue.

After weakly hitting a few keys, she said, "All I can tell you is that they were not admitted for emergency treatment." She sagged back in her chair while I was still saying thanks.

Immediately Heather punched in Fiona's number on her cell. "Good, you're home, then," she said when Fiona had answered. "How'd you get there? Figures. No, no, I don't mean anything by that. Yes, I'll see that Omar gets back to you as soon as possible. Where's Mae? Okay. You two get some rest, then. Talk to you later!" She smiled knowingly. "Mick Finney personally escorted them back to Fiona's place. Don't ask me how Maeve is going to negotiate through that crowded cottage in her wheelchair. But they're safe out of Manomet Manor, and that's what counts. Oh, here's Dick! Hello, darling."

Heather's big hearty husband had arrived just in time to help Joe out to the Mercedes. We'd had to leave Scruffy in the car, stretched out on the front seat, with a blanket tucked around him. Our favorite vet, looking as if someone had taken the air out of him—it was now four in the morning—said almost the same thing about Scruffy as Dr. Blitz had said about Joe. "Don't worry about this fella." Dick lifted the dog's eyelids one after the other. "He's a tough old survivor."

Who's he calling old? Scruffy sniffed scornfully. *He should have seen me topple that bad guy.* Pushing the dog over a bit so that I could get into the front seat, I held him half in my lap while Heather and Dick smooched good-bye, and Dick took off in his van. I noticed that Scruffy *was* getting a little white under his muzzle. Yet he was only five. A lot of good years left. Tears ran down my cheeks. I turned my head and brushed them away.

"Come on, I'm taking you and your guys home," Heather said. "You're dead on your feet. And you're getting weepy."

You can't hide tears from a friend.

Chapter Twenty-two

Once tucked into our bed, Joe fell into a sleep so restless that I didn't have to worry about his being concussed at all. Nevertheless, I shook him from time to time to make certain he wasn't in some kind of violent coma. Scruffy flopped on the floor at the foot of the bed with a hefty sigh, but once he went to sleep, his back feet began running as if he were on some kind of perpetual chase.

With my internal clock set to wake me every hour to check on Joe, I'd fall into merciful darkness, then a few minutes later start awake as if I'd had a caffeine overload. On one of these alerts, I realized that something else was bothering me. What had Faye Kane come here for? Obviously, she'd found my jacket, as attested to by the notebook and wallet. That damned victims' list! And my address, of course. I tried to meditate, to see the situation clairvoyantly, but my head was aching too much. All I kept seeing was that nurse's shoulder bag spilling out its contents onto the floor. What else might she have been up to that hadn't registered on my consciousness?

Maybe a glass of wine would help me relax. There was an open bottle of Chardonnay in the refrigerator. I took a glass off the shelf and opened the door. At that moment, I simply froze as piece after piece of a puzzle flashed across my mind's eye, that third eye in a clairvoyant's forehead.

I glanced at the clock, then called Fiona.

"I feel as if I just got to sleep. Oh my goodness, it's only five-thirty," she mumbled. "You must be in trouble again."

"I need you to dowse the house, Fiona," I said. "Faye Kane got in here while I was at the hospital. She poisoned something for sure. I can see that much, but I don't know what to be suspicious of. Should I just throw everything out? I must have fifteen or more tea blends alone. Oh, I'm so tired. I was just going to take a little wine, when it hit me—"

"Don't drink anything!" Fiona sounded completely awake now. "I'll be there in fifteen minutes. Mae's on the sofa, dead to the world—I don't think she'll miss me for a while. We called Brian first thing, and he's flying home as soon as possible."

I didn't know what to do with myself as I waited. Was it even safe to make coffee? Then I thought, *Open a fresh can and use unopened bottled water*, so that's what I did. I was never going to get the chance to sleep again anyway, and the strong brew boosted my flagging strength.

A few minutes later, I heard Fiona's Town Car crunching into the driveway. I was at the kitchen door to greet her as she hobbled up the porch stairs, clumping her owl-headed cane on every step, her crystal pendulum swinging from a chain around her neck. She seemed spryer than she'd been in many weeks. Escape from danger is its own kind of therapy. And then, of course, there was Mick, her new admirer.

"You can do this for yourself, you know," she said as she dowsed over my sugar bowl. "I always do this in restaurants, to make sure the food I've ordered will be good for my body."

"Doesn't the waiter look at you funny?"

"Better that than a case of salmonella, dearie. Besides, with a bit of glamour, the server won't even notice what you're about." Satisfied with the sugar, Fiona helped herself to a cup of coffee and sweetened it fearlessly with a heaping teaspoon of the white stuff. Continuing through my kitchen, her crystal swung in slow sedate arcs around boxes of cereal, canisters of coffee, tea, flour, and more sugar. "Let's have a look at that refrigerator."

While I took out everything, even jars of pickles and salad dressing, I related to Fiona all that had occurred after I was released from the hospital. Fiona smiled, nodded, and dowsed calmly on, humming to herself. I thought I recognized a few bars of "That Old Black Magic." The silver bangles on her arm tinkled quietly as she moved from suspect to suspect: ham, cheese, lettuce, tomatoes, eggs. Pretty difficult, I guessed, to poison an egg. The crystal doddered on.

Until it got to the opened half-gallon of orange juice, that is. As Fiona lifted the crystal pendulum over the bottle, it began to zigzag violently back and forth. It looped at crazy angles and bounced back against Fiona's breast. I almost imagined I heard it screaming faintly, but I realized that wasn't possible.

"Well, well, what have we here," Fiona said, lifting the carton with two fingers. "I'll just dump this into the sink, dearie."

"No, stop!" I moved to protect the juice. "I think I'd like to get that analyzed."

"What for? We both know it's poisoned, and who did the poisoning."

"But it's evidence!" I objected.

"Very bad karma, that's what it is. Stone and the others will have all the evidence they need very soon. I've been *calling* that expert on Pavulon back to America. It's been my little project, and I do think it's working. A few hairs from a shedding wolf, a pinch of the victim's grave dust. . . . One of Hazel's Household Recipes, you know. So don't you worry, dearie. Bodies will be exhumed, and that forensic person will find everything he needs in their tissues. So must it be."

I wondered where she got the wolf's hair but refrained from quibbling. Fiona in full glamour cannot be gainsaid. She pushed me aside with her cane, clumped to the sink, and dumped the orange juice directly into the drain. Good Goddess, was it burping and bubbling like Drano? Fiona turned the hot water on full throttle, and the poison ate its way to oblivion. She even rinsed out the carton, so there was no point in keeping that in case it still held traces of the poison. Now I would never know what it was. Oh well, perhaps ignorance would spare me from developing psychosomatic symptoms.

"Burn incense," Fiona commanded as she rapidly dowsed the remaining contents of my refrigerator. "I suggest cinnamon and myrrh. And while you're at it, sweep the kitchen with a straw broom—not one of those wimpy nylon things—and whisk the negativity right over the threshold to be neutralized by Mother Earth."

"Absolutely. Thanks, Fiona," I said belatedly. After all, she had driven her arthritic body over here after about an hour's sleep and dowsed every foodstuff in sight. But would I ever trust my own refrigerator? And what about that wine?

"Don't you fret, dearie. The wine's fine. Knowing you, I checked that one out first." Fiona zeroed in on my worries with her usual accuracy. Catching the pink light of dawn coming in through the kitchen windows, wisps of hair formed a halo around her carroty-gray corona of braids. Waving her owl-headed cane, she looked a perfect fairy godmother complete with wand. "Trust your instincts. That's why you've got 'em."

Faye Kane's bad vibes were thoroughly defused by the time I'd swept and swept and incensed the room, scrubbed the counters and table with sea salt. Also I tossed out the milk, in case. Then I fell on the bed beside Joe, who was still thrashing from side to side restlessly, and I knew no more of the world for several blissful hours.

The phone woke me at twelve-thirty. It was Serena Dove. "We have a situation here, and Rose seems to think you and your friends can be of assistance." Her tone was cool, but nevertheless I could detect the undercurrent of anxiety.

"Oh Good Goddess—Hari's gone?"

"An apt guess. Yes. I don't know how this could have happened. We're always so careful at St. Rita's."

"His father?"

"Must be. Rose was at Manomet Manor until dawn, helping with the rescue. What an awful thing! All those handicapped people. And I understand it was not an accident." As Serena continued to talk, I cradled the phone against my ear and pattered around making coffee. "When she came home, Hari was not in his bed. His pajamas were on the floor. Evidently he'd dressed in jeans and a jacket, and packed a few other clothing items in his backpack."

"Could Hari have got access to a phone? He may have called his father, you know. That's what happened when he and his mother stayed the night at my house before they went to you."

"It's possible. There's a wall phone in the kitchen, which is not locked up at night like the offices. I noticed a chair pulled over near it. Although I would venture to say that no one could get into St. Rita's at night without tripping an alarm, there are ways that a boy could have slipped out. The old coal chute in the cellar perhaps. Or out on the porch roof and down the maple tree."

"Rose must be wild. Her worst fear realized. . . ."

"Yes, she was even too upset to make this call. I've given her a calming draught, but it's hardly taken the edge off."

"But how could he have gotten over the wall?"

"A rope fire ladder from the third floor is missing. Will you come?"

"Of course, but it's my friend Fiona that we really need. She may be able to tell us where Abdul has taken Hari. Have you contacted the police?"

"Yes, but they're still greatly occupied with the Manor. They did send a cruiser, two officers, a man and a woman."

Barbie and Ken, I thought. "The trouble is, I have a sick guy here, Serena. As soon as I get someone to stay with him, I'll come over to help. Tell Rose I will be there, that we will bring Hari home."

"I pray that you're right," Serena said.

* * *

Phillipa was closest, just on the other side of Jenkins Park, She agreed to come at once. "Serena has reported this to the police?" was all she asked, and I assured her that Barbie and Ken were on it.

"Oh, you've met them," she said with a chuckle.

"Cute couple. They nearly arrested me."

"So . . . Kane and Wallace are in the hospital, and Stone tells me you may have put them there. We have some catching up to do."

When she hurried into my kitchen ten minutes later, she was carrying the usual basket of homemade goodies. *Oh joy—safe food,* I thought. Peeking inside the linen towel, I realized suddenly how hungry I was. Foccaccia! After I poured us both a mug of coffee, I broke off a large piece of the savory bread for instant energy.

"Forgive me. I'm ravenous," I mumbled through a delicious mouthful. "Mmmm. Olives and feta. Makes an excellent breakfast for us Greeks."

"Shipton? Greek?" she scoffed. "Just because you're engaged—"

I deflected the lecture on feminist individuality. "As soon as I have a spare moment, I'll definitely tell you the whole story. But for now, Wallace and Kane were here and up to no good when Joe brought me home from the hospital. Somehow Kane managed to knock Joe unconscious with my frying pan. I had to give Kane and Wallace a shot of their own medicine to subdue them. Oh, and I did a binding spell, too. Who knows? Anyway, Barbie and Ken toted the villains off to the hospital. I got a few hours' refreshing sleep, although a week would have been better. Joe's still sleeping, rather fitfully, and I don't dare leave him alone. I'll need you to wake him every hour or so, make sure he's not in a coma. And when he gets up, he'll need a little nourishment. Like me. And Scruffy's knocked out, too. He could use some scrambled eggs and wheat toast."

"Not to worry. If there's one thing I'm good at, it's feeding people. Animals, too. You go see what you can do for Rose. That bastard Abdul, a pox on him."

"Now, now. Thoughts are things," I remonstrated.

"I'm counting on it," Phillipa said. "You're calling Fiona, of course?"

"Of course."

Scruffy appeared in the doorway, leaning against the frame, and sighed deeply. *I gotta go pee now. Did someone say scrambled eggs?*

"Here's my noble and brave guardian," I said, leaning down to scratch Scruffy's sensitive chest. "And you deserve a treat. But I have to go out now, so Phil is going to feed you." Which reminded me to ask Phillipa, "Do you know where the D.A. has stashed Lucrezia and Caesare?"

"Stone won't tell me. Even though I assured him I wouldn't breathe a word."

"Imagine that! So little faith . . ."

As soon as I got into the Jeep, I punched in Fiona's number and talked to her as I drove, something I often glare at other drivers for doing.

"Oh, the poor little thing," Fiona said. "I know what it's like to lose a beloved child. She must be beside herself."

"How's Mae?"

"Brian's here. He's carrying her into their car as we speak. That man is a saint—I haven't heard him say one 'I told you so.' Mae's pretending to be just fine, but there are some mighty dark circles under her eyes. So I'm quite free to meet you at St Rita's."

"You must be exhausted, too. I thought you might rather dowse for Abdul and Hari at home."

"I could do that, but I feel it would be more comforting to Rose to watch me in action, so to speak. I don't know about Serena Dove, though."

"She'll be fine."

*   *   *

Lying on the living room sofa with a folded washcloth on her brow, hands crossed over her breast, Rose appeared to be in a pale swoon, like Juliet in the tomb. Several of the young women hovering about her were quickly dispatched elsewhere by Serena Dove. The ex-nun's wiry gray hair was looking a little wilder than usual, and her normally sweet smile had been replaced by an acerbic frown.

"Oh, Cass! At last!" Instantly Rose came to life, sat up, and let the cold cloth fall into her hands, where she began to knead it anxiously. "Rasheed's got Hari! What if he manages to get out of the country! You know he'll go straight to Saudi Arabia, and I'll never see my boy again!"

I took her in my arms and held her for a moment. She was as frail as my own daughter Cathy, but I felt such strength in her. "Fiona's on her way. Fiona's what we call 'a finder.' An uncanny ability to locate people and things."

Rose sat up a little straighter as I let her go. "I remember the day of Hari's custody hearing, that extraordinary humming spell." Her voice was even more raspy than usual, definitely affected by stress.

"How exactly does Mrs. Ritchie do her finding?" asked Serena. She gracefully motioned toward a sideboard setup of coffee in a thermal pitcher and some sandwiches. "Please, have something to keep up your strength." I smiled my gratitude, ashamed to be so hungry in the midst of Rose's agony, and needing even more a continual boost of caffeine. Being sleep-deprived had given me a numb, spacey feeling, as if I were a zombie or one of the Stepford wives.

I shook my head, trying to clear my brain of sci-fi images. "Fiona dowses with a pendulum. Over a map." That sounded rather lame even to my ears.

"This I have to see," Serena said.

And see it she did, when Fiona hobbled in a half hour later looking like a swirl of autumn leaves in her coat-sweater of many colors and gypsy patchwork skirt. Her green reticule hung by its long strap over her shoulder, several folded maps sticking out of the top. Drawing Rose into her plump arms, she said, "Chin up, my little dearie. We will find your boy, I promise you that."

After greeting Serena with a cryptic remark about St. Francis de Sales, patron saint of writers, Fiona accepted a cup of coffee from the sideboard. *Was Serena a writer? How did Fiona know?* Two pencils were sticking up out of my friend's crown of braids—the sign of a moderately pixilated mood but not the complete madness of a three-pencil day, Her silver bracelets jingled as she waved her cane imperiously over the coffee table. "This will do fine. Perhaps someone will be good enough to clear off the toys and magazines?"

Apparently fallen under Fiona's spell, Serena hastened to comply. Fiona drew a small rocker up to the cleared table, unfolded a map of the South Shore, and smoothed it out, peering through her gold-rimmed half-tracks at the familiar terrain. After removing a crystal pendant from around her neck, she breathed a mist on it, the better to polish the glittering stone with the hem of her sweater. I'd seen Fiona dowse many times in the past few years, but this was the first I'd ever noticed that she murmured a few words over the crystal. A potent new rhyme? One of Hazel's old spells? I would have to grill her about this later.

Rose leaned forward from her seat on the couch, elbows on knees, her chin resting on her hands, an expression somewhere between hope and fear on her face. Serena sat upright in a straight chair near the sideboard, hands folded in her lap as if holding a rosary, a little removed from the strange scene unfolding in St. Rita's living room, but her bright, quick eyes missing no detail.

The crystal swung erratically over the map, settling on no special location. After a few minutes of this, Fiona folded up the South Shore with a deep sigh and took out a map of Boston and Environs. This she smoothed out as she had the first, then held up the pendant above the city. Again the crystal would not fix on one place. It zigged and zagged and behaved in an annoyingly inconsistent manner.

"What does that mean?" Rose cried out, only her cry was more like a croak.

"You must be calm, dear." Serena moved to sit beside Rose, stroked her hand, then held it in a firm grip. "This reminds me of *sortes biblicae*. The supplicant opens the Good Book at random and lays a finger on the text, there to receive the Divine Answer. Of course, it's quite different from dowsing in substance. Yet in spirit . . ."

"And then there's the Ouija board, but I can't say I'm a big fan of that. What else have you?" I couldn't help leafing through the maps in Fiona's reticule, which now rested beside the rocker.

"Massachusetts. As a general rule, though, the smaller the scale, the less accurate the reading." The new map was laid down, and Fiona began again. This time the crystal seemed to take on a sedate new persona, moving back and forth gracefully in smaller and smaller arcs until it came nearly to rest at Beverly, just above Salem.

"What's in Beverly?" Serena wondered.

"I have no idea," I said. "Would you be willing to try the *sortes biblicae*?"

"Oh, good idea!" Fiona clapped her hands amid a tinkle of silver bangles. "I've never seen that one."

"Not in *Hazel's Book of Household Recipes*, then?" Seeing tears welling in Rose's eyes, I felt ashamed of my light comments. This was not, after all, just an exercise in extrasensory perceptions. This was a young mother brokenhearted over the loss of her child. "Right, let's do try that, Serena. You're the *maven* here, so to speak."

A rather large gilt-embossed, illustrated Bible, of the kind that was fashionable in Victorian times, lay open on a lectern set near the bow windows, probably a hangover from St. Rita's day. With a small, demure smile, Serena crossed over to the handsome book and closed it gently. "Who will do the honors, do you think?"

"Why, you will of course," Fiona said. "It's a question of affinity."

Serena crossed herself, murmured a blessing, and laid her hand flat on the Bible. Taking a deep breath, she opened it, keeping her gaze on Rose, who looked back steadily, although she trembled. Serena's finger moved down the page slowly, then stopped. She put on the glasses that were hanging around her neck on a braided hemp cord, and she read: "I heard also the noise of the wings of the living creatures that touched one another, and the noise of the wheels over against them, and a noise of a great rushing. Ezekiel 3:13." Serena and Fiona looked at each other in bewilderment. Then Serena said, "Well, obviously, this will need some interpretation."

"Oh, I know! I know what that means," Rose cried hoarsely, a bright flush in her cheeks. "Airport! Beverly Municipal Airport! I was there once with Rasheed when we were courting. He had a pilot's license then, and he took me for a grand ride all the way to Boston Harbor. There's a charter company has an office and planes at that airport."

"Rose, I think you've hit on something very plausible here." I was already punching in my home number. "Does your husband still have a pilot's license?"

Her burst excitement dwindled as fast as air from a punctured balloon. She drew in a ragged breath. "I don't know. He never mentioned it, I think not since Hari was born."

"Phil!" I spoke softly into my cell phone, walking over toward the bow windows. "How's Joe?" Phillipa replied that he was still sleeping. " 'Still sleeping' is good, as long as he's not unconscious. Better have a look. Yes, we have news. Fiona's here, and we've fixed on a location."

"Don't worry about Joe," Phillipa assured me. "He's thrashing around, so not in a coma. On a scale of one to ten, how do you credit this find?"

"Eleven," I said. "Because we did some other searches, too—on the psychic computers we have on hand here. I thought you'd be able to get through to Stone much better than I. That desk sergeant always gives me the runaround."

"I wonder why. And here you are calling in with a perfectly legitimate tip from the Psychic Friends Network."

"Will you call?"

"Of course. Where is that bastard kidnapper, as you see it?"

"We have to move on this right away. Abdul may be at the Beverly Municipal Airport in the process of renting a plane either with or without a pilot. At least, we hope he's still there. Stone should get the Beverly cops moving on this before Abdul takes off for parts unknown."

"I take it that Abdul may have a license? He'd have to file a flight plan."

"Yeah, sure. But then he could change his mind and maybe head for Canada?"

"Okay, I'm going to light a fire under Stone. Where will you be?"

"Are you kidding?"

"Who's going with you."

"Rose. Maybe Fiona."

"Keep your cell on. Blessed be."

"You bet." I turned back to the ring of anxious faces. "Phil will get to Stone, and we trust Stone will get to the Beverly Police Department—before Abdul makes his move."

"Cass, I have to get to Hari myself. Will you take me?"

"Yes, of course. I just told Phil I'd be on my way. Fiona?"

Fiona was already packing up her maps. "I wouldn't miss this trip for the world." Slinging her reticule over her shoulder, she grabbed her cane and pointed it like a sword as she charged toward the door. *Remarkably spry,* I thought, *for someone who was crippled with arthritis just a few weeks ago.*

"I'll pray for you," Serena said. "The Lord will protect you and Hari, Rose. I feel that in my bones."

"I'll say a few words myself," Fiona said. "Let's go."

"Oh, I hope you're right, Serena," Rose said. "Thank you for everything you've done—and are doing. Maybe . . . maybe I'll be bringing Hari home with me later." Leaving the doyenne of St. Rita's with a hasty hug, the slight young woman practically pushed us both out the door, where we clambered into the Jeep and sped off.

Chapter Twenty-three

I glided through the crowded highways with surprising ease. Even traffic lights gave us a green thumbs-up. "Move over, Luke Skywalker," Fiona said as I wove through yet another glut of commuters on Route 95. The trip took only an hour and a half, and I'd be surprised if that in itself did not involve some magic. The Force was definitely with us.

Phillipa called while we were still south of Boston. I handed the phone to Fiona so that I could keep both hands on the wheel, a wise move at the speed I was traveling. Fiona repeated Phillipa's words as she heard them: "Stone's been in touch with the Beverly cops, and they're on their way to the airport. Meanwhile, all outgoing charter flights have been delayed until the planes' occupants can be identified and cleared. A photo of the boy and his father that Rose left with Serena has been faxed to Beverly. They know what they're looking for, a bearded Saudi with five-year-old boy answering to 'Hari.' Phil wants to know, how are *you* doing, Cass?"

"You can answer that one."

"Cass thinks she's racing at Daytona, but other than that . . ." Fiona said.

"Ask Phil what she knows about the airport." I zoomed past a bevy of tractor-trailers laboring uphill.

Fiona conveyed the question, then repeated Phillipa's answer. "Small municipal airport, mainly used for charter, instructional, and corporate flights, a few military planes, and also as a 'reliever' for Logan."

"Ask her where it is."

"She says she's never been there, just follow the signs." Fiona relayed this unhelpful tip, then listened for a moment. "Yes, Phil, we'll call you as soon as we get there. And if there are any developments, you keep in touch. We're on tenterhooks, whatever they are." She punched off.

"So they won't let any planes leave, right?" Rose leaned over from the backseat, her voice ragged and anxious. "But what if he's gone already?"

"If he'd flown the coop, I wouldn't have dowsed him in Beverly," Fiona said with more assurance than I believe she felt. Nevertheless, Rose asked us some version of these two questions about every ten minutes. By the time we crossed the city line, I was half-crazed with patient answering.

"Do you remember where the airport is?" I asked Rose. I was hoping not to stop for directions.

"I'm not at all sure. So many years since I've been here."

"Take a right at the next intersection," Fiona directed me.

"Are you sure?"

"Trust me. Bear left at the fork."

"How exactly are you navigating, Fiona?"

"Don't ask. Oh, look," Fiona cried with glee as I followed her directions. "There's a little green airplane sign."

The phone rang again. Fiona answered. "Oh, yes, I see. All right. I'll tell her."

"Tell me what?" Rose and I questioned in unison.

"Alas, dearie. Now don't get upset, you'll need all your wits about you." Fiona had turned and was patting Rose's hand. "I'm afraid they haven't found Hari and his father. Apparently, a man who fit Abdul's description was in the charter office making arrangements when two cruisers arrived. No boy with him, but Hari may have been in the café. The guy in the charter office said the bearded man just melted away as soon as he heard the sirens."

Rose in the backseat wailed, "Oh my God, he's gotten away."

While Rose continued to moan and cry, I concentrated on following the green signs. A few minutes later, we were driving into the little airport. Cruisers with flashing lights made it easy to spot the office of Aviators of New England, where small planes could be rented. I braked hastily, and we all jumped out.

Rose was incoherent and Fiona was gazing about in a distracted manner, so it was left to me to explain who we were to the uniform officer outside the charter outfit's door. There was another officer inside, and the rest were off searching the premises.

The hefty, red-faced, blond officer gave his name as Eric Gunderson. "So, this guy who kidnapped the kid is an Arab, right? Some kind of terrorist maybe?"

I hastened to dash his hopes. "No, not a terrorist. Just an ordinary kidnapper. His name is Rasheed Abdul, and this young woman is his wife, Rose Fiorello, the missing boy's mother." Rose tried to smile at the man, her face tearstained and tense. I put my arm around her and continued. "Abdul must have arrived and left in a car. Did anyone see him and the child, perhaps notice what make of car he was driving?" My earlier encounter with Abdul was returning to my mind's eye. "Wait, I think I know. . . . He's probably driving a black pickup truck. Do you think you could send out a bulletin to that effect, maybe stop him before he gets too far away?" Out of the corner of my eye, I saw Fiona had spread out one of her maps on the cruiser's fender and was bent over it, dowsing with her crystal.

"I dunno. Been some time since he left." Officer Gunderson caught sight of Fiona. "What the hell's she doing?"

I didn't care for his offhand manner, so I said, "Of course, we

don't absolutely know that terrorism is *not* involved." It had occurred to me that I could up the ante with a few obscuring nega-
tives. Why should I play fair with a guy who had once tried to
knock the lights out of Scruffy?

Gunderson snapped to attention and hurried to confer with his
partner, who had just emerged from the charter office. The resulting APB described a possible terrorist situation, an Arab pilot
traveling in a black pickup, holding a five-year-old boy hostage.
The Beverly Police Chief notified the FBI that they were in pursuit of a suspected terrorist who may have left a bomb somewhere in the airport.

Fiona had put away her dowsing kit. We three heard the bulletin broadcast on the cruiser's radio with varying reactions, Rose
trying to explain to Gunderson that Abdul couldn't be a terrorist,
he was an accountant, a CPA, while I attempted to keep her
quiet.

Fiona, who had her answer, simply smiled and nodded her
head before leaning over to tap Gunderson smartly on the shoulder. "Abdul's heading north. Route 95, Salisbury, border of New
Hampshire." I noticed that she had drawn herself up into full
glamour. Naturally, he accepted her information without question. Later he would probably wonder what had possessed him,
but who cared if the result was Hari's rescue?

I have to confess to a twinge of conscience when the decision
was made to shut down the airport for a thorough bomb search.
Still, it's always a treat to see those beautiful bomb-sniffing dogs
in action, intent and dedicated German shepherds. And what was
the loss to the world if a couple of corporate jets were late taking
off?

Fortunately, we were not forced to evacuate, so I marshaled
my little crew to the café, where we sipped restorative coffee
served by a very nervous counterman. I ordered a few sandwiches, too, ones that had been made up earlier when the server
hadn't been distracted by the fear of being blown up at any moment. Rose could only nibble on packaged crackers, but Fiona

and I tucked into ham and cheese with a good appetite. Then we waited. And waited. And waited. I may even have dozed a little—I was at that point quite exhausted.

I came to life when Fiona called Phillipa. "So you heard about that already? Well, I can't imagine how they got the idea that terrorism might be involved," she said. "But you know how people are these days about bearded Arab types. The FBI, too? Well, they *should* be involved. After all, this *is* a kidnapping. Yes, Salisbury was my call. Dowsed it clear as day. We're in the café now, waiting for news." She motioned the phone toward me, but I shook my head. No way did I want to be cross-examined by Phillipa about how the FBI got into this.

"Ask her about Joe," I whispered.

She did, and relayed the reply. "Phil says he's woken up at last, he's fine, but he has a hell of a headache and wants to know what's going on here. She's making a beautiful frittata."

She offered the phone a second time, but again I shook my head. "Cass says she'll be in touch later. Yes, dear. Of course we'll keep a low profile. No, we won't embarrass Stone. I wish you were here, too. Thank you, I'll tell her."

"Heather and Deidre send their love and prayers," Fiona said. "Now, Rose, I have a good feeling about this. There's a rest room right across the walkway. Why don't you wash your pretty face and freshen up a bit. You go with her, Cass. I'll hold the fort. If there's any word, I'll run right after you."

As I shepherded Rose across to the Ladies, I saw out of the corner of my eye that Fiona was taking a half pint of Scotch out of her reticule and pouring a dollop into the remains of her coffee. It was always a source of amazement to see what Fiona could pull out of that old green carryall. I couldn't blame her for taking a wee nip, but if I'd had a drop of the stuff myself, I would have gone straight into oblivion. It's a fearsome responsibility being the Designated Driver.

Rose and I used the facilities, then splashed our faces with cold water, which felt very good indeed—vital and refreshing. I saw that Rose's normally high color was back, and her eyes were brighter. *Dear Mother of All, surely we will have good news soon*, I thought.

We stepped into the walkway. Rose paused to tuck her hair behind her ears. Slowly, in my mind's eye, a golden light evolved and surrounded the two of us. If a light can be described as loving, this one was pure love and more, indescribably warm and reassuring, even joyous. A place one yearned to stay—but couldn't, not yet. *Surely we are blessed.*

Gradually the light faded away, but I was still in its golden aura when I took Rose's hand and guided her back to our café table. Fiona beamed at us. Gunderson was standing beside her, also smiling broadly. "We got him," he said, looking most at Rose. "The boy is safe. Your son is fine." I could tell how pleased he was to be the bearer of good news for a change.

I think Rose would have fainted then, if I had not been beside her with arms ready to hold her up. We sat her down carefully and got her to put her head between her knees until the lightheadedness passed. She was laughing and crying at the same time. "Oh, thank God, thank God. When will I see him? Will they bring him here to me?"

They would, and they did. Hari was whining and fretful, terrified for his father, whom he'd last seen being dragged away in handcuffs by uniformed men with drawn guns. But he was also anxious to be in his mother's reassuring arms again, and Rose's face when she enfolded him was a glory to behold.

As I learned later with some satisfaction, Abdul had a tedious and frightening time extricating himself from the suspicion of being involved in some terrorist plot. Good enough for him!

Chapter Twenty-four

It may not be a Wiccan festival, but it should be. Thanksgiving is a celebration of earth and a holiday of the heart. No gift-giving frenzy, no greeting cards to old acquaintances in which one attempts to compact the year's highlights into three pithy sentences. Just a plain old family dinner party, as traditional or nouveau as one wishes, in honor of the year's harvest. For me, it truly was a time for some quiet reflection about my blessings, such as my upcoming wedding to the love of my life and my narrow escape from death at the hands of sex-crazed medics at the Manor.

I was thankful, too, to be preparing the feast in my own home for my own family (well, not all of them, but Yule was coming!) instead of being a guest single at Deidre's. I looked forward to the unique flavor of Grandma's Nine Herbs Stuffing, which I would prepare from her own secret recipe. I'd save some for Phillipa to taste; it would be fun to see her try (and I bet, fail) to name the ingredients. My grandma had been a sorceress in the kitchen with an offbeat way of flavoring traditional dishes

Phillipa and Stone were spending Thanksgiving in Connecticut visiting with her brother Dan Gold, a cardiologist, and his "blended" family, a young wife, his wife's teenage sister, a new baby, and two older sons by his first marriage. "It's like trying to sort out the characters in a Russian novel. I've had to draw a family tree with bio notes just to keep straight the ex-wives, current wives, children, stepchildren and assorted in-laws of my two brothers," Phillipa had complained to me. "I do like to avoid any familial faux pas, like calling the third wife by the second wife's name." It was quite a sacrifice for Phillipa to give up the chance to whip up something dazzling on her own trophy Viking range, but family fealty had won out this year.

I have to admit I felt smug about cooking for my own little circle: Joe, Rose, Hari, Fiona, Heather, and Dick. (The perfect housekeeper for Heather had not yet answered our call, and she herself was unprepared to wrestle with tradition.) Then Becky and Ron decided to join us, a bonus blessing. On other years, they'd spent this holiday at Ron's parents', which Becky confessed always gave her the feeling of brittle refinement with undercurrents of foreboding, as if she were dining on stage in *An Inspector Calls*. Having separated herself from her in-laws' high-powered corporate law firm, Becky now felt free to let drop the occasional critique of life in Lowell Country. And to have a holiday meal with her own mom.

Nine people jammed into my dining-space-for-eight would have been a cozy group, gathered around the free-range, organic turkey to which Heather had given her approval. But, thanks to Deidre, there were ten celebrants wedged knee to knee, not to mention two dogs underneath the table, since we'd be entertaining Honeycomb as well.

Deidre had sprung this one on me a few days before the holiday. "You know, I had wanted to invite Fiona here. My dining room seats twelve or more comfortably. But I thought, what with missing her grandniece and all, it might give her sad thoughts to be among young children."

"And besides, I asked her first." I was spin-drying fresh herbs, the kitchen phone cradled between shoulder and cheek.

"So you did. The thing is, I would have invited Mick Finney, too."

"That's because you're an unregenerate matchmaker, which I am not."

"Mick Finney's smitten with Fiona, but he's shy."

"There's nothing shy about sending a gal a dozen long-stemmed red roses."

"I mean, in person, he's shy about expressing his deep attraction to her. Poor Mick, such a lonely man. I bet he had no one to share this lovely family holiday."

"Cut that out, Deidre!" I took out my chopping knife and got to work on the herbs.

"What's that whacking noise?" she asked.

"I'm mincing herbs for Grandma's stuffing."

"You can buy stuffing all prepared in a bag, you know. Just add hot water and margarine. We call items like that *convenience foods*, Cass, in case you haven't heard of them. So . . . poor Mick, he's probably going to nuke a Hungry Man Frozen Turkey Dinner with Extra Mashed Potatoes and that pathetic little square of cornbread."

"He'll be counting his blessings that he can watch consecutive football games and knock back a few beers without any feminine interference. Why don't you have Will invite him to *your* place with that roomy dining room?"

"Because—as if you didn't know—I think Mick's ardor could be like a healing balm to Fiona. Mark my words, Fiona would be dancing whatever the hell that Scots dance is if she just had a sincere, sexy guy courting her."

"*Fling*, Dee. It's called a Highland Fling. And I sure would like to see Fiona throwing herself into that." Deidre knew she could nail me with that word "healing." Still I demurred. "But how do you know that Fiona will welcome his advances? We wouldn't want to be responsible for some sad shooting accident involving Mick-on-the-make."

"I just know. You can tell from their auras that they're made for each other."

"Deidre! I didn't know you could read auras."

"I can't. But if I could, I know those two would be surrounded with a lovely green light. Or maybe red."

"Or a nice tartan aura. Okay. You win. I'll invite Mick. And Hecate help you if this ruins the Norman Rockwell festive family scene I'm arranging here."

"Trust me. They'll both thank you—if not now, eventually. Whoops! Gotta run. Will Junior and Jenny will be home any moment."

I had to hand it to Deidre. She knew how to handle a closing. Get that agreement signed, then get out fast. As soon as we'd hung up, I called Mick, and I have to admit that he sounded most appreciative. Could he bring a bottle of single malt Scotch? *Sure.* Next I called the Farmer's Fancy Organic Foods Market and upped my order from a fifteen-pound to a twenty-pound bird. Mick Finney was a big man who looked like he had an appetite to match.

A twenty-pound roast turkey is a truly impressive sight, and the stuffing was nearly as good as Grandma's. "Thanksgiving is one of the reasons I haven't brought myself to become a vegetarian," Heather defended herself as she bit into the succulent breast meat. "Somehow a rice-stuffed pumpkin as the entrée or a tofurky doesn't quite fill the bill."

"I like meat," Fiona said. "I come from a long line of unapologetic carnivores. In Scotland the growing season is short and unpredictable. If men didn't bring home fish and game, their families would starve. But I don't want to have to kill anything myself. No *animal*, that is."

We who knew her well were used to Fiona's quirky pronouncements, but they seemed to leave Ron in a constant state of astonishment, while Mick merely beamed admiration.

"If every woman carried a pistol in her handbag and didn't hesitate to use it, I wouldn't be surprised if crime were practically wiped out," Fiona told Ron as she refilled his glass with the amazing Scotch Mick had brought to the festivities.

Still later she assured him that "your mother-in-law can't help being drawn into criminal plots—it's her karma, just as it's your karma to be drawn into corporate plots. It's what you decide to do about it that will count in your next incarnation. Have you thought who you'd like to come back as? I'd like to be the captain of a spaceship myself."

When Ron stumbled off later to my bedroom to "catch the scores," I didn't know if it was Mick's Scotch or Fiona's conversation that made him seek a quiet corner and a cold cloth for his brow.

Thanksgiving was a favorite with Scruffy, too, and Honeycomb was his favorite visitor. Their festivities were somewhat marred, however, by their being followed around by Hari, who even sat under the table with them in order to "play doggie," demanding of his mother that his meal be served on the floor. Much as I needed the elbow-room up top, however, I drew the line at putting that kind of temptation in front of two hungry dogs.

Listen, Toots, I hope you don't expect me to share my tasty food finds with this greedy little person. Deep sighs and complaints continued to drift up from under the table.

Later, when Scruffy and Honeycomb were fed their portion of turkey leg and other good things, Rose had to scoop Hari away from the dog dishes as he prepared to join them. "Look, Mama! I can eat with no hands like a doggie."

"Dogs prefer an unvaried diet of nutritionally balanced dog food," Heather reminded me, eyeing the ceramic bowls lavish with Thanksgiving tidbits.

We'd had this argument many times before. "It's a holiday, Heather. I'm sharing the bounty of earth with our canine companions. Lighten up!"

Scruffy licked up the last smidge of turkey flavor as if trying to remove the GOOD DOG painted on the bottom of his dish. *You ought to report her to the SPCA for what she feeds Honeycomb. That stuff they eat at her house tastes like twigs and bark.*

"Speaking of sharing with our canine companions," Dick said, "Heather's been working night and day to keep everything going. The Morgan Manse is no small enterprise—all those dogs, all those rooms. We have a woman who comes in once a week, but that just slicks the surface. And I'm afraid I'm not as much help as I would like—long hours at the Wee Angels Hospital, you know. We're desperately in need of full-time help, but Heather assures me that rescue is coming, she just doesn't know who or when. I don't know if there's anything you can do. . . ."

"We'll put a fire under it, so to speak," Fiona said. "Don't worry about a thing. Why don't you men go for a nice walk, now. Take Ron with you, too. I suspect he needs a breath of air." Shooed out by Fiona, Joe, Dick, Mick, and Ron took Hari and the dogs for a ball game on the beach, for which we were all grateful.

After the rest of the food and dishes had been cleared away, Becky holed up with Rose in a living room corner discussing Abdul and the complexities of divorce. My daughter had agreed to take on Rose as a client, pro bono, which was exactly what I had wished. Becky didn't anticipate much difficulty in obtaining full custody of Hari from a suspected terrorist.

"Dick's worried about you, Heather, dear. You need to start calling the domestic services agency," Fiona said. "Plymouth has one, doesn't it?"

"Yes. Finch's French Maids and Escort Service. Unfortunately, one of the Flaming Finches runs the place. Not Wanda, though. But, anyway, I thought, since we put in a psychic call for the perfect household help for me, that I ought to wait and see what happens," Heather said.

"I don't think Finch's French is the right place. After the debacle at Pryde's, the family may be holding a grudge on Wanda's behalf," I chipped in. "What's in Braintree?"

"The Mop Brigade of Braintree. In Westport, it's the Whistling Maids, Caretakers & Cooks of Cohasset."

"'A whistling maid and a crowing hen always come to a very bad end.' One of those early antifeminist proverbs," I said. "Anyone for a nice cup of digestive tea?"

"*Never* wait to see what happens. *Always* give the pot a stir," Fiona instructed. "Not even magic happens by magic."

"Okay," Heather agreed. "I'll start calling around on Monday. After all, I have to get everything shipshape for Cass's wedding— just one short month away!"

Shipshape. Little did we know how prescient *that* was.

Following Thanksgiving it did seem like one greased downhill slide to Yule. So many details to be wrapped up. So many minor catastrophes to be averted. And this was just a small family wedding. What kind of endurance would a person need, I wondered, to make it through a great catered affair? This was not the stuff of which I was made.

But never mind the trivia of a florist who was allergic to dogs, a very pregnant photographer, and caterers moonlighting as astrologers who were aghast to discover that there were several dates in December when it would be dangerous to work with knives and stoves. At least the major matters were proceeding just fine. Cathy was coming east with Irene, Adam from Atlanta with Freddie. Heather offered to put up Freddie at the Morgan Manse in the girl's former favorite yellow roses bedroom with the private bathroom and monster tub. Becky and Ron could drive home to Boston after the wedding, and Tip would be staying with his father. Cathy, Irene, and Adam would stay with me. It was all manageable. I just had to keep saying to myself, "Most things work out."

Not surprisingly, just three weeks before the wedding, the obligatory Greenpeace emergency whisked Joe away amid his fervent promises that nothing on earth would keep him from getting home in time for the ceremonies (we were planning two in the same day). The *Rainbow Warrior's* "minor" mission was to glide into Sète harbor in France where a suspect ship might be unloading the fruits of illegal logging in Liberia. Once the logs from unsustainable, out-of-control logging were identified, Greenpeace activists would paint them in bright yellow letters with the legend *Liberian Crime.*

"And I suppose the gendarmes will just stand around smiling and drinking the local *vin rouge* while you stigmatize those ill-gotten logs?"

"They *assure* me this will be a fast hit and a quick getaway." My beloved had that glad glint in his eye. Hanging around while I fussed and fumed over wedding minutiae was no way as attractive as sailing the seas to France on a mission to save endangered forests. I rather wished I could tag along.

But instead of voicing these sympathetic thoughts, I said, "Do you realize that I have ordered hundreds of long-stemmed red roses to stand dramatically in crystal vases? How long do you suppose those babies can keep from their velvet heads from drooping if you're late?" The red roses were meant to complement my near-white velvet dress (I called the color *"pearl"*) and Heather's Victorian living room, where the actual ceremonies would take place. The reception—or raucous party—to follow would spill into her conservatory.

"I swear on my mother's head I'll be back in time."

"I hope the Greek gods are not paying attention to this display of hubris. Does your mother know that you readily call the Fates down upon her?"

I felt rather relieved that Joe's family had decided not to fly over for the ceremony. I suspected this had something to do with Joe's civil divorce not being recognized by the Greek Orthodox church. Then, too, *double trouble*, he was marrying a divorced woman in rites that would include a handfasting.

Fortunately, Joe had his own strong faith that seemed to be untroubled by his departure from orthodox ways or my Wiccan path. "Not to worry, sweetheart," he assured me. "Mama will always welcome you warmly. We Greeks have a certain flexibility."

Perhaps Joe was right. After he'd sailed for France, a large package arrived addressed to "Mr. and Mrs." *Should I fear the Greeks when they come bearing wedding gifts?* I wondered as I tore through the sturdy wrappings. Inside, beautifully wrapped, was a silver-framed icon called "Life-Giving Well" that depicted the

Holy Mother above a chalice of cascading blue water, surrounded by smaller figures—saints and sinners, I assumed. Quite magical, like the Queen of Cups in Phillipa's Tarot. Also in the package was a handmade book of recipes exquisitely lettered with drawings of herbs and a sketch of the parts of a lamb. Unfortunately, the text was all Greek to me, but Joe would translate when he returned.

In lieu of family, Joe had invited several Greenpeace buddies who might or might not be available on The Date, which was December 22nd, Yule in the Wiccan cycle of the year.

The "fast hit and quick getaway" went pretty much as I had predicted, with several of the activists hauled away in vans by the gendarmes on December 10th. Joe wasn't among them, but he and other loyal shipmates decided they must wait for their comrades to be released. The companies who were selling the Liberian logs asked the French police to keep the Greenpeace guys in jail as long as possible—48 hours before they must either be brought before a judge or released. Or, as I viewed it, two days into my nervous breakdown across the Atlantic in Plymouth. When the activists finally paid their fine and got out of jail, there remained only a week in which to sail home, winter storms permitting.

Joe's ship would dock in New York on December 21st, which was cutting it pretty close. I should have been in a fair state of panic, but actually a marvelous, unbridal calm had come upon me. I knew in my heart that everything was going to be just wonderful. December was already becoming a magical month of reunions for me.

Tip had arrived first. He'd shot up several inches in the way of teenagers, but would likely be of medium height when he finished growing. Slim but muscular, he was nicely bronzed from working outdoors after school all year. His dark hair had been allowed to grow long, and he wore it in a neat ponytail. Although his voice had changed, his laugh was still the same, sometimes a high crazy lilt and at other times a deep chuckle ending in a cough, just like his father's. The shape of the man he would be was emerging from the boy.

"Hi. Are you the lady who advertised for a handyman?" He greeted me as he had the first time we met, his smile broad, his eyes taking on that Asian look.

"Oh, Tip. I'm *so* glad to see you!" I hugged him warmly while Scruffy danced up on his hind legs to lick the boy's face. "Are you hungry? I was just making lunch."

It's the boy, the one who plays ball! Dogs never forget a good friend. Tip got right down to Scruffy's level and greeted him with praise and pats.

Then, while he chatted on happily about living with his bachelor uncle, I made chicken sandwiches, put them on plates for the two of us, and poured Tip a glass of milk. "How are things with your father?" What I really wondered was, is the man still drinking?

"Oh, you know. He's glad to have me around to get a few chores done before winter. That leg of his has been giving him trouble, and there's no one else to help."

I had mixed feelings. I'd love to have Tip move back to Plymouth, but I knew he'd have a better life in Wiscasset, stay in school and graduate, study music, and be the person he was meant to be. Once I had fantasized about adopting Tip, having him live with me so that I could protect him from his unreliable parents. Seeing him almost grown up reminded me that it's the way of nature for the young to be encouraged to fly off in new directions.

"Going to finish the year in Maine?" I poured myself a cup of ginger tea.

"Pa wants me to stay here and get a job with him playing Indian at Plimouth Plantation. But I've promised Coach I'd be back for the spring track meet, and Uncle J. is always after me to hit the books. I like school, you know." He smiled shyly, as if confessing to a weakness. "And I have some great buddies in Wiscasset."

"I'm glad. You'll make us all proud, I know."

*   *   *

Adam and Freddie arrived at dinnertime. They'd driven all the way from Atlanta in his silver-gray Lexus. I have to confess that the first thought through my brain was, where did they spend the night? Well, time enough to learn the details later. No longer looking like a computer nerd, my tall, fair son was turned out now like an ad from *Gentleman's Quarterly*—casual but expensive. My gorgeous green-eyed Adam. Freddie was right about him being a hunk.

Freddie herself was quite a surprise. Somehow since she'd graduated, she'd got it all together and developed her own unique look, still punkish, but with style. Her pixie haircut was a softer black, a few jelled peaks but no orange or purple streaks. Her makeup, as always, emphasized her amber eyes, but the whole effect was somehow lighter, the brows dark but natural-looking. And her lipstick, thank Goddess, was a moist, deep rose instead of a slab of brown. The miniscule skirt hadn't changed, but her outfit exuded a whole different quality, especially the long black leather coat and high boots.

Obviously relishing my surprise, Freddie winked at me and grinned. "Yo, Cass. Ain't it great what a steady paycheck will turn out?"

"Adam, dear! Freddie, you look stunning!" I exclaimed. It did not escape my attention that Adam alone brought all the bags from the car and was rewarded by a slow, sexy smile from Freddie. The tips of her rose-painted fingernails (all the same color!) just grazed the sleeve of his sheepskin jacket. In an instant maternal alert, I began to wonder if I was looking at the future here. But weren't they poles apart, not only in age and experience, but also in attitude and taste. I wondered, for instance, what CDs they could both agree on to play on the ride north. Alternating perhaps between heavy metal and Bach fugues? It was definitely time for my clairvoyance to kick in and answer a few burning questions.

My son's favorite pot roast was simmering in the slow-cooker.

Freddie set the table while I nuked some potatoes and took out the coleslaw I'd made earlier. "You must be exhausted from all that driving," I prodded.

"Not too bad," Adam said, "We stayed in Atlantic City last night. Freddie thought it would be fun if we tried our luck at one of the casinos."

"Oh, and how did that go? Lose your shirts, did you?"

"Hey, Ma, total surprise! Freddie hit that crazy money machine that spits out a shower of greenbacks. Whistles and bells, people yelling and clapping. What a blast!"

Freddie kept her gaze on her plate and avoided my pointed look. "How wonderful for you. A girl can always use some ready cash."

"Hey, like, I was bound to give it a try, Cass, you know what I mean?" She pushed a few shreds of coleslaw around the edge of her plate. "It's not, like, I'm going to make gambling my career or anything. Not when I've got this awesome gig with Iconomics."

"Freddie's been great. I'm real proud of her." Adam reached for another helping of pot roast, seemingly oblivious that his casual praise had Freddie blushing to her eyebrows. "She's got this knack for troubleshooting. Whenever we run a big program for the first time, there's always a bunch of kinks we have to iron out. Finding the flawed logic path seems to be your girl's specialty."

"I'm not at all surprised. I've rarely met a young lady as talented as Freddie."

She avoided my gaze, still studying her plate, then looked up suddenly and grinned, "I'm not all thumbs like I used to be. Haven't crashed a thing lately."

"Good to hear," I said. "Control, that's the ticket. And not in casinos, my dear. Sometimes being really talented can be hazardous to your health and freedom."

Seeing Adam's quick, questioning look, Freddie explained. "Cass is afraid I might develop, like, a genie-type talent with the slots. If I start breaking the bank at Monte Carlo and get noticed, the management would want to stuff me back in the bottle, you know what I mean? Remember, I mentioned that I have this rapport with machines?"

I thought that was putting it mildly. This was a girl with psychometric powers that could completely screw up any system she put her mind to, a gift that had saved our lives last year when she addled a bomb timer while we were both tied up waiting for it to go *boom* in a big way. *That* part of the scenario had never come out in the newspaper accounts.

"Has Adam ever seen what you can do to a spoon?"

Freddie shot me a warning glance. "It's just a parlor trick, Cass. I wouldn't want to, like, bore him with that kid stuff."

Sure she wouldn't. But someday it would happen. Adam would get a glimpse of Freddie's true genius. And then what?

After dinner we drove over to Heather's and got Freddie settled in that yellow suite she used to like so much. But its glamor couldn't compare to being with Adam, I saw from her expression as we got ready to drive home without her.

"Hey, good news," Dick said, while we were all standing in a knot at the door. "CCC got us someone to help around here."

"CCC? Got you who?"

"Caretakers & Cooks of Cohasset," Heather said. "I took Fiona's advice and made a few calls. Inquired about a cook-housekeeper who could do a few garden chores, too, and also help care for the family dogs, never more than a dozen at a time."

Adam laughed. "I'm surprised they found someone to fit that profile. What's she like? Former mud wrestler? VA nurse? Bail bondswoman?"

"*He.* He's a retired merchant mariner," Dick said. "Captain Jack. He says he figures the dogs won't be any worse than some of his former shipmates. Very colorful character. We just love the parrot."

Parrot? I had a quick flashback to Heather playing Jimmy Buffet CDs at top volume while we lazed in her pool last July. "Yes, but can he cook? I mean, other than *cheeseburgers in paradise?*"

Heather grinned. "You won't believe it. He's a positive sorcerer in the kitchen. The galley, he calls it. That chowder is the best I've ever had. Biscuits and pies to die for! Also he cleans, polishes silver, gardens, and can tune up a car. And he's got this funny whistle he does, sort of extra high-pitched. Says he learned it from the dolphins."

Freddie, Adam, and I were clearly enthralled. "What's the big deal about a whistle?" Freddie wanted to know.

"It's magic with the dogs. And I think I know magic when I see it," Heather affirmed. "Absolutely stops them in their tracks, you'd think you were at an obedience trial. Yes, I think Captain Jack may just be Captain Right. Plus, that parrot of his is *so* cute—and smart! 'Call me Ishmael,' he says. In fact, Ish is quite the conversationalist."

"Mostly nautical," Dick said..

"Or naughty," Heather added.

Freddie gave me a raised eyebrow.

"After her last housekeeper went into witness protection, Heather needed help badly." I explained. "So we sent out a call at Samhain."

"Cool. But did you, like, call for a parrot named Ishmael, too?"

"We try to leave our spells open-ended, so we never really know how they will work out. The infinite cosmos has answers we would never dream of. The first time we tried a calling we were expecting, maybe, endangered turtles, but we got a pair of eagles instead. And Joe, too! Joe was the bonus."

"Awesome. I gotta give this a try," Freddie said. "Wow, it's good to be back in witchville where the possibilities run wild."

"Are you two speaking in tongues, or what?" Adam was shaking his head, trying to make sense of us.

"Right on." I hugged Freddie good-bye, and Adam did the same. I noted that her face over his shoulder had that cat-got-the-canary expression.

"Hey, Ma—what's with the deep sighs?" Adam asked as we drove home.

"Was I sighing? Just a little tired, I guess." I'd just have to let this Freddie-and-Adam situation take its course without any nudges from me. That's the hardest thing, that you can't and shouldn't make another person change course because you think it's best. All change comes from within. Bummer.

Chapter Twenty-five

The next day, in an icy December rain, Adam drove me to Logan, maneuvering through impassible construction areas like a pro. We found Cathy shivering against a column in front of the Arrivals door. Wearing a pink quilted down jacket over a long flowered dress and smoking a pastel cigarette, she looked fragile enough to float away on a wisp of smoke at any moment. Soignée Irene in a supple black leather jacket over a striped tee and black jeans waved cheerfully as she shoved their assorted luggage toward the curb. Adam jumped out to help. We hugged and screamed and got everyone settled in the Lexus.

"Love the wheels, Adam." Cathy leaned over her brother's shoulder to inspect the dashboard computer whose lovely female voice had offered directions and a map as we drove into town. No matter that the map didn't take into account the numerous detours around torn-up roads—it was still very impressive. "So, Mother . . . where's the bridegroom?"

"In France, last I heard. Assisting the activists who are painting *Liberian Crime* in yellow letters on logs that were illegally harvested. I expect they're all housed in a French jail by now."

"Greenpeace, I assume. Admirable." Irene was gazing out the window with interest. "Boston in the rain. I was hoping for snow."

"If it gets just two degrees colder, your wish will be granted. *My* wish is that we get home before that happens."

"Aren't you nervous about Joe?" Cathy put her hand on my shoulder and gave me a sweet, light kiss on the cheek. I laid my hand over her china doll fingers, feeling the slim gold ring that was a new addition to her left hand. But I didn't inquire about its significance. I would look at this as another test of my ability to let go. If she wanted my counsel, Cathy would ask for it. Somewhere in a book of Zen I read that one should not give advice unless it's requested three times. Not being a Buddhist, I thought one request was as much as I could manage.

"I worry that he may be stuck in jail, not that he'll leave me waiting at the altar. He'll call and give me his schedule as soon as he gets the chance. Sometimes he sends an e-mail note on the ship's computer. Anyway, crazy as it may seem, I'm feeling marvelously calm. Maybe I've been drinking too much kava tea."

"Mother really knows her way around herbs," Cathy told Irene. "Uppers, downers, potions, poisons, and possets."

" 'Here's flowers for you,' " Irene quoted the Bard. " 'Hot lavender, mints, savory, marjoram . . .' "

"I wouldn't expect Ma to get the jitters over an ordinary wedding after her recent narrow escape from the Angel of Death." Adam smiled wickedly as he let the cat out of the sack. "This is one cool lady." Tipped off by Becky, Adam and Freddie had used the Internet to track down the entire sordid story of Kane, Wallace, and the murders at Manomet Manor, far and away a more exciting tale than the sanitized version I had given them. As he veered through traffic and construction tie-ups, Adam treated Cathy and Irene to his own colorful version of those events.

"I'm so impressed," Irene said. "Your mother is a positive heroine."

"Really, Mother, you should have called me or something," Cathy complained.

"I thought the story would be better told in person," I side-stepped. "Only Adam beat me to it."

Adam smiled his disbelief. Sometimes I thought he knew me the best of all my children. "I think Ma works on a need-to-know basis."

I've always thought that our wedding was the best party ever. Not only because everyone dear to me was gathering in one place at one time. Or because being formally united with the love of your life is a white-hot experience that makes all others pale by comparison. It was all that and something more—magic, pure and simple.

I feel sorry for couples who simply decide to live together with no fanfare. There are certain moments in life too important to let slip by without flowers, music, incense, vows, laughter, tears, dancing, feasting, toasts, wishes, kisses, hugs—the works!

Even the weather blessed us. It was one of those brilliant December days when the sunshine seems to be brighter, the sky bluer, and the air crisper than anyone has the right to expect in midwinter. Joe's last-minute arrival turned out to be part of the charm; he drove from Logan to Plymouth on the morning of our wedding. Before he arrived, I had the chance to don my pearl velvet dress, a sheath with a delicately beaded jacket, and all the elegant satin undergarments that went with it. Even though my sandy hair is the wrong color for it, I wore it in the Grecian style Joe likes with a circlet of tiny white flowers and green laurel leaves, all fresh and fragrant.

"*Jesu Christos*, sweetheart, you are *so* beautiful!" was his most satisfactory reaction as he pulled me into his arms. We were in the bedroom, kissing a passionate hello. Then I came to my senses and pushed him to arm's length. "Don't mess me," I cried. "Cathy and Irene did my makeup. Maybe a touch too the-atrical? How do you like these eyes?"

"Gorgeous as always. Hey, I guess I'd better shower and get

changed. I hope it isn't bad luck for you see me in my new suit and fantastic gray silk shirt before the wedding?"

"Absolutely not. Our day, our rules." He looked marvelous to me already—dark curly hair, just flecked with gray, square chin, Mediterranean eyes, brawny build—my dream guy. As always, a rush of energy and excitement had come in the door with him. I wished I could detect auras, because Joe's must have been a leaping fantastic show like the northern lights.

Now I know why the bride and groom are discouraged from seeing each other before the ceremony. Because when Joe presented me with the wedding gift he'd been hiding in his duffel bag, an emerald pendant that matched my engagement ring, and he fastened it with a kiss on the nape of my neck, we were soon wrapped up in a major clinch and maybe headed for more. Fortunately, Becky knocked discreetly on the bedroom door in the nick of time. "Hey, are you guys decent yet? Heather called to say it's time we got over there for the pre-ceremony champagne bash."

"We'll be out in a jiffy. Where's Scruffy?" I disentangled myself from Joe's arms and repaired my lipstick with a shade not chosen by Cathy, hoping she wouldn't notice.

"Your fresh dog jumped into the wedding car ten minutes ago and is fogging up the windows. Getting impatient, like the rest of us. I expect he'll be honking my horn at any moment." The "wedding car" was no stretch limo, only Becky's BMW, beautifully waxed and agleam for the occasion.

So, okay, maybe I can't be quite objective about it. But I will always know that a kind of blissful glamour embraced Joe and me and the entire wedding company. And what an eclectic party it was! Our circle of five and their families, my own extended family, including, of course, Tip and Freddie, Scruffy and the rambunctious Honeycomb. Three of Joe's Greenpeace buddies who weren't at that moment saving the planet, Mick Finney, Rose and Hari, Maeve in a walker, Brian looking proud and worried, Euphemia managing with two canes, and our newest friends,

Captain Jack and Ishmael the Parrot, made up the small but select guest list.

Until our wedding day, Joe and I hadn't met the captain, so Heather coaxed him away from the kitchen for a few minutes. A small gray-haired fellow of indeterminate age, with merry blue eyes and a grizzled chin, he wore faded jeans, a striped canvas apron of many pockets that might have been meant for a carpenter, and a rather seedy captain's hat at a rakish angle. I detected the scent of some spicy pipe tobacco and a whiff of rum. Perhaps he was dousing Phillipa's wedding cake with rum. Or having a wee nip to keep up his strength. As Heather had led us to expect, a large green bird was perched on the captain's shoulder, to the delight of Hari and the three older Ryan children (Baby Anne was spending the day with her grandmother).

I had to ignore wicked Phillipa, who leaned over to softly hum "He's Popeye the Sailor Man" in my ear. "Hey, we called him here," I murmured. "He must be the perfect solution."

Scruffy and the parrot, however, did not hit it off. When my Best Dog trotted into the living room in his jaunty black bow tie, Ishmael suddenly screamed, "Thar she blows, boys! Wok! Wok!"

Flustered by the sudden appearance of a squawking bird, Scruffy backed up in alarm. Ishmael hopped off the captain's shoulder and flapped insolently past the dog's nose. Then he fluttered away around the room, crying out wildly, managing with clipped wings to hop his way up to the top of a Chippendale highboy. Leaping higher than he ever had for a frisbee, Scruffy snapped at the parrot's tail and came away with one green feather. He spat it out of his mouth and held it down with one proprietary paw.

Just wait till that feathered freak lights somewhere. I'm gonna get that sucker and have him for a snack. If he's not too tough to chew. Scruffy leapt up a few more times, severely endangering Heather's Waterford lamps, before Joe could clip a leash on to his collar and insist upon a mannerly *sit-stay*.

Meanwhile, Ishmael continued to scream. "Pirates! Pirates!

Break out the muskets, me hearties," followed by a string of salty curses.

"I bet you never heard language like that on a Greenpeace ship," I whispered to Joe, who was chuckling quietly. Ishmael's vocabulary was amazing.

Captain Jack smiled affectionately. "Come on now, Ish. How many times do I have to tell you not to go teasing the dogs? We got ourselves a nice berth here, but the dogs come with it."

"Belay that order!" Ish muttered as he jumped back onto his companion's shoulder, where he continued to give Scruffy the evil eye in beady parrot fashion until the captain returned to the kitchen, closely followed by Phillipa, whose curiosity about kitchen witchery was insatiable. Whatever was going on in there, the aromas were certainly savory. It promised to be a wedding luncheon to remember.

In a small receiving room between the front door and the large parlor, a trio of musicians hired by Heather were warming up. Strains of Medieval and Renaissance tunes wafted over us. Someone began singing "Who but my lady Greensleeves" in a clear, bell-like voice, accompanied, I thought, by a lute and a recorder.

Fortunately for the decorum of the occasion, Ish was confined to a covered cage during the ceremonies. The Reverend Peacedale officiated at a formal service, which took place in Heather's living room, in front of the fireplace. To his credit, the pastor seemed not to be discomforted by a Yule log merrily blazing behind him. On the other hand, he didn't linger over the service, either, but recited his part in quite a sprightly fashion.

My informal circle of bridesmaids surrounded me, each wearing her characteristic colors: Deidre dressed in an ankle-length baby blue frock, Phillipa aswirl in one of her dramatic black dresses relieved only by a striking gold Isis pendant, Heather looking slender and lithe in a russet Ultrasuede pants suit, and Fiona impressive in a shimmering sheath of many colors, silver bangles jingling, and her reticule close by. I supposed her pistol was at the ready in case anybody burst into the room at the last minute to prevent the nuptials, à la Jane Eyre.

And as for me, the bride resplendent, in the fragrant aura of my bridal bouquet of red rosebuds and rosemary, never have I felt I had that glamour spell so nearly right as when I stood beside Joe for us to be legally pronounced man and wife. Nor had Joe ever looked as handsome to me as he did that moment. I couldn't take my gaze away from his Aegean eyes that seemed to speak to me of a love beyond words.

Having asked me many questions about Wicca, its ceremonies, and handfasting in particular in our earlier talks, the Reverend Peacedale was obviously disappointed that another commitment prevented him from witnessing the event itself. With hearty handshakes all around, he rushed off. Perhaps just as well, because the champagne was already flowing rather freely. Heather had always been a liberal hostess, and Dick was quite her match. Perhaps I *could* glimpse the occasional aura, after all, because when those two were together—hospitable Cancer and convivial Leo—their discernible glow of warmth embraced us all.

Fiona presided over the handfasting, of course, but since she'd never opted to be ordained a high priestess by mail-order, she couldn't have performed the legal ceremony. Her authority was undiminished, however, by this minor technicality, as she cast the circle that we three stood within. Surrounding us in a second circle were my four bridesmaids and Adam, as Joe's best man. The scent of myrrh, the flickering light of many white bayberry candles, and tall crystal vases of red roses filled the room with sweetness and light as well as representing the four elements of air, fire, water, and earth. The rest of the party formed a third larger circle holding hands as a symbol of the unbroken protection. My back was to the north, Joe's to the south, and Fiona's to the west. The ceremony began at the half hour to ensure that good fortune would be sweeping upward to the full hour.

Joe and I had braided the three-stranded handfasting cord in our wedding colors: green for life, red for love, and white for spirit. In the majesty of her full glamour, Fiona bound us together, our hands clasped to form a figure eight, symbol of eternity. For Wiccans, "tying the knot" is literal not figurative. Fiona charged us to be joined in perfect love and perfect trust, to nurture and comfort each other in whatever life might bring our way, always seeking to enhance one another's growth in spirit. Although some handfastings last only for a year and a day, after which the union may be renewed, the ceremony can also bind a couple for eternity. The vows Joe and I had written for the occasion were magic words that fused us for all of this life and the lives to come.

Perhaps no one but Heather and I noticed Scruffy stealthily creeping from the third circle to the second. Best Dog! Nevertheless, Heather clapped a firm hand on his collar lest he disrupt the service.

Then it was time for Joe and me to jump the broom, age-old symbol of the jump into a new life. I like to think we managed this as gracefully as could be expected of two fortysomethings bound together by a braided cord, our coordinated leap possibly reminiscent of a sack race.

After that, everyone cried out "So must it be!" and the feasting and dancing began. The captain had turned out a magnificent seafood buffet that Phillipa was taste-testing with professional zeal. "I'm impressed, and I don't impress easily," she said. .

Across the room, Heather caught the expression on Phillipa's face and mouthed "ha ha."

The trio of musicians had moved into the conservatory amid the sturdy palms in pots that had managed to survive Heather's houseful of canine companions (tucked up in their comfortable kennel for the day). At one point in the party, Tip played a clarinet solo he'd been practicing, quite a beautiful plaintive piece. I was so proud of him! Proud of them all, indeed, even with those few small wrinkles of worry about Freddie's attraction to Adam,

Becky's future with Ron, Cathy's with Irene, Rose's divorce, and Tip's struggle to stay in school.

"Everything okay, sweetheart?" Joe asked, observing me briskly shaking off negativity, which must have looked much the same as if I were shaking off bugs. Maybe I was letting go a bit, too. Possibly I could allow the creative life force of the universe to take over my concerns while Joe and I were on our honeymoon. Yes, good idea.

Well, not quite. Stone and Phillipa cornered us for a few grave moments of discussing the coming trials of Faye Kane and Randolph Wallace. All that ugly business was to begin on January 15th, and I was going to be called as a prosecution witness.

Euphemia, too. Invited to join our conference, the crime-fiction fan squeaked with glee. "Imagine me nearly being the victim of a real murder spree!" She struggled off to tell Rose the wonderful news.

"You'll be back from your trip by then, right?" Stone demanded of me and Joe.

"As for your trial outfit, Cass," Phillipa added. " I always think a black picture hat and seamed stockings strike the right note with a jury. Do you have any real pearls?"

"Sounds like something out of an old Judy Holiday film," I said.

"Oh? Who's Judy Holiday?" Phillipa smirked.

"Just promise to be there in case I need a humming spell," I said.

"So, where in the world will you be?" Having dispatched Will to take the children to "see the doggies in their little houses," Deidre had wandered over to hear the latest from Stone.

"Would you believe that our destination is going to be Joe's surprise?" I said.

"I want to be sure we truly escape." Joe slipped his arm around my waist, and I leaned on his shoulder. Okay, he would run the show. For a few blissful days.

"How in Hades are you supposed to pack?" Deidre cried.

"Joe wants me to learn to travel light." I winked at the two women. "Like a Greenpeace bride should. Poncho, jeans, shirts, boots. Travel Smith's all-purpose black dress and crushable sun hat.

"Somehow she's managed to fill a bulging garment bag and a supersize suitcase with those few items." Joe's first complaint of our marriage.

"You don't suppose, do you, that Fiona couldn't find you in your secret rendezvous?" Deidre's smile twinkled with mischief.

Joe was undaunted. "Watch out, gals. I have my own mojo, you know." He flashed the gold cufflinks that I'd given him as a wedding gift. Between the pentagrams at his wrists (which were also Christmas stars) and the cross dangling on his chest, he certainly had all bases covered.

"All I know," I said demurely, "is that I've been asked to bring my passport, but that might simply be for identification."

"I think you've hit on a clue there." Heather threw herself onto a wicker loveseat, legs dangling over the edge. The party was winding down, and the hostess was zonked. "Clever Cass! There's never a mystery she can't solve, no matter how much danger she brings on the rest of us." She sighed heavily. "And why do I have the feeling that it will ever be thus?"

"Cass is my savior," Rose cried. "Cathy and I have had such a nice long talk about the old days at school—we were in the senior play together, do you remember that? Anyway, in case she didn't realize how wonderful you've been, I told her all our adventures."

"Oh, great," I said. "Rose, dear, something you will learn about being a parent. Most children want their mother to be Donna Reed not Wonder Woman."

"Who's Donna Reed?"

I groaned, and I was not alone. "Okay, guys. I'm going to get changed now, and not into my Wonder Woman hotpants. Joe wants to get going before dark."

The shortest day of the year! From now on, the sun would gain power, encouraged by our Yule rituals and all festivals of light everywhere. In the early darkness, snow began to fall. Soon a swirl of wet flakes glistened on every branch of every tree on Heather's estate, a lacy fairyland, a mysterious moonscape, an ice queen's silver palace. We gazed out from the long windows with wonder, closed into the ambiance of green oasis in the conservatory and warm reds in the Victorian parlor.

My children and their significant others, with Freddie and Tip, gathered around me for a major hugging session that soon had me sniffling and nearly ruining Cathy's extraordinary eye makeup.

"Fly carefully," Becky ordered.

"And you don't even know where you're going!" Freddie exclaimed with a knowing little wink. "How cool is that!"

Meanwhile, good-natured Will Ryan and his crew of Yule elves were cleaning off the cars and attaching Goddess-knows-what to the rear bumper of Joe's inevitable rental, although he had traded up to a Buick for the occasion..

It was time for us to leave. We were spending our wedding night at the Ritz so that we could fly out at practically dawn tomorrow for points unknown, or so Joe thought. He still had much to learn about being married to a clairvoyant. Not that I'd had a tiny moving picture in my head revealing our honeymoon destination, but I did see clearly, in my mind's eye, where he was hiding those airline tickets. In the lining of his travel kit, a kind of neat hidden pocket. New Zealand! It would be glorious summer there. I stuffed two pairs of shorts and an extra swimsuit into my already bulging suitcase.

The worst was saying good-bye to Scruffy, whom I was leaving in the Devlins' tender care. I clipped the leash on to his collar and handed it to Heather.

That's okay, don't worry about me, Toots. You two go ahead and have fun while I'm left here starving on a diet of twigs and bark.

"It's only for a little while, just a couple of weeks," I whined. No one can make you feel as guilty as a companion dog who looks at you with those reproachful eyes from under a fringe of fur. "It will do you good to have other dogs to romp with."

I'll probably be riddled with fleas by the time you get back. Or ticks. Or hookworm. Ack Ack. Heather put a consoling hand on Scruffy's neck, and Honeycomb nudged his flank sympathetically, but he was still coughing as we drove away. Everyone waved madly at us from Heather's front door, our Buick dangling Deidre's dream-catchers and good-luck charms from the bumper.

Inside the car, propped up on the backseat, were two of Diedre's handmade dolls dressed in copies of our wedding out-fits. What would we do with them, Joe wanted to know. I said I'd find a place for them in my luggage. I didn't say that it would be taking a chance to abandon our magic poppets. This was no time to trifle with serious spellwork. I'd already put rose petals in all of our shoes, so that we'd walk with love and luck wherever we went.

And so we did!

If you enjoyed
*The Divine Circle of
Ladies Making Mischief,*
don't miss Dolores Stewart Riccio's next novel
about the adventures of Cass Shipton
and her divine circle of friends,
coming soon from Kensington!

Turn the page for a special preview . . .

Chapter One

"*Double, double, toil and trouble . . .*" Phillipa grinned wickedly as she lay down the tenth card from the Rider-Waite deck, last of the layout; it was called *The Moon*. "I wouldn't take on any new crusades if I were you, Cass. From start to finish, this reading counsels you to watch your step." She leaned over the layout, dark wings of her hair falling forward, her expression disapproving, like a garage mechanic sizing up a faulty carburetor. A bunch of swords and wands in my cards, so what? I was beginning to be sorry that I'd asked her to read the tarot for me. Three phases of the moon looking down upon a howling wolf and a smiling dog, what was so bad about that?

"It's a card of hidden foes and unforeseen perils. The wolf, now—that's a symbol of untamed creation. The dog, on the other hand, adapts to mankind insofar as it suits his own interests, sort of like your dog Scruffy. And see this rugged path through hostile country? Not to mention this crayfish popping out from the pool of the Cosmic Mind." Phillipa's blunt fingernail pointed to various pictorial elements. "What did you tell me you were doing this Samhain? I mean, apart from our own circle ceremony."

"Church. I've been invited to give a talk at the Garden of Gethsemane Ladies' League on the origins of Halloween in our

Samhain. I really loathe giving speeches, but I feel I ought to represent Wicca in a favorable light whenever I have the chance."

"*Fire burn, and cauldron bubble*," my hostess intoned, giving a quick stir to the pot of pear and mango chutney simmering on her Viking range, wafting the spicy aroma throughout the room. I thought there must be extra calories in the very air of Phillipa's state-of-the-art kitchen. Not to mention the Fall Fruit Breads we were sampling with our tea, the theme of her next bimonthly cable cooking show, *Kitchen Magic*. As Colette wrote, and Phillipa was fond of quoting on and off the air, "'If you aren't up to a little magic, you shouldn't waste your time trying to cook'"

Phillipa returned to the long marble table and gave my cards another gloomy look before gathering them up. "Five of Wands, Seven of Swords. Maybe the Ladies are planning an exorcism or something. Rid you of the cursed demons that possess you, my dear."

"Not at all," I said. "The Reverend Peacedale couldn't be more ecumenical-minded. I suspect he's quite interested in the mystic experience *per se*. My clairvoyant episodes, I mean. And he understands that the ancient nature religions predate the advent of Satan and therefore have nothing devilish about them."

"Well, don't say you weren't warned."

Which is what I thought about later, while having my stomach pumped out at Jordan Hospital. The Ladies' League Hospitality Hour had been as disastrous as my lugubrious friend possibly could have predicted. Only the strong hands of my bridegroom, Joe Ulysses, holding me back by one shoulder and a robust nurse on the other side had kept me from pulling the gagging, scratching tube out of my throat and to hell with it. Probably one of the worst hours of my life. I really was tempted to call up a few impish entities I'd read about to avenge my misery, but I am pledged to work on the white side of Wicca.

I wasn't the only one enduring the unendurable. Several members of the League and the minister's wife were also at the hospital, and as I learned later, one of the older spinsters whose passion was chocolate—Lydia Craig—wouldn't be making it to the All Saints Day service on November 1st. Poison hemlock causes weakness, nausea, vomiting, difficult breathing, and if enough of it is ingested, paralysis and death. And those mystery brownies had been cleverly laced with the stuff. It was almost enough to turn a gal off chocolate forever.

I recalled how Mrs. Peacedale—Patty—had made a face when she nibbled at her brownie, muttering that the baking soda had not been properly sifted into the flour. I, too, had thought they were rather musty or mousey tasting despite a liberal dose of vanilla. But any brownies would suffer in comparison to Phillipa's.

Then, when everyone began to feel ill, the herbal lore in my brain clicked in. I guessed immediately what we'd eaten and told the paramedics. "I'm certain it was poison hemlock. That mousey aftertaste," I'd said weakly. Due to my conviction, we all got our stomachs pumped out immediately, while I was mentally kicking myself for my stupidity. I'd eaten one too many bites of that fetid brownie, purely out of politeness.

As the endless day at Jordan Hospital wore on, and it was obvious that I would never eat again, I urged Joe to go home to feed himself and Scruffy. "Don't worry about me," I said faintly, laying on the guilt. "You two have a good meal."

His Aegean blue eyes looked worried and somewhat reproachful. "How could this happen? And at a church social, for God's sake? Can't you go anywhere without being drawn into danger?"

"Is this the pot calling the kettle *black ass?*" I suggested. As a ship's engineer for Greenpeace, Joe continually sails into his own share of perilous misadventures.

"And I thought that, once we were married, you'd be happy to stay at home and tend to the weaving," he complained, grinning sheepishly. After a few restorative kisses, he left, with touching reluctance, and the evening nurse appeared.

"Hi. My name is Brenda. Are we feeling better now, Mrs. Ulysses?" she inquired briskly while she took my blood pressure. Although assuming an air of motherly authority, she was at least

ten years younger than I, a pale girl with slightly protruding eyes
and fine brown hair falling out of its coil. "You were lucky, you
know, honey. You didn't eat too much, and it didn't get too far.
Was that your husband who just left? Nice tan for this time of
year. Tanning salon?"

"No, Greenpeace. He travels the world in search of environmental hazards, often in tropical climes. And it's *Ms.* Shipton," I
mumbled. My throat was still sore. "My good luck was being the
guest speaker at the League. People kept asking me questions,
so I was delayed in getting to the hospitality table until after almost everyone else. And I didn't finish my brownie, which didn't
taste very good."

She checked my bracelet I.D. "Oh, yes. Shipton. I see. I
wouldn't mind being a Mrs. myself, but that's just me. What was
the talk about, honey?"

"Nature spirituality religions in pagan times. The origins of
Halloween. And modern-day Wicca."

"Is that, like, witches, curses, and all?" Nurse Brenda glanced
at my face again as if she might have missed some telltale sign,
such as green skin or a wart on my nose. Soon she'd connect
Shipton with our circle's notoriety in becoming involved in local
crimes.

Speaking of which, any minute now, the circle would be alerted.
Phillipa would probably hear the news first and call Fiona, Heather,
and Deidre. The circle would be swarming in here bringing their
various healing arts, none of which would include anything as
cursed as gastric lavage, ugh. A few stomach-calming herbs, a little white light, a homey lecture from Fiona.

"Wiccans, actually," I corrected Brenda. "So, have they discovered who brought the lethal brownies to the Ladies' League
yet?"

"I can't imagine *who* would try to poison a nice group of church
ladies. Two detectives are working their way down the hall right
now, questioning the victims who are well enough to provide information. They'll get to you pretty soon, and you can ask them

if an arrest is imminent." Brenda cast a calculating look my way. Perhaps I had made her personal list of suspects—either because of the Wiccan connection or my herbal business *Cassandra Shipton, Earthlore Herbal Preparations and Cruelty-Free Cosmetics.*

Besides *whodunit?*, the other big question on my mind, which I did not voice aloud, was how a person with clairvoyant skills like myself could munch up a poisoned brownie without a clue? Admittedly, I could hardly ever summon up my visions at will. They came and went by their own mysterious plan, hardly ever with glad tidings or a winning lottery number.

I was relieved to see it was Stone Stern and his partner, Billy Mann, who arrived at my room soon after Brenda bustled away. Phillipa's husband is a tall, scholarly looking man, surprisingly gentle for one in his profession. "Cass, what in the world?" Stone took my hand and squeezed it gently. There was real warmth in those gray eyes behind oval, metal-framed glasses. "I don't mean to scold you when you're in a weakened state, but why do I always find you in the midst of mayhem and murder?"

"Same question Joe often asks me. Obviously, it's my karma. Does Mrs. Peacedale know who donated the hemlock treats? Did Bevvy Besant eat the damned things? She's the Hospitality Chairperson, so she might have an idea who brought them. And how many victims were there, anyway?"

"Relax, Cass. Mundane as my talents may be, I'll do the investigating. But no, the minister's wife doesn't know who donated the brownies to the hospitality table. And yes, Mrs. Besant is here in the hospital but indisposed at the moment. Thirteen persons in all were admitted to the hospital, including a teen-aged boy delivering office supplies who copped a brownie out of the church kitchen. Tough on him but a good thing, actually. Narrowed the poison field down to the brownies, although you helped with that, too, so I heard. Nevertheless, every item served will be tested."

"Oh, oh—Bevvy's getting pumped, the poor baby," I murmured. "And what about poor Lydia Craig, she seemed like a sprightly old lady. The poison took her rather fast, didn't it? Has her family arrived?"

"Yes, it was all over quickly. Speedier than Socrates, in fact. But relatively painless as poisons go. The ancient Greeks considered it a humane method of execution. Weakness of the limbs followed by paralysis of the breathing apparatus. She must have eaten quite a few of those brownies, although all the survivors mentioned a kind of "musty" or "bitter" flavor. Apparently, the Craig woman was known to have a big yen for chocolate. Have the Craig family members been notified yet, Billy?"

Billy, a beefy, red-cheeked guy who looked as if he'd been sent down from Central Casting to play an Irish cop, had been leaning on the door frame, studying in his notes with a puzzled frown. At the mention of his name, however, he looked up and grinned. "Hey, Cass. How'ya doing? Reverend Peacedale and a uniform are breaking the news to the Craigs. I understand the old lady was a spinster, no immediate family, but some nephews and a niece who are local."

"So, Cass," Stone continued, "can *you* shed any light at all on the poisonings?"

"Did the incident have anything to do with your being the guest of honor?" Billy asked. He removed a pencil stump wedged behind his ear and poised it above his notebook.

I hadn't thought of that. Could anyone be crazy enough to register their protest to Wicca by poisoning the brownies? "Maybe. But I don't really feel that was the motive. And beyond that, I haven't a clue. Sorry." And I was sorry. I really wanted to help Stone. What I needed here was a helpful little vision showing me why, when, and above all, who. "Maybe something will come to me later."

"No one seems to know anything," Billy complained. "We can pair up every single one of those sweets with a church member *except* the brownies. They simply appeared out of nowhere in the kitchen, and the coffee-hour hostesses set them out on the buffet."

"Like magic." Stone winked at me, squeezed my hand again, then stepped back to allow my so-called dinner tray to be placed in front of me. After the orderly left, Stone said, "Before you eat any of that stuff, I should warn you that Phil's on her way." Then he and Billy departed to see if Bevvy was talking yet.

"Drink it, you mean," I muttered to myself, eyeing my tray. Insipid broth, industrial tea, pale apple juice, and some kind of weird gelatin, Laboratory Lime perhaps.

My next visitor was Selwyn ("call me Wyn") Peacedale, pastor of the Garden of Gethsemane Presbyterian Church of Plymouth, which was located just around the corner from my house, an antique saltbox overlooking the Atlantic. I've always thought Wyn resembles a heavenly cherub who has aged a bit, but today his round cheeks and dimples were lost in grief. He took my hand in a pastoral way; his was feverishly damp, mine was icy cold. "How're you doing, Cass? What a terrible thing this is! I'm so sorry that you were a victim in this vicious attack on the church. As it happened, I had to leave to attend to some pressing parish matters right after your most informative talk, or I probably would have been poisoned myself. I love chocolate stuff, you know. But you, just a visitor to Gethsemane . . ."

"Not exactly the first time. I attended the Donahue funeral—standing room only at that one. Anyway, I'm alive, that's the main thing. Poor Lydia Craig. It must have been terrible telling her family. And how's Patty?"

"Patty's doing well physically, I believe. Like you, she's been treated, had her whiffs of oxygen, and now she's having a little liquid supper. But she's very upset about what happened, just to think that one of our own may have done something like this. There are always some disagreements and strained relations, of course, but . . ." He sighed heavily. "As for counseling the Craigs, I've visited the niece and nephew who are living here in Plymouth. There's another nephew in Marshfield. The niece offered to notify him and various cousins." He sighed again and flushed slightly. "I believe Lydia's left the church quite a bit of money. At least that's what she told me last Christmas when I was seeking contributions toward some renovations. I could hardly believe it, given her usual modest donations, but she said it was a *fait accompli*, and I would be mighty surprised, but not to call the contractors just yet, as she intended to live a good long while. Well, well . . . poor Lydia. 'Tomorrow is promised to no one,' as they say. Such a cruel end to her expectations." He was quiet then, looking out the window at the October darkness, lips moving silently. For a moment, he seemed to have forgotten where he was. Then a look of apprehension crossed his face, and he remembered he'd been talking to me. "I trust this bequest won't cause a problem. With the relatives, that is."

"From what I've seen of inheritance, I would say, steel yourself, Wyn." It still hurt me to speak, so I said no more.

"Patty and I will pray about it. And for you, too, Cass, may the Lord bless and keep you." He trudged out with disconsolate steps for a pastor who'd just got a fortune to spend on his church. Right in the vestibule exhibited on an easel, I'd seen an architect's drawing of a grand new entrance and an addition. Wyn called it his "heart's wish made visible," and I'd said that's a magic visualization, same as we do.

As predicted, the circle descended *en masse* a few minutes later, bringing a discernible wave of warmth and energy into my room.

"Don't touch that slop," Phillipa commanded immediately, unpacking the small hamper she carried on her arm. "I've brought you a thermos of my own double chicken-beef herbed broth, jellied pomegranate juice with a touch of port wine, and some Assam tea."

"What, no calves' foot jelly?" I whined. The broth smelled heavenly rich.

"Phil finds it really hard to get decent calves' feet these days." Tall, lithe Heather Devlin pushed past Phillipa to give me a hug, her long bronze braid swinging halfway down the back of her khaki jacket, like some modern-day Maid Marian. "Look, I've brought you one of my best candles. Light this, my dear, and you'll breathe in the ocean's healing power."

The candle was greenish and looked like a tide pool, being filled with tiny crustaceans and shells coated with barnacles. If I lit the thing, in a thrice Brenda would be rushing into my room with a fire extinguisher. But it's the thought that counts. "Thoughts are things," was my grandma's favorite saying, and it's become one of my guiding lights.

"And *I've* brought you an amulet, a little gargoyle to frighten away the bad vibes." Deidre Ryan was trying to lean over me and fasten her handiwork to one of my bed's white enamel posts but she's a petite gal and was having to stand on her tiptoes.

Heather took the ghoulish artifact out of Deidre's hand and tied it up above the nurse's buzzer. "Nice eyes," she commented. "I like that angry red glare."

"Now, girls," Fiona Ritchie took over the room with her new wise-woman glamour. In the slight shift of perception caused by the glamour, her normally plump, rather frumpish self had metamorphosed into a regal, Minerva-like person to whom anyone would want to listen attentively. It was an enviable talent.

"How does she do that?" Deidre whispered in my ear.

"I think it's akin to *presence,* the kind of aura that some actors are able to project," I whispered back.

"If you had dowsed your food, as I taught you to do, you would have detected the poison," Fiona scolded.

"Fiona, it was a church social! How would it have looked if I took out a pendulum and let it swing over the cookies?"

"Exceptional people have to learn to tolerate some puzzlement among the mundanes. Do you know," Fiona continued, "that there are some religious sects that claim their true believers can handle snakes or drink poison without harm? In ancient times, priestesses of the Great Mother, too, were snake-handlers. No, no—don't look so alarmed. It's not a test I want us to try. From my studies, I think harmony is the key, and disharmony equals dis-ease. No lectures today, however." Her deep warm hug was like medicine itself, and I basked in it. "But on Samhain, we'll talk of this again. Meanwhile . . . " Out of the pocket of her coat-sweater of many colors, Fiona fished a compact iPod. "Here are some magical tunes to help restore the harmony. Play it later, when you're alone. I want to see you dancing out of here by tomorrow."

Dancing after hemlock poisoning? Sure, why not. Just don't ask me to make friends with snakes.

The "magic tunes" turned out to a tract of medieval music played at my wedding to Joe last Yule. And bringing with it memories of our enchanted honeymoon in New Zealand, it did indeed make me feel like dancing.